UNUSUALLY STUPID POLITICIANS

Washington's Weak in Review

Kathryn Petras and Ross Petras

VILLARD
NEW YORK

A Villard Books Trade Paperback Original

Copyright © 2007 by Kathryn Petras and Ross Petras

Published in the United States by Villard Books, an imprint of
The Random House Publishing Group, a division of
Random House, Inc., New York.

VILLARD and "V" CIRCLED Design are registered trademarks of
Random House, Inc.

Library of Congress Cataloging-in-Publication Data

Petras, Kathryn.
Unusually stupid politicians: Washington's weak in review / Kathryn
Petras and Ross Petras.
p.   cm.
ISBN 978-0-8129-7751-6
1. Politicians—United States—Anecdotes. 2. United States—
Politics and government—Anecdotes. 3. Stupidity—
Anecdotes. 4. Stupidity—Humor. I. Petras, Ross. II. Title.
PN6231.P6P48 2007
320.973—dc22   2007017352

Printed in the United States of America

www.villard.com

2 4 6 8 9 7 5 3 1

Book design by Susan Turner

Note: This book contains material on politicians behaving in their normal manner. Some of them continued to behave so after this book went to press. We regret that we are unable to keep up with them in real time—the book is as accurate as we could make it up to its final editing and publication.

CONTENTS

INTRODUCTION
xi

1 POLITICIANS AT WORK
3

2 INSIDE THE POLITICAL MIND
ATTITUDES, THEORIES, AND INSIGHTS
35

3 POLITICAL SKILLS AND TALENTS
66

4 THE POLITICAL PERSONALITY
POLITICIANS ACTING, BEING, AND DOING
110

5 POLITICAL COMMUNICATION
144

6 POLITICAL CAMPAIGNS
167

7 POLITICAL FAMILIES
199

8 BUREAUCRACY
216

**9 YOUR GOVERNMENT AT WORK FIGHTING TERROR
AS USUAL AND TO THE BEST OF ITS ABILITY,**
WHICH ISN'T NECESSARILY THAT COMFORTING
(IF YOU KNOW WHAT WE MEAN)
234

10 POLITICAL PUNDITS
270

Introduction

BACK IN THE 1800S, MARK TWAIN WROTE THE FAMOUS "Suppose you were an idiot. And suppose you were a member of Congress. But I repeat myself."

We are happy to report that the United States has made great strides in the over 100 years since Twain wrote those words.

First of all, in deference to the politically correct among us, Twain would no longer be able to say "idiot." He might offend someone . . . like, say, a congressman or an idiot. But we re—oh, never mind.

Second, in Twain's day congressional idiocy was confined to white males . . . since they were the only people who were allowed to be voted into Congress. So when Twain said "member of Congress," he meant men. White men. Today, we're so much fairer. We let anyone into *any* government position, as long as he or she has the votes—and, more important, the money to get the votes. Virtually anybody can become a U.S. politician or bureaucrat, and, judging by the record, virtually anybody does. So we're proud to say that political idiocy today knows no boundaries—neither race, color, creed, religion, political affiliation, nor national origin matters anymore.

Third, instead of confining that idiotic condition to Congress, Twain would now realize that idiocy is *everywhere* in the U.S. political system. Just look at the news on an average evening. Representatives and senators are idiots, *state* representatives and *state* senators are idiots; mayors, town councilpeople, bureaucrats, even *presidents* can be idiots.

So look how far we've come.

Approach this book, then, not as a negative foray into the foibles of American democracy, but as a *celebration*. A celebration of American diversity, where stupidity, vapidity, greed, arrogance, hypocrisy, gluttony, pig-headedness, and cloth-headedness are no hindrance to high position and governmental authority.

In fact, they just might help.

A lot.

A whole lot.

So let's begin celebrating . . .

ONE

POLITICIANS AT WORK

POLITICIANS ARE PUBLIC SERVANTS. IN OTHER WORDS, THEY serve the public. They do what the public wants them to do . . . which, if you look at the record, could mean that the public wants them to take lots of taxpayer money, take lots of vacations, and enact useless, dumb laws.

But isn't that being cynical?

IT'S A TOUGH CONGRESSIONAL LIFE:
THE INCREDIBLY HARD WORKLOAD OF OUR PUBLIC SERVANTS ON CAPITOL HILL

Senators and representatives do not have it easy. Sure, they get some perks and their salaries really aren't that bad. But they work hard for the money—merely for the betterment of U.S. citizens like us.

We think it's time to give credit to these hardworking public servants. After all, just look at the facts:

FACT #1: *In 2006, congressmen were working nearly THREE DAYS a week! (Well, more like two, actually, but it was spread over three days . . .)*

We're tired just thinking about it, but, yes, it's true. The congressional workweek began late Tuesday and lasted until Thursday afternoon. (Of course, the House was in recess for many weeks, but that's not the point.) And this workweek was followed for the whole year—not counting the month-long August recess, the two-week April recess, and the other weeks they get off in February, March, and June. . . .

FACT #2: *And NOW, as of January 2007, they actually have to work (gasp) FIVE WHOLE DAYS a week! (Well, almost five whole days . . .)*

House members now have to be in the Capitol each Monday by 6:30 P.M. and aren't done with their workweek until Friday at about 2 P.M.

Can you imagine having to work Monday (well, late Monday) through Friday (well, mid-Friday)? And they got some of their holidays cut as well. For example, instead of a six-weekday Memorial Day holiday, they'll only get Memorial Day off. (You know, like most Americans.)

It's all due to the new Democrat-run House. The Democrats wanted to make sure work got done—and extending the workweek seemed to be the logical first choice. But some representatives think it represents something more insidious . . .

As Representative Jack Kingston (R-GA)—who used to fly home on Thursday and return to D.C. on Tuesday—astutely pointed out: "Keeping us up here eats away at families. Marriages suffer. The Democrats could care less about families—that's what this says."

FACT #3: *The above fact notwithstanding, the House started out the new longer workweek by cutting it one day short . . . to watch a VITAL college football game!*

The much-vaunted "longer workweek so we can get things done" plan got sidelined in the VERY FIRST WEEK.

Of course, all that was on the agenda was voting on raising the minimum wage and changes in homeland security legislation. This was clearly not as important as the big national college championship football game between Florida and Ohio State. So the new minority leader, Representative John Boehner (R-OH), asked for Monday off so members (including himself) could attend the game. One of the chief opponents of the prior Republican-led Congress's three-day workweek, House Majority Leader Steny Hoyer (D-MD), took to the floor to back up Boehner, explaining, "There is a very important event happening Monday night, particularly for those who live in Ohio and Florida."

The House got Monday off. And Florida won.

FACT #4: *Even before the grueling new five-day-week schedule, on September 22, 2006, the Senate actually had to work on a Friday . . . for 10 whole minutes!*

The poor men and women usually never worked on Fridays, so imagine how difficult it must have been to have to go to work. And they had to stay there for 10 entire minutes. The mind boggles. It also boggles to realize what was going on while they decided to adjourn at 9:40 in the morning—little things like, um, a war in Iraq, a deficit that keeps growing, and gasoline prices going through the roof. But, hey, there was an election coming up and campaigning takes time, you know . . .

Presumably that's also why on nine workdays, the House

met for a teeny bit more than 10 minutes (11 minutes). And the Senate had three workdays that lasted less than *one* minute!

GREAT AMERICANS:
POLS DOING GREAT THINGS

Politicians do a lot more than grub money for themselves—they *contribute* to our American society. Here are some of the greatest recent contributions made by some of our greatest politicians, heroes all. Let's give our heartfelt thanks to these great Americans and their earthshaking achievements, which have truly made America a *better* place.

THANKS TO THE LEGAL WIZARDRY OF BUSH ADVISER JOHN YOO . . .

. . . the president of the United States now has the legal power to torture children—and crush little boys' testicles!

Yes, thank God, it's true. A big squishy hug to John Yoo, formerly deputy assistant to the U.S. attorney general (and now a proud professor at the University of California at Berkeley, helping to train young minds). Because of his hard work, we now have official legal memos, including one notorious one of 2002, that give the president unlimited powers to torture captive suspects anyway he (or she) wants—and to go to war, for that matter, anywhere, anytime, and against anyone. Professor Yoo wants us to know that he's not just talking about cracking the bones of a few grown-ups, either. This great American wants to make sure the president can, for example, crush the testicles of a terror suspect's little children. Here the great American legal mind explains:

> Q: "If the president deems that he's got to torture somebody, including by crushing the testicles of the person's child, there is no law that can stop him?"

Yoo: "No treaty."

Q: "Also no law by Congress. That is what you wrote in the August 2002 memo."

Yoo: "I think it depends on why the president thinks he needs to do that."

As we can see, if the president thinks it's okay to smash some testicles, it's okay. Thank you, John Yoo, for giving our president the *freedom* to crush.

THANKS TO CHILD-FRIENDLY MISSISSIPPI GOVERNOR HALEY BARBOUR . . .

. . . *more middle-school kids can buy and smoke cigarettes!*

People in favor of childhood smoking will applaud the efforts of Governor Haley Barbour, who won a long court battle to withdraw funding for Mississippi's antismoking program. At last!

Some may accuse the governor of doing this as a favor to his longtime clients when he was a tobacco industry lobbyist (Barbour served as a lobbyist for tobacco clients from 1998 to 2002. His firm, Barbour, Griffin & Rogers, was paid a total of $3.8 million by the tobacco companies, according to reports obtained by the U.S. Senate Office of Records). We say that's being *cynical*. The governor himself explained it was a matter of bureaucratic *principle*. He actually initially opposed the program for technical administrative reasons . . . or so he said. He explained that it was funded by the courts and instead should be funded by the legislature; and more to the point, it needed legislative approval. Of course, once the legislature approved the program, the governor vetoed it anyway, but that's just *quibbling*.

And so, a deep and heartfelt thank-you to a great American; especially from the tobacco sellers of America, and from all kids (and their parents!) who favor starting the smoking habit as soon as possible after grade school.

THANKS TO THE HEROIC EFFORTS OF REPRESENTATIVE RICHARD W. POMBO . . .
. . . *Americans may soon be free to kill any endangered species they want!*

Anyone with an irresistible yen for machine-gunning a grizzly has got to love hardworking Representative Pombo (R-CA), who has been struggling to help America by abolishing the Endangered Species Act, which he says puts "rats and shellfish" ahead of people. (Pombo happens to be a rancher when he's not legislating, but we're sure this crusade has *nothing* to do with pesky endangered species on his land.)

Pombo's proposed legislation phases out protection for *all* wildlife by 2015. Unfortunately, Pombo hasn't succeeded yet in passing this into law, but he's been trying hard. He almost made it in 2006. Meanwhile, our intrepid congressman has succeeded in eliminating habitat protection on 150 million acres of wilderness areas. He's also lifted a 25-year moratorium on offshore oil drilling.

Thanks to the selfless efforts of Pombo, perhaps soon American oil drillers, corporate ranchers, and mining company presidents will rest easy, and all of us will have the freedom to gun down a walrus or a whooping crane whenever we feel like it.

THANKS TO FRUGALLY MINDED CONGRESSMAN JIM SENSENBRENNER . . .
. . . *it's now much harder for Americans in debt to declare bankruptcy—even for medical reasons or due to Hurricane Katrina!*

You're up to your ears in debt due to a heart condition or a home-destroying hurricane? Buck up and get a job!

Yes, fellow Americans, we're fortunate that Congressman Sensenbrenner (R-WI) believes in the old-fashioned American virtues of frugality and hard work, virtues that made America great. The good congressman, who happens to be a multimillionaire by inheritance (his great-grandfather invented the Kotex sanitary napkin) and who also happens to truly utilize and enjoy his perks of office (he was recently named a top freebie junketeer in Congress), has won approval for a bill that makes it much harder for Americans in debt to declare bankruptcy. This bill was roundly denounced by consumer groups but strongly backed by credit card giants, who even in a record year of profits wanted to reduce potential losses. Our stalwart "no exceptions" congressman also refused to consider an exemption for victims of Hurricane Katrina—and even boldly voted against an aid package for the same victims.

A heartfelt thank-you, from *all* of us "old-fashioned" Americans, particularly those of us who own banks and credit card companies.

THANKS TO FAIR-MINDED SENATOR ARLEN SPECTER . . .
. . . it may soon be easier for corrupt Enron-type executives to cheat fellow Americans!

Senator Specter (R-PA), longtime member of the Senate Judiciary Committee, has proposed bold legislation calling for a "rollback" of tactics used by federal prosecutors to fight corporate wrongdoing at firms like Enron and Arthur Andersen. Simply put, he wants to be *fairer* to corporations and corporate bigwigs being investigated by the feds, by cutting back on investigations and making it more difficult for prosecutors to recruit corporate whistle-blowers.

And so we bestow a warm thank-you, from all American corporate wrongdoers, particularly those of us who have stolen more than a few mil from our employees and share-holders.

THANKS TO EVER-SO-ENERGETIC REPRESENTATIVE JOHN MURTHA . . .

. . . Americans won't get as much job training, veterans won't get as much health care, and there will be even less flood control!

In 2006, the good congressman Murtha (D-PA) spent much of his time battling and cutting government spending on job training, blocking $150 million in health care for veterans (including those just back from the fighting in Iraq), and cutting back on federal flood control.

Murtha certainly knows where to put all that money he saved the federal government—not in the pockets of the taxpayer, of course, but in the pockets of Halliburton and fellow contracting corporations. Murtha opposed spending to investigate contractor fraud in Iraq—leaving companies like Halliburton free to overcharge. And give out "honorariums" to deserving congresspeople.

As Murtha puts it: "deal making is what Congress is all about."

And so we salute John Murtha, who may not be an incorruptible congressman but is certainly a deal-making one—an American hero not quite in the mold of Mr. Smith from that Frank Capra classic *Mr. Smith Goes to Washington.*

THANKS TO THE GREAT HUMANITARIAN AMBASSADOR JOHN BOLTON . . .

. . . the U.S. showed how it isn't against slavery in our hemisphere!

He may have left the United Nations, but Americans can be proud that before he left, Ambassador John "What's wrong with the KKK, anyway?" Bolton went on record as opposing—yes, *opposing*—a U.N. antislavery resolution.

This clearly *locked in* a good impression for the rest of the world: Americans don't hate slavery. Good PR move, John.

When a number of Caribbean countries got together in December 2006 to propose a commemorative resolution before the U.N. on the abolition of the slave trade in the Western Hemisphere, Ambassador Bolton announced that he absolutely refused to sign. Why? *For a very important moral reason.* According to an official letter from the American delegation, the United States objected to some wording in the resolution; namely, it preferred the words "the emphasis" to "emphasizing" in the document. And so it refused to sign, rendering the resolution effectively dead, given time constraints.

Unfortunately, after some loud members of Congress (especially the Congressional Black Caucus) kicked up a storm, Bolton was forced to sign on.

But nevertheless, we salute this intrepid ambassador, who, in the best tradition of such esteemed American envoys as Averell Harriman and Benjamin Franklin, clearly showed the world where we as Americans stand. Or at least where a few of us stand.

DEALING WITH CONSTITUENTS:
POLITICIANS AT THEIR WARMEST AND FUZZIEST

Good politicians understand that they are not the bosses, but the *servants* of the people. And so they always, always, show *respect* for the voters.

Warm and Fuzzy Pol: Representative Jo Ann Emerson (R-MO)

Wonderful Way of Showing Respect for the Voters: Ended letter sent to a constituent with "i think you are an asshole."

POLS ON THEIR JOBS—JOB QUALIFICATIONS

Some confidence-building words from the man in charge of defense and Iraq:

> "I would confess I'm no expert on Iraq."
> "I'm no expert on military matters."
>
> —Secretary of Defense ROBERT GATES to Congress during confirmation hearings

....

Some confidence-building words from a man who was in charge of defense and Iraq:

> "I am not going to give you a number for it because it's not my business to do intelligent work."
>
> —Secretary of Defense DONALD RUMSFELD, asked while testifying before Congress to estimate the number of Iraqi insurgents

....

Some confidence-building words from the man in charge of the United States government:

> "I would say [the highlight of my presidency] was when I caught a 7.5-pound perch in my lake."
>
> —President GEORGE W. BUSH to a German newspaper reporter

....

Some confidence-building words from a Supreme Court justice:

> "I really don't want to be a judge. I don't want to be judged. I don't like judging other people."
>
> —Justice CLARENCE THOMAS in a lecture at Holy Cross College

....

Some confidence-building words from a man who headed the CIA:

> "I couldn't get a job with the CIA today. I am not qualified."
>
> —CIA director PORTER GOSS shortly before being appointed

Emerson personally signed the letter, which was responding to a citizen's question on testimony by oil executives before the Senate. She even included a handwritten message at the bottom of the letter: "PS—please forgive the delay in responding." (She later said she had no idea how the offending line got added and immediately launched an investigation.)

Warm and Fuzzy Pol: Susan Sheybani, assistant to Bush campaign spokesman Terry Holt

Wonderful Way of Showing Respect for the Voters: Respectfully asked of working-class Americans, "Why don't they get new jobs if they're unhappy, or go on Prozac?"

This was said during a discussion of low-quality jobs for American workers. Nevertheless, Bush won the election. Sheybani's supporters insist that it was a very funny joke she made. Hilarious!

We *love* compassionate conservative jokes. Which reminds us: This cripple and this retard were walking, and . . .

Warm and Fuzzy Pol: Richard Riordan, as California secretary of education

Wonderful Way of Showing Respect for the Voters: When asked by a little girl if he knew what her name meant, Riordan nicely replied, "It means stupid, dirty girl."

The girl's name was Isis, which actually doesn't mean stupid. But we think the name "Richard Riordan" may mean "wide-assed idiot" in Albanian. Riordan—a man who really seems to understand children—explained this as a "joke."

Warm and Fuzzy Pol: Mervyn Dymally, Democratic assemblyman, California

Wonderful Way of Showing Respect for the Voters: Canceled demonstration in support of little girl dissed and humiliated by secretary of education because of color of little girl's skin

In a wonderful example of American politics at its best, after Richard Riordan called a little girl named Isis stupid and dirty, Democratic state assemblyman Mervyn Dymally called for him to step down, telling the San Jose *Mercury News* the child was a "little African-American girl."

"Would he [Riordan] have done that to a white girl?" Dymally asked rhetorically.

The answer was yes, Riordan would have done that to a white girl. And he did. Little Isis was white. So Dymally promptly canceled the civil rights demonstration he was planning.

Rhetorical question: Would he (Dymally) have cared if a maligned little girl was white?

We know *that* answer.

VERY VITAL LEGISLATION:
THINGS WE'RE SO GLAD THE GOVERNMENT DID

Why bother with health-care legislation (it's complicated and fraught with controversy) when you can deal with other important things—like Peeps and cheerleaders and all that other *interesting* (and non-voter-alienating) stuff?

Herewith some very vital moments in recent legislative history.

Vital Legislation: A resolution "recognizing the contributions of the Christmas tree industry to the United States economy," and urging the Department of Agriculture to promote "awareness of the importance of the Christmas-tree industry"

Proud Sponsor: Representative Virginia Foxx (R-NC)

Why Needed: In a word, plastics. Or two words, plastic trees. But let's not be cynical. According to a Foxx spokesperson, "Congresswoman Foxx is a believer in traditional family values, and the Christmas tree is a symbol of that." Foxx's family, probably by a pure coincidence, happens to run a nursery that sells Christmas trees.

Vital Legislation: A resolution "concerning the national cheerleading championship of the University of Central Florida Varsity Cheerleading Team"

Proud Sponsor: Representative Tom Feeney (R-FL)

Why Needed: If we didn't encourage cheerleaders, where would our country be? (Interestingly, shortly after this, Feeney sponsored a bill aimed at dramatically limiting the sentencing discretion of federal judges—earning the condemnation of both conservative *and* liberal judges; this leads us to wonder if Representative Feeney is best off sticking to cheerleaders.)

Vital Legislation: A Motion Honoring Marshmallow Peeps

Proud Sponsor: Representative Pat Toomey (R-PA)

Why Needed: Marshmallow Peeps are, in the words of Representative Toomey, "one of the most recognized and celebrated products" of Just Born, Incorporated, of Pennsylvania, which in 2004 was celebrating its fiftieth anniversary.

Vital Legislation: A resolution to honor the "thousands of Freemasons in every state in the nation . . . for their many contributions"

Proud Sponsor: Representative Paul Gillmor (R-OH)

Why Needed: Many Freemasons vote. Many Freemasons live in Ohio. Representative Gillmor is from Ohio.

Vital Legislation: A long list, including: a resolution commending civil servants, a resolution establishing Financial Literacy for Youth Month, a bill naming a post office, and our personal favorite . . . a bill for nurturing "the development and planning of certain policies, schedules and programs for postmasters."

Proud Sponsor: Senator Daniel Akaka (D-HI)
Why Needed: We're not sure; for one thing, can't postmasters develop schedules on their own?

Vital Legislation: Legislation to improve access at Rocky Mountain National Park's Twin Owls Trailhead—among the *only* bills sponsored by . . .
Proud Sponsor: Senator Wayne Allard (R-CO)
Why Needed: We have a funny feeling it all has to do with a friend or acquaintance of Allard's—i.e., read this statement by Allard:

> "I am pleased to announce that my legislation to improve access at Rocky Mountain National Park's Twin Owls Trailhead has been signed into law by the President. This is the culmination of over a year's worth of hard work to protect the historic character of the MacGregor Ranch while improving access to the park for its users. This legislation allows us to be good stewards of our public lands, while also protecting private property rights. It shows that we can safeguard our national parks, while taking into account the concerns of private landowners."

Vital Work: Maintaining Texas dildo ban
Proud Adjudicator: Supreme Court of the United States

Why Needed: We had a question or two about this; and about the Supreme Court's decision in October 2006 to maintain Texas's ban on "devices including a dildo or artificial vagina, designed or marked as useful primarily for the stimulation of human genital organs." It seems that with all the vital questions facing the court on surveillance, torture, the First Amendment, marriage debates, etc., the issue of whether or not Texans can buy dildos in Austin is relatively minor, and anyway, if the Texans want to buy one or two, why not?

Vital Work: Legislation banning the sale of sexual devices
Proud Sponsor: State Representative Guy Ralph Davenport (R) of South Carolina
Why Needed: Because sex should be all natural? We reproduce part of this bill below to show the general tenor of the work considered under Davenport's tutelage in the South Carolina legislature.

(C) As used in this article:
  (1) "sexual conduct" means:
    (a) vaginal, anal, or oral intercourse, whether actual or simulated, normal or perverted, whether between human beings, animals, or a combination thereof;
    (b) masturbation, excretory functions, or lewd exhibition, actual or simulated, of the genitals, pubic hair, anus, vulva, or female breast nipples including male or female genitals in a state of sexual stimulation or arousal or covered male genitals in a discernably turgid state;
    (c) an act or condition that depicts actual or simulated bestiality, sado-masochistic abuse, mean-

ing flagellation or torture by or upon a person who is nude or clad in undergarments or in a costume which reveals the pubic hair, anus, vulva, genitals, or female breast nipples, or the condition of being fettered, bound, or otherwise physically restrained on the part of the one so clothed;

(d) an act or condition that depicts actual or simulated touching, caressing, or fondling of, or other similar physical contact with, the covered or exposed genitals, pubic or anal regions, or female breast nipple, whether alone or between humans, animals, or a human and an animal, of the same or opposite sex, in an act of actual or apparent sexual stimulation or gratification; or

(e) an act or condition that depicts the insertion of any part of a person's body, other than the male sexual organ, or of any object into another person's anus or vagina, except when done as part of a recognized medical procedure.

(2) "patently offensive" means obviously and clearly disagreeable, objectionable, repugnant, displeasing, distasteful, or obnoxious to contemporary standards of decency and propriety within the community.

(3) "prurient interest" means a shameful or morbid interest in nudity, sex, or excretion and is reflective of an arousal of lewd and lascivious desires and thoughts.

(4) "person" means any individual, corporation, partnership, association, firm, club, or other legal or commercial entity.

(5) "knowingly" means having general knowledge of the content of the subject material or performance, or failing after reasonable opportunity to exercise rea-

sonable inspection which would have disclosed the character of the material or performance.

(D) Obscenity must be judged with reference to ordinary adults except that it must be judged with reference to children or other especially susceptible audiences or clearly defined deviant sexual groups if it appears from the character of the material or the circumstances of its dissemination to be especially for or directed to children or these audiences or groups.

(E) As used in this article, "community standards" used in determining prurient appeal and patent offensiveness are the standards of the area from which the jury is drawn.

(F) It is unlawful for any person knowingly to create, buy, procure, or process obscene material or a sexual device with the purpose and intent of disseminating it.

(G) It is unlawful for a person to advertise or otherwise promote the sale of sexual devices or material represented or held out by them as obscene.

(H) A person who violates this section is guilty of a felony and, upon conviction, must be imprisoned not more than five years or fined not more than ten thousand dollars, or both.

(I) Obscene material and sexual devices disseminated, procured, or promoted in violation of this section is contraband and may be seized by appropriate law enforcement authorities.

DUBIOUS DECISIONS

Politicians are elected because of their decision-making abilities and good judgment. We elect them and trust them to make the right decisions about our towns, cities, states, and nation. Here are three recent shining examples of local deci-sion makers making decisions: mayors with superlatively *good* judgment.

We need more men like these . . .

MAYOR CLEVERLY USES OFFICIAL CREDIT CARD AT STRIP CLUB

Mayor Mike Smith of New Lenox, Illinois, used his offi-cial mayor's credit card to pick up the tab for $1,500—at the strip club VIP's, in Chicago.

"It was just very poor judgment to put it on that card," admitted Mayor Smith. "Naturally, when you're out at a bachelor party having a good time, you're going to find that . . . everyone has had a few drinks, and with drinks, sometimes discretion goes out the window. I'm no different than anybody else, I'm human. Nobody was stepping up to the table to pay the bill." So what else could the poor guy do? We wonder how much he tipped . . .

MAYOR CLEVERLY ASKS POLICE ESCORT TO STOP FOUR SCHOOL BUSES BECAUSE HE WANTS A HUG

On an impulse, Mayor Frank Melton of Jackson, Missis-sippi, told his police escort to pull four local Callaway High School buses over on an interstate highway. The buses were taking students home from school.

The reason: The mayor wanted a hug. "It's been such a stressful two weeks," Melton said. "I wanted to shake their hands. I wanted to touch them. That's all it was . . . I went through the buses and shook their hand and hugged them and told them how proud I was of them . . . I told the kids to have a great weekend and a safe weekend," he said. "I didn't do anything stupid or illegal."

He added that there were no safety hazards, since the drivers pulled off the interstate onto the median strip.

"I reserve the right to go into our schools. I reserve the right to encourage kids. I reserve the right as the mayor," he said.

Right?

MAYOR CLEVERLY ALLOWS *THONG GIRL 3* TO BE FILMED IN HIS OFFICE

Mayor Don Wright of Gallatin, Texas, decided to allow the makers of *Thong Girl 3* to film in his office . . . on a Sunday.

The mayor stated that he supported filmmaking for economic development, and only had a "general idea" of what the movie was about. "This is a chance for our people to get in the movies and make some money. I was excited about it." Thong Girl is a "risqué superheroine" who wears a red thong and "polices the skies with an iron fist." The mayor added that when he looked at the *Thong Girl* website, he was "surprised. . . . I didn't have a clue."

Interestingly, several months earlier the mayor displayed his better judgment in another incident: He cleverly asked a female employee if her breasts were implants. She sued him for harassment.

THAT'S WHY THEY CALL THEM JUNKETS—
OR, POLS WITH A TRIP JONES

Politicians and junkets go together like junkies and junk. Politicians don't *need* to go on junkets, but they're addictive. And they're fun! (And sometimes illegal.)

That doesn't stop our intrepid politicians, though. When offered a chance to further their understanding of, say, a beachfront spa in Malaysia, they make the sacrifice and go.

Kinda makes you want to sing God bless America, doesn't it?

The Most Brazen Junket(s) Award goes to . . .
Representative Jim Kolbe (R-AZ)

. . . for racking up nearly $40,000 worth of free trips between June and November of 2006—more than any other member of the Arizona delegation—*after* he announced he was going to retire. For virtually no useful reason, Kolbe visited Turkey, Italy, Poland, England, Canada, Spain, and Belgium.

The Most Creative Junket Award goes to . . .
Representative John Sweeney (R-NY)

. . . for holding a fun "Congressional Winter Challenge" in which he and his guests all pretended to be Olympic athletes!

This gets big points for being—shockingly—the only taxpayer-funded "Pretend Olympics" junket we've ever seen reported.

More specifically, Sweeney invited 53 lucky people to join him at the Lake Placid Olympic facilities to compete in skiing, bobsledding, and hockey—all paid for by New York taxpayers. And if the notion of a "pretend Olympics" isn't creative enough, it also wasn't connected with *anything* remotely political. (Talk about creative!) Sadly, Sweeney's fun challenge appears to have violated a number of House gift and travel rules—including a prohibition against purely recreational travel.

The Most Blatant "You Scratch My Back, I'll Scratch Yours" Junket Award goes to . . .
Representative Alan Mollohan (D-WV)

. . . for going on a five-day trip with his wife and two top aides to Bilbao, Spain, just a month after passing funds on to the group that paid for said trip.

Mollohan got a very nice trip to sunny Spain courtesy of TMC Technologies 30 days or so after TMC got a $5 million contract courtesy of Mollohan's earmark. Mere coincidence, of course.

THE "HOOTS, MAN, I CANNA REMEMBER" JUNKET AWARD GOES TO . . .

Representative Tom Feeney (R-FL) and *Representative Bob Ney (R-OH)*

. . . for taking a golf trip to Scotland and somehow forgetting who paid for it.

It could happen to anyone, couldn't it? Well, perhaps not. But it *did* happen to two different congressmen on two different occasions. In each case, the representative in question went on a trip to Scotland, apparently for fun on the links, and in each case, the representative in question claimed that the trip was paid for by the National Center for Public Policy Research.

But the center wasn't on the same page. They didn't pay for the trip, they said. Oops. Turns out super-lobbyist Jack Abramoff paid for the trip. Feeney didn't explain the oversight, but Ney came up with a truly logical explanation: he had been *duped* by Abramoff. (No. We don't get it, either.)

THE "NEWARK, NEW JERSEY, CAPITAL OF THE WORLD" JUNKET AWARD GOES TO . . .

Newark mayor Sharpe James

. . . for promoting Newark in such logical places as the Bahamas, the Virgin Islands, Puerto Rico, the Dominican Republic, Rio de Janeiro, and South Beach, Florida.

James had an annual travel budget of $25,000, but added another $150,000 in travel expenses. His rationale? "As the last of the civil rights mayors in America, I had to travel and sell this city and tell the world about the Newark success story."

We're sure it's merely coincidental that all the places in which James felt the need to promote Newark were sunny vacation spots.

THE "I'M A FISCAL WATCHDOG" JUNKET AWARD GOES TO . . .
New York state comptroller Alan Hevesi (D)
. . . for watching out for New York's taxpayer dollars by taking two first-class trips to Las Vegas and two others to Tel Aviv using those taxpayer dollars.

Hevesi knows how to save a buck, no doubt about it. This is a good thing for a state comptroller usually—but it's not quite as good when the saving comes at the expense of the taxpayer. In 2006, the money manager saved dough out of his own pocket by flying first class to Vegas twice (to the tune of $2,265.30 for the round-trip ticket the first time, $3,796.60 the second). His spokesman, David Neustadt, offered this non sequitur by way of explanation: "Under Alan Hevesi, the state pension fund has gone from $95 billion to $140 billion." (Yes. Minus $6,061.90.)

Hevesi also flew first class to Tel Aviv twice—with his aide. The cost to taxpayers? $29,941.70. This time his spokesman said he had no information on the reason for the trips. But did we mention that the state pension fund went from $95 billion to $140 billion?

THE "THE FAMILY THAT TRAVELS TOGETHER" JUNKET
AWARD GOES TO . . .
Representative Eliot Engel (D-NY)
. . . for making sure that his family gets to see the world in style.

Never let it be said that Engel forgets the little people—if said little people are family members, that is. This family-minded junketeer has spread the wealth. He and his wife went to top-notch resorts in San Juan, Las Vegas, Wyoming, and Florida—paid by special interest groups. He and his daughter took a $5,300 jaunt to New Orleans. He and his son took free trips to Seattle, London, and Jerusalem. And he didn't forget his dear ol' mom! Engel and his 83-year-old mother enjoyed some quality son-mother time during a nine-day, $8,000 trip to the Bellagio in Vegas, not to mention a spa in La Jolla, California.

AND ALSO GOES TO . . .
Representative John T. Doolittle (R-CA)
. . . for taking his 12-year-old daughter on a $29,400 junket to South Korea and Malaysia—including a stop at the Berjaya Beach & Spa Resort on the Malaysian island of Langkawi, where they enjoyed the attentions of a personal butler, got massages, and rode water scooters on Burau Bay.

AND ALSO GOES TO (YES, FOLKS, IT'S A TRIFECTA!) . . .
Representative Vito Fossella (R-NY)
. . . for spending $53,000 in campaign funds for family trips to Las Vegas, Palm Springs, Vail, and Florida. (Not one to stint on the extras, Fossella also used the funds to pay for ski lift tickets, ski lessons, and scenic railway trips. Whadda guy!) When questioned about the possible misuse of campaign funds, Fossella cogently explained, "mistakes have been made." He reimbursed the campaign for some of the costs.

NECESSARY CONGRESSIONAL OFFICE "ENHANCEMENTS"—
PAID FOR BY TAXPAYER MONEY

Let's face it: When you work for the government as a public servant, you *need* certain things. No, not brooms, but plasma TVs. To get your job done correctly, you need them badly. And you're willing to pay for them . . . or, rather, let the public pay for them.

Buyer	Vital Enhancement	Cost	Reason
Rep. David Dreier (R-CA)	Plasma-screen TV	$5,763	It's a cool TV.
Rep. David Dreier (R-CA)	Nice new rugs	$1,338	According to spokeswoman Jo Maney, rugs were needed to mitigate the noise created by traffic on the marble and tile foyers in his Cannon Building and district offices.
Rep. John Murtha (D-PA)	Plasma-screen TV	$5,926	"Inexpensive" way to have cool videoconferencing ability, much cooler than standard TVs
Rep. Solomon Ortiz (D-TX)	Two 43-inch plasma-screen monitors and a 43-inch plasma-screen TV	$5,799 per monitor $7,309 for TV	Also for video-conferencing, three times cooler than Murtha's
Rep. Tom DeLay (R-TX)	ViewSonic flat-screen monitor	$2,078	For computer presentations. Our question: Now that he's out of office, who gets the monitor?

LIVING LARGE—

OR, IF YOU HAVE EXPENSIVE TASTES, HAVE WE GOT SOME GOVERNMENT AGENCIES FOR YOU!

The days of the poor, hard-toiling public or nonprofit servant who gets little for his or her efforts are, blessedly, long gone. Nowadays working for certain departments in the public sector or for nonprofits funded by the feds can provide you with some mighty nice accoutrements.

Where? And what? you may ask. We're glad you did.

WORK FOR THE HEALTH AND HUMAN SERVICES DEPARTMENT AND USE A LUXURY PRIVATE JET!

Health and Human Services secretary Mike Leavitt is one happy high-flying public servant—and we do mean high-flying. He gets to use a luxury Gulfstream III 14-seat private jet whenever he wants. Well, actually the jet is leased by the Centers for Disease Control and Prevention (CDC) to be used for emergencies only. But Leavitt is a bit . . . cavalier, shall we say, when it comes to defining the word "emergency."

In the first seven months of 2006, Leavitt had a number of "emergencies" that apparently required use of the luxury jet—to the tune of $720,000 worth of taxpayer dollars, or about $38,000 per flight. Nineteen "emergencies" like: attending news conferences, meeting with state officials, and promoting President Bush's Medicare prescription drug plan.

He was so busy on those "emergency" assignments that the CDC actually had to find *another* plane to use when faced with two bona fide emergencies (an anthrax case in Pennsylvania and a lab accident in San Juan, Puerto Rico, in which a person was exposed to radioactive material). But, hey, at least we all can relax knowing that Leavitt was comfy.

WORK FOR NASA AND NEVER FLY COMMERCIAL AGAIN!

No, we're not talking space shuttles here, but a plain old normal seven-airplane fleet—available for special official occasions related to a mission, transportation of equipment, or research.

But the folks at NASA seem to stretch the rules a little. Eighty-six percent of the time, they're using the planes for regular business—business meetings, bringing spectators to shuttle launches, going on executive retreats . . . in other words, things that don't seem quite that special.

The cost? $25 million in 2003 and 2004. And even though the Government Accountability Office has been recommending a reduction in NASA's fleet and travel budget, NASA officials actually want to go the other route and *expand* the fleet . . . for another $77 million. Gotta love those flyboys!

WORK FOR THE U.S. POSTAL SERVICE AND STAY IN LUXURY HOTEL SUITES, GET EXPENSIVE MEALS, AND TIP LAVISHLY!

Neither rain nor snow blah blah blah. Notice that the U.S. Postal Service (USPS) creed doesn't mention limos, 400-square-foot hotel suites, or gifts for *American Idol* runners-up.

Then again the slogan is intended to apply to those folk who deliver the mail, not postal service spokespersons. Like, say, Azeezaly Jaffer, vice president for public affairs and communications, to pluck a name out of the air.

Jaffer lived high on the hog in his 20-plus years at the USPS before he resigned in 2006. The USPS Office of Inspector General investigated him for the period of January 2003 to December 2005. In that time, Jaffer got a load of unusually nice perks, including a stay at a 400-square-foot Grand Hyatt suite during an official USPS event (cost: $8,252); $12,863 worth of meals at one suburban restaurant; a $5,000 meal at a D.C. restaurant (including a tip of 44%); trips to Los Angeles to meet with Warner Bros. reps, ostensibly as part of a stamp promotion program; and a party in appreciation of *American Idol* runner-up and rural postal carrier Vonzell Solomon—which was termed an "employee appreciation" event. Jaffer also gave Solomon expensive luggage . . . which allegedly came from a closet in which he kept other swag, such as pearls, digital cameras, and Movado watches—all detritus from USPS National Executive Committee events.

This is a guy who claimed that all postal service costs "fall into two basic categories: the actual costs of moving each piece of mail and the contribution each piece of mail makes to support [the USPS's] coast-to-coast network. That's not special postal accounting, that's the law."

WORK FOR THE NONPROFIT LEGAL SERVICES CORPORATION AND GET POSH MEETING SPACE (THAT YOU DON'T USE), NICE BUFFET SPREADS, AND MORE!

The Legal Services Corporation (LSC) isn't a government agency, but it does get a nice chunk of federal money—$330.8 million in 2006—to help out local nonprofit legal aid organizations around the country who offer free legal aid to the poor.

Apparently some of that $330.8 mil, though, is helping out LSC board members. Some examples: They've got ritzy headquarters on Washington's K Street—which they might be overpaying for by as much as $1.8 million. And they don't use their office for meetings, but instead go to the upscale Melrose Hotel because they want "convenience" and don't want to "feel confined." Naturally, they charge their meals there, getting such things as a $59-per-person entrée buffet and $14 "Death by Chocolate" dessert spreads. And board members just voted to raise their meal allowance by 200%. They fly first class when they have to leave D.C.; they've hired a chauffeur and car for traveling around the capital (why use a taxi?) and, speaking of taxis, someone spent $200 on a taxi ride in Ireland.

All this at the same time that the LSC reports it has had to reject about half its applicants . . . because it doesn't have enough resources.

WORK FOR THE BUREAU OF ALCOHOL, TOBACCO, FIREARMS AND EXPLOSIVES AND GET A VERY NICE OFFICE SUITE—PLUS A FLAT-SCREEN TV IN YOUR PERSONAL BATHROOM!

We all know that working for the ATF must be so horribly grueling . . . so no wonder former director Carl Truscott had to make things a little nicer for himself.

Making things nicer, in this case, meant that Truscott was forced to order design changes to the plans for the new ATF headquarters, more specifically, plans for his suite. Changes he wanted included wood floors and paneling that cost about $243,000, a retractable TV monitor, a $65,000 conference table, remote-controlled doors, and the ever-important bathroom with telephone (natch) and flat-screen TV.

But Truscott was a fair-minded fellow—he also wanted the Joint Operation Center (a nexus for agents in the field) and the gym to be mighty snazzy, too. Where the Joint Operation Center was concerned, he felt the original design was "not elaborate" enough, so he proposed a "Star Wars–type center," with a glass-enclosed VIP viewing room, another flat-screen TV, closed-circuit TV, and a theater-style layout. As for the gym? He wanted $137,000 worth of new equipment and, a must, of course, executive showers.

Shockingly, there were numerous anonymous complaints about Truscott and his desire to overspend. And, sadly, Truscott's visionary design plans wound up not being implemented. No wonder he resigned—just before the government released a report about his intended (and costly) design changes. Then again, how could he be expected to work at the ATF without that flat-screen TV by the toilet?

MONEYMAKING TIPS FROM MONEYMAKING POLITICIANS

You *too* can live like a politician! You *too* can get rich! Let's let politicians tell you how. Many of them seem to be absolute financial masters—with skills far beyond that of a Warren Buffett.

Herewith some simple ideas. Follow them and you'll have the money you dream of. (Or you'll be in jail.)

HOT MONEYMAKING TIP: *Buy house from lobbyist-run sham charity at under-market price in exchange for potential political favors.*

Representative Jim Ryun (R-KS) bought a house on Capitol Hill at $100,000 below market value—at a time when the D.C. market was red hot and houses were actually selling *above* market value. But Ryun was a savvy real estate investor: He didn't bother with brokers, but bought his house from the U.S. Family Network, a "charity" connected with Tom DeLay and Jack Abramoff.

HOT MONEYMAKING TIP: *Buy land. Arrange to have Congress approve multimillion-dollar bridge to be built near that land.*

Land is always a good investment—especially if it "happens" to lie near a major construction project, like, say . . . a

WHY YOU WANT A GOVERNMENT CREDIT CARD

If you've got an urge to splurge with your plastic, may we suggest you try to get your hands on a federal employee credit card? They seem like a great way to buy whatever you want—and on Uncle Sam's tab, to boot.

For example, U.S. Department of Agriculture employees have had a bang-up time with their government-issued credit cards. An audit looking at only 300 employees' purchases found that about 15% of them spent $5.8 million on nongovernment things like Ozzy Osbourne concert tickets, lingerie, tattoos, and bartender school tuition.

And it was similar at the Defense Department. Air Force and Navy personnel spent $69,000 on cruises, $48,250 on gambling, and $79,950 on "gentlemen's clubs" and prostitutes.

bridge that will link Nevada and Arizona. Senate Majority Leader Harry Reid (D-NV) did just that—bought a chunk of Arizona land that wasn't a bad investment on its own. Then he earmarked $18 million in federal funds for a bridge that would cross the Colorado River. Luckily for Reid's investment, the bridge would be only a few miles from his 160-acre plot of undeveloped land. Talk about your lucky breaks!

(Note: Reid's office referred reporters to a local developer who said that it was "ludicrous" to say the bridge would affect land values. But another investor who had bought land near Reid's said the proposed bridge "has already had a positive influence" on his property's value. Who to believe? Well, we know who *we* believe.)

HOT MONEYMAKING TIP: *Buy land. Arrange to have Congress approve multimillion-dollar highway to be built near it.*

Yes, this is a bit of a variation on the above. But it's not a *bridge,* it's a major *highway* that earns you your big bucks. Former House Speaker Dennis Hastert (R-IL) used this as his investment plan: he used a trust to buy 138 acres of farmland and transferred that land to a real estate development company to be used for a residential development that included over 1,600 houses, a public school, and commercial and retail businesses. And guess what? The land "happens" to be about 5.5 miles from the proposed Prairie Parkway highway—a project he strongly promoted in the House and for which he got $207 million in earmarks. Yet another brilliant real estate buying move! Who'd have guessed there might be a highway near that old farmland? Super-investor Denny Hastert, that's who!

And he is super—his partners in the trust only made a 144% profit on their estimate. Hastert's was 500%. And the highway still hasn't been built!

HOT MONEYMAKING TIP: *Buy war-related stock. Start war.*

This requires a bit more of an effort on the investor's part, since starting a war is a little difficult for many. But not for, say, hmm . . . Vice President Dick Cheney. In just one year— from 2004 to 2005 to be precise—Cheney's 433,333 stock options in Halliburton increased 3,000%, from a mere $241,498 to a rather healthy $8 million plus. This took place while Halliburton was making billions in no-bid/no-audit government contracts—over $10 billion for Iraq War–related work.

Let us be fair here, though. This nice return on investment wasn't only because of the war in Iraq. A small amount was also from post–Hurricane Katrina government contracts.

(Cheney also receives a deferred salary from Halliburton of about $200,000 a year and a pension to boot.)

In spite of his apparent moneymaking skills, Cheney insists that he's not making the windfall it appears. As he said in 2003, "Since I left Halliburton to become George Bush's vice president, I've severed all my ties with the company, gotten rid of all my financial interest. I have no financial interest in Halliburton of any kind and haven't had, now, for over three years."

For some reason, he didn't mention the fact that Halliburton has been paying him a deferred salary of about $200,000; oh, and that pension, too. Not to mention the stock options, of course.

Frankly, we think he's being a bit too modest.

HOT MONEYMAKING TIP: *Set up nonprofits. Get federal funds for nonprofits. Have nonprofits pay you and your cronies.*

But, you're thinking, nonprofits are *non*profit. In other words, there is no profit involved, right? Wrong. Wrong, that is, if you're Senator Robert Menendez (D-NJ), who can show us how to put the "profit" back into *nonprofit.* He arranged for a nonprofit community agency to get millions in federal assistance AND had that nonprofit agency rent a nice building he happened to own . . . for $300,000. Nice and simple.

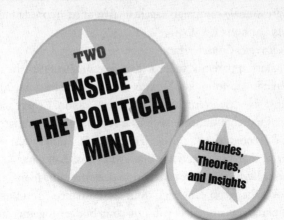

TWO

INSIDE THE POLITICAL MIND

Attitudes, Theories, and Insights

THE POLITICAL BRAIN IS A FASCINATING ONE.

Some politicians' brains, like Lincoln's, are filled with deep and profound thoughts. But the more average political brain seems filled with other things . . .

WHEN BAD THINGS HAPPEN TO GOOD AMERICANS—
OR, HOW SATAN REALLY *TRULY* AFFECTS U.S. POLITICS

Many politicians delve deep when something bad happens . . . to themselves, to their constituents, to the country. They look for complex causes and apply their superior political intellect to determining just why the "bad thing" occurred.

You might be surprised to discover what exactly is behind certain events.

Problem: Failure of conservative Republican John Jacob's congressional campaign against five-term representative Chris Cannon (R-UT)

Obvious Cause: Satan

Satan apparently took a deep personal interest in the campaign of John Jacob, who ran for Congress in 2006 against five-term representative Chris Cannon. "There's another force that wants to keep us from going to Washington, D.C.," Jacob said. "It's the devil is what it is. I don't want you to print that, but it feels like that's what it is." Satan has acted financially, hurting Jacob's business deals, freezing loans, and making the Jacob campaign difficult to finance. "You know, you plan, you organize, you put your budget together and when you have 10 things fall through, not just one, there's some other, something else that is happening," Jacob said. Asked if he actually believed that "something else" was indeed Satan, Jacob said: "I don't know who else it would be if it wasn't him. . . ."

Problem: 9/11 attacks

Obvious Cause: God's wrath

According to Senator James Inhofe (R-OK), the 9/11 attacks were quite obviously divine retribution. Simply put, God was mad about U.S. foreign policy. Apparently He felt we weren't defending Israel enough. In his (Inhofe's, not God's) words, "One of the reasons I believe the spiritual door was opened for an attack against the United States of America is that the policy of our government has been to ask the Israelis, and demand it with pressure, not to retaliate in a significant way against the terrorist strikes that have been launched against them."

Frankly, we would have preferred God had sent a brief note or something instead of an attack.

Problem: 9/11 attacks

Obvious Causes: Hillary Clinton, Ted Kennedy, Nancy Pelosi, Barbara Boxer, George Soros, Michael Moore, Bill Moyers, and Noam Chomsky

According to pundit Dinesh D'Souza's brilliant, incisive, *secular* analysis, it wasn't actually God but *liberals* who caused 9/11. These liberals (and some others) who represent the "left wing" of the Democratic Party got the Islamic world angry at the United States, and produced in the Middle East "a visceral rage—some of it based on legitimate concerns, some of it based on wrongful prejudice—but all of it fueled and encouraged by the cultural left. Thus without the cultural left, 9/11 would not have happened."

Q.E.D. That's good enough for us. (Wait a sec—Hillary is left-wing?)

Problem: Rise in Birmingham, Alabama, crime rate

Obvious Cause: Satan

Birmingham Police Chief Annetta Nunn is a devout Christian—which could be the reason she has attracted the attention of Satan. As Nunn points out, when Christians speak boldly, "Satan is going to attack." So she wonders if her own behavior and actions, including singing hymns at the funerals of three slain officers, and making speeches and writing articles mentioning God, have given the devil a personal reason for raising the homicide rate in Birmingham.

Problem: Radical Islam, smudges

Obvious Cause: Fake god, an idol

According to Lieutenant General William Boykin, the reason for radical Islam, and specifically, the *Black Hawk Down*–inspiring incident in Mogadishu, Somalia, was an idol.

"Ladies and gentlemen, this is your enemy," Boykin said

at an Oklahoma church in 2002, according to the *Los Angeles Times*. "It is the principalities of darkness. It is a demonic presence in that city that God revealed to me as the enemy." He showed a dark shadowy smudge—"a strange dark mark"—on an aerial photograph of Mogadishu as "proof." But not to worry! That smudge won't attack America. Boykin recounted his conversation with a Mogadishu warlord: "Well, you know what? I knew that my God was bigger than his. I knew that my God was a real God and his was an idol." And so God—or the president (we're not sure that the two aren't confused in Boykin's mind)—in order to protect America gave Boykin a promotion . . . to the position of deputy undersecretary of defense. We must say it's *comforting* having such nuanced intellectual firepower at the Pentagon protecting us from strange dark smudges.

THE NOT TERRIBLY BRIGHT POLITICAL CAUCUS:
A GRAB BAG OF STUPIDITY

The following politicians, we surmise, are not stupid, regardless of their behavior as indicated below. We're *sure* that if asked to take an IQ test, each one would score at least in the double digits. But perhaps we're being harsh. Let us amend that to say we are sure that each one would score in the *high* double digits.

UH—ISN'T THERE A CONTRADICTION SOMEWHERE IN THERE, JUDGE DRAYTON?

Drayton Nabers, in a campaign ad while he was running for chief justice of the Alabama Supreme Court, declared the following:

> "I will interpret the law strictly as it is written without inserting my own personal opinion. . . . I will fight

against abortion because this is against my strong Christian values."

Nabers, who was famous for posting the Ten Commandments in his courtroom, lost the election in a squeaker—by three percentage points, that one-digit number perhaps representing a significant portion of his IQ.

DEAR CONGRESSMAN MEZVINSKY—DO YOU MEAN TO SAY YOU ACTUALLY INVESTED IN ONE OF THOSE NIGERIAN E-MAIL SCAMS?

"I am Widow Mbumba James, former wife of the esteemed and tragically deceased Minister of Finance and I am in urgent need of your most felicitous help. I recently found deposited in my account 89 million US dollars and . . ."

We've all gotten these e-mails and deleted them, but former congressman Ed "Brains" Mezvinsky (D-IA)—big buddies to Hil and Bill, with son big buds with Chel—somehow actually *believed* them. Didn't he wonder *at all*, like, why Widow James selected him, of all people? Didn't he even think that maybe, just maybe, it wasn't, like, *true*?

Evidently not. And the good congressman fell for these e-mails, not just once, but many, many times. In fact, Mezvinsky fell for "just about every different kind of African-based scam we've ever seen," according to federal prosecutor Bob Zauzmer. And then the former congressman actually began *stealing* from clients and even his own mother-in-law to finance his "investments." Prosecutors claimed Mezvinsky used his ties to the Clinton family to convince others to give him money. "He was always looking for the home run. He was always trying to find the business deal that would make him as wealthy as all the people in his social circle," said Zauzmer. And what better way than to let some Widow James use your account to deposit $89 million and give you a cool $8.9 million as a fee?

Unfortunately, as most people were able to figure out all by themselves without actually contacting the good Widow, these were *all* scams. Meanwhile, Mezvinsky's son, Marc, is seriously dating Chelsea Clinton—but if marriage is on the horizon, the elder Mezvinsky won't be able to make the wedding. He's in jail, serving a seven-year sentence for fraud.

And now, Mezvinsky's wife, Marjorie Margolies-Mezvinsky, a former television reporter, has won a seat in Congress herself (D-PA). Which is why we recently sent her this e-mail: "Dear Marjorie—we are poor/rich orphans who happen to be in possession of the sum of 130 million dollars US for which we need your most gracious help. . . ."

CONGRESSMAN PATRICK KENNEDY CAN'T REMEMBER WHERE HIS CAMPAIGN HEADQUARTERS ARE

Congressman Kennedy (D-RI) is not famous as the "intellect of the House of Representatives." During his first campaign, he couldn't remember where his campaign headquarters were when asked by radio call-in voters. During a speech at the House, he lamented middle-class America's inability to "make mends meet." He also said: "I myself have educated myself about the severity of the Articles of Impeachment, and I want to share with my colleagues and the American people some of the thoughts that I have learned."

WE THINK YOU'VE STRUCK OUT, SENATOR JAMES BUNNING

The best line on the good Republican senator from Kentucky comes from *Time* magazine: "He has shown little interest in legislation that doesn't concern baseball."

Problem: Kentucky doesn't even have a major league team.

Bunning is famous in the Senate for being a bonehead—to such an extent that political observers wondered if he had Alzheimer's or dementia (he didn't—he even had a news conference and provided doctors' reports to prove it). "His is a tragic case of descent into senility," said one congressional staffer, "except without the 'descent' bit."

Bunning's genius extended to telling a group of GOP fund-raisers that his Italian-American opponent Daniel Mongiardo looked like Saddam Hussein's sons; to saying that al-Qaeda was out to get him (see page 264); and, best of all, to his pitifully stupid attempt to win his debate with Mongiardo. He said he had legislative business in Washington so he couldn't go back to Kentucky for the debate—ignoring or forgetting the fact that the Senate was in recess. Then, with Bunning participating in the debate via satellite, it became obvious to virtually everyone that he was *woodenly reading from a teleprompter,* violating the rules of the debate—and moreover, looking even less terribly bright.

Representative Lynn A. Westmoreland (R-GA) Wants a Bill to Require Display of the Ten Commandments in the U.S. Capitol . . . but Can't Remember What They Are

> TV host Steve Colbert: "What are the Ten Commandments?"
> Westmoreland: "You mean all of them?—Um . . . Don't murder. Don't lie. Don't steal. Um . . . I can't name them all."

So THAT'S why he wants them displayed!

Representative Dana Rohrabacher Speculates on Global Warming—It Could be Dinosaur Farts

Representative Dana Rohrabacher (R-CA), a defender of convicted felon-lobbyist Jack Abramoff ("He's a very honest man. A fine man") and who was affiliated with the "Left-Right Festival of Mind Liberation," is clearly an *independent* thinker.

He offered the world—and a House Science Committee hearing—his well thought out speculations as to previous causes of planetary warming: "We don't know what those other cycles were caused by in the past. It could be dinosaur flatulence."

Carrying this reason to its logical conclusion: Could Al Gore be wrong? Could today's global warming be caused, not by coal and oil, but by *human* farting? Shouldn't the eminent scientists being aggressively questioned by Rohrabacher's committee be looking into this?

FASCINATING INTELLECTUAL INSIGHTS FROM XENOPHOBIC RACIST POLITICIANS, POLITICAL PUNDITS, AND GENERAL PARANOIACS—

OR, ARE WE BEING TOO HARSH?

Politicians are not just lawmakers. They are great THINK-ERS. And they think GREAT THOUGHTS. Deep thoughts. Thoughts that make you think.

Fascinating Intellectual Insight: Jewish, Arab, and Korean shop owners all sell wilted lettuce to black people.

Political Genius: Civil rights leader and U.N. ambassador Andrew Young

Ever wonder why fresh arugula is not a soul food? According to Andrew Young, it's all because of the Jews—

nefariously acting in concert with Arabs and Koreans. These nasty ethnic groups simply won't let black people have fresh greens. Or fresh bread, for that matter. In a recent speech, Young informed the world that Jewish, Arab, and Korean shop owners had "ripped off" inner-city communities for years, "selling us stale bread, and bad meat and wilted vegetables."

Fascinating Intellectual Insight: The religion of Islam is evil, evil, evil. All of it. Or them.

Political Genius: Representative Tom Tancredo (R-CO)

Tancredo modestly proposed that the entire civilization of Islam is "a civilization bent on destroying ours." Not to be outdone, he urged the pope not to apologize for calling Islam "evil." He also cleverly proposed to bomb Mecca after any new terrorist attack on the United States. The conservative *National Review* concluded that "Tom Tancredo is an idiot."

Fascinating Intellectual Insight: Muslim jihadists are worse than the gooks!

Political Pundit Genius: Syndicated political columnist Mark Steyn

Steyn stated in his deep analysis of the Iraqi quagmire that "basically, if you want to find an exit strategy for Iraq, then pretty soon, you're going to . . . have to be finding an exit strategy for a lot of other places because those jihadists, they're not like the gooks in Vietnam. They're not just going to be content to take over Vietnam. If America pulls out of Iraq, they're going to follow us wherever we go."

Boy, and to think we once were worried about the gooks! And the Chinks!

Fascinating Intellectual Insight: We must keep all immigrants out of America, especially ragheads, to prevent their taking over Congress.

Political Genius: Representative Virgil Goode (R-VA)

First, Congressman Goode had a problem with fellow representative Keith Ellison (D-MN) being sworn into Congress using the Koran (horror of horrors!). Then he opined that "I am for restricting immigration so that we don't have a majority of Muslims elected to the United States House of Representatives." Or, as he later clarified, "If American citizens don't wake up and adopt the Virgil Goode position on immigration there will likely be many more Muslims elected to office and demanding the use of the Quran."

Then Goode maybe got a little nervous . . .

REPORTER: "So you do believe there're too many Middle Easterners here now?"
GOODE: "No, I—I said there were—and the Diversity Visa program needs to be ended. It shouldn't have been adopted to begin with, in my opinion."
REPORTER: "But do you think there are too many Middle Easterners in the United States right now?"
GOODE: "Uh—I'm not gonna say 'yes' or 'no' on that. I'd like to know the exact number. I don't have the exact numbers."

Our question: How many is too many?

Fascinating Intellectual Insight: People descended from house slaves are better in government than people descended from field slaves.

Political Genius: Don Samuels, Minneapolis City Council

Samuels argued that he was more effective in serving the city's blacks because he was descended from "house slaves" in the South, rather than "field slaves"—the type who picked cotton. He rather easily won reelection; maybe some people knew their place?

Fascinating Intellectual Insight: Women in the U.S. military have major problems with their sexuality—and their thighs.

Political Genius: Senator James Webb (D-VA)

In a *Washingtonian* magazine article entitled "Women Can't Fight," the former secretary of the Navy explained: "Many women appear to be having problems with their sexuality. . . . What kind of woman would seek out the Academy routine?" He explained that women just don't have leadership potential: "I have never met a woman, including the dozens of female midshipmen I encountered during my recent semester as a professor at the Naval Academy, whom I would trust to provide those men with combat leadership." Even when they *do* lead, apparently they should have Webb behind them. "What the whole world may not know is that women did not attain these positions in the same way that men historically have. . . . Women will not be leading men inside the brigade this year. They will be managing them, buttressed by the officers who hurried them along. And the morale of the brigade will demonstrate this distinction far better than this article ever could."

As for thighs, Webb also allegedly referred to female midshipmen as "thunder thighs."

Fascinating Intellectual Insight: Use a livestock fence to keep out human livestock, uh, Mexicans.

Political Genius: Representative Steve King (R-IA)

King not only advocated a new electrified fence to keep out those Mexican varmints, he actually "designed" one—and showed a model of it to fellow congressmen. His fence uses "the kind of current that would not kill somebody." King assured listeners that is would work just fine; after all, "we do this with livestock all the time."

Fascinating Intellectual Insight: The sun revolves around the earth—and dastardly Jews have kept that truth from the public.

Political Geniuses: Georgia state representative Ben Bridges (R) and Texas state representative Warren Chisum (R)

Chisum circulated a memo to all members of the Texas House of Representatives along with a letter from fellow law-maker Ben Bridges of Georgia. The memo offered a fascinating fact: Evolution is a plot by secretive Kabbalistic Jews to keep us from the truth, and so it shouldn't be taught in schools. In their words:

> Indisputable evidence—long hidden but now available to everyone—demonstrates conclusively that so-called "secular evolution science" is the Big-Bang 15-billion-year alternate "creation scenario" of the Pharisee Religion. This scenario is derived concept-for-concept from Rabbinic writings in the mystic "holy book" Kabbala dating back at least two millennia.

Chisum recommended a website dealing with these "facts." The website also helpfully points out that Copernicus was wrong: The sun rotates around the earth . . . something we've long suspected.

THE INTELLECTUAL POLITICIAN—

OR, POLITICIANS SHARE THEIR KNOWLEDGE IN MANY DIFFERENT AREAS

To become a politician, one usually has to go to law school, or college, or at least high school. Yes, politicians are an educated bunch. Read some insights below—and *learn*.

POLITICIANS SHARE THEIR KNOWLEDGE OF . . .
Perfect English

"Selling out my country, my state, that is beyond my amprehension. . . . Ain't no way I'm going to do it."
—SENATOR CONRAD BURNS (R-MT)

Q: "Do you think your ethical problems have contributed to the negative view that Americans have of the Republican Party and Congress right now?"
REPRESENTATIVE TOM DELAY (R-TX): "I haven't had no ethical problems."

"People are less aware of literary, poetry and history than in previous times. Literary and history give speech depth and quality."
—SENATOR ROBERT TORRICELLI (D-NJ), discussing the reasons he published two books on great speech makers and their speeches

"Tudors Needed."
—CONGRESSMAN JIM BACCHUS (D-FL), in a letter to other representatives looking for volunteers to tutor underachieving high school students

"One thing is clear, is relations between America and Russia are good, and they're important that they be good."
—PRESIDENT GEORGE W. BUSH in Strelna, Russia

POLITICIANS SHARE THEIR KNOWLEDGE OF . . .
Political History

Missouri state representative Jim Avery (R) weighed in on the 1803 Louisiana Purchase during a legislative debate about the Confederate flag. Avery was apparently convinced that the United States fought with France over the Purchase—and he wasn't just talking about haggling over price:

> "Well, we fought over it. We fought over it, right? . . .
> You don't think there were any lives lost in that? It was
> a friendly thing?"

(Avery seems to have overlooked a key word in the term "Louisiana Purchase," i.e., "purchase." Which means "to buy," not "to battle." A simple mistake . . .)

Texas House Speaker Tom Craddick (R) helped middle school students better understand the setup of the U.S. Congress . . . by telling them that there were 454 members in the House and 60 in the Senate. (Well, he's close-ish, but no cigar. Actually, there are 435 members in the House and 100 in the Senate.)

Vice President Al Gore was doing a press event at Monticello, Virginia. When faced with busts of George Washington and Benjamin Franklin, Gore turned to the curator and asked, "Who are these people?"

(Answer: Washington is often called "The Father of Our Country" since he was the first president and Franklin is often referred to as "Ben." He was pretty big back then, too.)

POLITICIANS SHARE THEIR KNOWLEDGE OF . . .
Irrefutable Logic

> "I can only impregnate. I can't get pregnant myself."
> —MISSISSIPPI STATE REPRESENTATIVE STEVE HOLLAND (D);
> and please note that Steve is *not* short for "Stephanie"

"When a storm hits, the best place to be is out of the path of the storm."
—HOMELAND SECURITY SECRETARY MICHAEL CHERTOFF, on what he learned from Hurricane Katrina

"[This is] the most expensive redevelopment project the country has ever seen. I would think, and predict, that it is going to cost money."
—SENATE MAJORITY LEADER BILL FRIST (R-TN), on the possibility of a tax increase to pay for Hurricane Katrina

"Those who enter the country illegally violate the law."
—PRESIDENT GEORGE W. BUSH

"When you're hunting for someone and you haven't found them, you haven't found them."
—SECRETARY OF DEFENSE DONALD RUMSFELD, on the hunt for Osama bin Laden

"If the Republican Party does not make substantial changes to their policies, they will largely remain the same."
—REPRESENTATIVE CORRINE BROWN (D-FL)

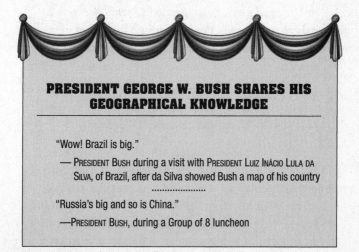

PRESIDENT GEORGE W. BUSH SHARES HIS GEOGRAPHICAL KNOWLEDGE

"Wow! Brazil is big."

— PRESIDENT BUSH during a visit with PRESIDENT LUIZ INÁCIO LULA DA SILVA, of Brazil, after da Silva showed Bush a map of his country

....

"Russia's big and so is China."

—PRESIDENT BUSH, during a Group of 8 luncheon

DEEP THOUGHTS ON HOMOSEXUALITY, COURTESY OF OUR POLITICAL LEADERS

Gay rights is a major issue. Should gays have the right to be married? Should gays be protected under antidiscrimination laws?

Many politicians have thought deeply on these issues—and have come up with profound, well-thought-out insights on homosexuality in the United States today.

SENATOR JAMES INHOFE: *He is proud that in "the recorded history" of his entire family, there is* not one *homosexual.*

Wow! Not one!

On June 6, 2006, in a speech on the Senate floor about the proposed Federal Marriage Amendment, the good Senator Inhofe (R-OK) shared with all of America his wonderful news—on the floor of the Senate in front of a photograph of him and his family.

> "As you see here, and I think this is maybe the most important prop we'll have during the entire debate, my wife and I have been married 47 years. We have 20 kids and grandkids. I'm really proud to say that in the recorded history of our family, we've never had a divorce or any kind of homosexual relationship."

Out of all of those people, too! Even Vice President Cheney can't say that. Inhofe also pointed out the evil designs of those who lobby against heterosexual beliefs:

> "The homosexual marriage lobby, as well as the polygamist lobby, they share the same goal of essentially breaking down all state-regulated marriage requirements to just one, and that one is consent. In doing so, they're paving the way for illegal protection of such practices as homosexual marriage, unrestricted

sexual conduct between adults and children, group marriage, incest, and, you know, if it feels good, do it."

Senator John McCain: *There should be—shouldn't be—should be—shouldn't be—gay marriage.*

Senator John "Straight-Shooter" McCain hasn't been shooting so, uh, *straight* recently. McCain has a dilemma. Is gay marriage evil and disgusting—and hence good fodder for getting votes from the conservative heterosexual right? Or is gay marriage tolerable and understandable—and hence good fodder for getting votes from the liberal heterosexual left and the gay conservative right?

Or maybe it's *both*?

Here's a tough, no-holds-barred, cover-all-bases answer from our "tell 'em like it is" senator on this tricky topic of gay marriage.

> **Commentator George Stephanopoulos:** "Are you against civil unions for gay couples?"
> **McCain:** "No, I'm not."
> **Stephanopoulos:** "So you're for civil unions?"
> **McCain:** "No."

Gay people everywhere are sleeping better after hearing this ringing endorsement for gay rights. (And so for that matter are conservatives, for this ringing denunciation of gay marriage.)

Mayor (and senatorial candidate) Stephen Laffey: *"I have never once seen a happy homosexual."*

We have—but we're probably not as *observant*.

Cranston, Rhode Island, mayor (until 2007) and Republican primary candidate for the U.S. Senate penned some humor columns back in his days at Bowdoin College in Maine. In a campus Republican publication, Laffey wrote, "I have never once seen a happy homosexual. This is not to say there aren't any; I simply haven't seen one in my lifetime. Maybe they are all in the closet. All the homosexuals I've seen are sickly and decrepit, their eyes devoid of life."

MAYOR (AND SENATORIAL CANDIDATE) STEPHEN LAFFEY: *Gays are destroying pop music.*

Not content with the "dead homosexual theme," Laffey also weighed in philosophically on the cause of the decline of pop music in America and England. Seems to have something to do with homosexuals, too. And communists. But we repeat ourselves.

"Why is the pop music of today so bad?" wrote Laffey. "Because it is communist to the very core. It's turning the children of America into sissies and preying on the minds of every American, making them weaker and weaker."

"Weaker and weaker." "Sissies" code for gay? We think so.

Boy George popped up as a topic, adding to our suspicions . . .

"And how about this humanoid (I'd hesitate to say person, and I would never use the word MAN) Boy George," wrote Laffey. "It wears girl's clothes and puts on makeup. When I hear it sing, 'Do you really want to hurt me, do you really want to make me cry,' I say to myself, YES, I want to punch your lights out, pal, and break your ribs. I say let's get those pinkos out of the music business and replace them with some tough conservatives."

Interestingly, Laffey commented that he never drank in college—i.e., these observations came from an absolutely untainted mind. Laffey also stated: "I never did coke. . . . I never smoked a doobie."

REPRESENTATIVE MARILYN MUSGRAVE: *The most important issue America faces is the looming specter of gay marriage.*

Forget Iraq. Forget terrorism. Forget global warming.

Marilyn Musgrave (R-CO) knows what's important. And she recently introduced a constitutional amendment to protect America. She proposes to outlaw gay marriage constitutionally. This is what she calls "the most important issue that we face today."

According to fellow congressperson Barney Frank (D-MA), "She doesn't like the idea of one gay person. So obviously the idea of two of us hanging out makes her very unhappy."

Musgrave has been applauded for her hard, firm positions on this issue, as well as for her attempts to legalize concealed weapons. In May 2006, she received an endorsement from the Ku Klux Klan.

SENATOR (NOW MAJOR LOBBYIST) RICK SANTORUM: *Gay sex equals bigamy equals collapse of universe as we know it.*

Gay sex leads to virtually anything. It's anarchic, chaotic, a looming black hole threatening to rip the very fabric of society—and perhaps the universe itself.

Former senator Santorum (R-PA) explains (italics ours):

> "If the Supreme Court says that you have the right to consensual (gay) sex within your home, then you have the right to bigamy, you have the right to polygamy, you have the right to incest, you have the right to adultery. *You have the right to anything.* Does that undermine the fabric of our society? I would argue yes, it does."

Santorum added, however, these *very tolerant* words: "That's not to pick on homosexuality. It's not, you know, man on child, man on dog, or whatever the case may be."

GOVERNOR ARNOLD SCHWARZENEGGER: *I think that gay marriage should be between a man and a woman.*

What more is there to say?

HOW TO SPOT A HOMOSEXUAL: TIPS FROM THE U.S. ARMY

The U.S. Army, under President Bill Clinton, inaugurated its "Don't Ask, Don't Tell" policy: If you're gay, don't tell the Army and you can stay in the Army.

But the Army cleverly has its methods of finding out anyway. After getting anonymous e-mails stating that a decorated sergeant and Arabic language specialist, Bleu Copas, was gay, the Army called him in for questioning in 2006. Then they asked their famous "trick gay-question"—it works every time.

The Army asked Mr. Copas: *Are you involved in community theater?*

UH, DIDN'T THE UNION WIN, GUYS? THE GRAND HIGH EXALTED UPHOLDERS OF THE CONFEDERACY AWARDS

Apparently, for some people the South never really lost the War Between the States. And so we award *Grand High Exalted Upholders of the Confederacy Awards* to some of our most *backward-looking* politicians. (Here's to 1862 and President Jeff Davis, guys!)

First, the top "General Robert E. Lee Club" awards go to two great Confederates:

GENERAL ROBERT E. LEE CLUB MEMBER #1: *Richard "The South Will Rise Again" Quinn, Senator John McCain's South Carolina state field manager, 2000, as recently as 2005 identified as McCain spokesperson*

. . . for many, many services above and beyond the call of Dixie duty, including: editorship of the neo-Confederate magazine *Southern Partisan* (which has featured ads for T-shirts applauding the assassination of Abraham Lincoln); organizing a rally of 6,000 people in support of flying the Confederate flag over the South Carolina statehouse; calling Nelson Mandela a "terrorist"; and best of all, dressing up McCain volunteers in Confederate army uniforms to hand out McCain flyers.

As for Martin Luther King Day, Quinn was agin' it, stating:

> "King Day should have been rejected because its purpose is vitriolic and profane. By celebrating King as the incarnation of all they admire, they [black leaders] have chosen to glorify the histrionic rather than the heroic and by inference they spurned the brightest and the best among their own race. Ignoring the real heroes in our nation's life, the blacks have chosen a man who represents not their emancipation, not their sacrifices and bravery in service to their country; rather, they have chosen a man whose role in history was to lead his people into a perpetual dependence on the welfare state, a terrible bondage of body and soul."

GENERAL ROBERT E. LEE CLUB MEMBER #2: *Bill "Billy Reb" Back, vice chairman of the California Republican Party*
... for publicly stating what we thought we'd never hear from a modern politico: The United States would be a better place if the Confederate South had won the Civil War.

He penned a brilliant nostalgic article titled "What if the South Had Won the Civil War?" and kindly decided to share it via e-mail with his California Republican colleagues. The problem was with the conclusion of the article—Back decided that it was too bad the South didn't win. If they had, everything would have been a lot better. For some reason, this annoyed many Republicans, particularly black Republicans who presumably would still have been slaves. One of them, Shannon Reeves, angrily wrote:

> His article concludes that problems with race relations in America are the result of slaves being freed through Reconstruction, and black migration out of the south as a result of desegregation. This article trivialized slavery and it trivialized the impacts of slavery on my ancestors and people of African descent. The notion that this country would be better off if my ancestors had remained enslaved, and considered less than whole people, is personally offensive, abhorrent, and vile.

> Back later apologized, saying he didn't really "mean it."

And now, all those other winners of our honorary Confederacy awards:

HONORARY CONFEDERATE #1: *Senator Saxby "Look Away, Look Away!" Chambliss (R-GA)*
. . . for stating, at a closed Senate Armed Services Committee meeting, "We need better intelligence. If we had better intelligence in the Civil War we'd be quoting Jefferson Davis, not Lincoln." The senator's office says he never used the word "we." Question: What word *could* he have used?

HONORARY CONFEDERATE #2: *Attorney General John Ashcroft*
. . . for praising the neo-Confederate *Southern Partisan* magazine: "Your magazine also helps set the record straight.

You've got a heritage of doing that, of defending Southern patriots like [Robert E.] Lee, [Stonewall] Jackson, and [Jefferson] Davis. Traditionalists must do more. I've got to do more. We've all got to stand up and speak in this respect or else we'll be taught that these people were giving their lives, subscribing their sacred fortunes and their honor, to some perverted agenda."

HONORARY CONFEDERATE #3: *District Judge Timothy Ellender of Terrebonne Parish, Louisiana*

. . . for showing up at a Halloween party wearing blackface, an Afro wig, prison jumpsuit, and shackles.

HONORARY CONFEDERATE #4: *Senator Trent "Pass the Sheet" Lott (R-MS)*

. . . for stating, at a meeting of the Council of Conservative Citizens, an alleged white supremacist group, that "the people in this room stand for the right principles and the right philosophy. . . . Let's take it in the right direction and our children will be the beneficiaries!" The direction implied seems to be back to 1862, although Trent tried to wiggle out by explaining he didn't really mean that. He meant something else.

HONORARY CONFEDERATE #5: *Senator Joe "I'm Jes' a Shit-Kickin' Red State Boy" Biden (D-DE)*

. . . for praising Senator Barack Obama (D-IL) as "the first mainstream African American who is articulate and bright and clean and a nice-looking guy." Unfortunately for his Confed creds, a few years back ol' Joeboy actually opposed efforts to fly the Confederate flag over the statehouse in South Carolina. Could Biden actually be a Union spy?

THE CREATIVE POLITICIAN:
FAVORITE SEX SCENES FROM POLITICIAN/ PUNDIT NOVELISTS

Politicians aren't only thinkers, they're also creative. As such, many express themselves in the form of novels. It's a chance to write something other than some dull new law or policy.

And what some of them write is certainly far from dull. Where else could one read lyrical descriptions of sex with bears, or with deer?

Meet the Author: I. Lewis "Scooter" Libby, former chief of staff to Vice President Dick Cheney

Novel: The Apprentice

The polymath Libby is not only a writer, but a lawyer and a prominent (convicted) former government official, once known at the White House as "Dick Cheney's Dick Cheney," and also by the nickname "Germ-Boy"—for obsessing over mandatory preemptive vaccination against smallpox. In his novel, the imaginative Germ-Boy (who allegedly helped think up a certain war in his spare time) offers traditional family-friendly dollops of incest, homoeroticism, bestiality, lice, mucus, torture, urine, excrement, armpits, pubic hair, pus, pedophilia, corpse robbery—and, of course, de rigueur menstrual blood.

Our Favorite Sex Scenes

He could feel her heart beneath his hands. He moved his hands slowly lower still and she arched her back to help him and her lower leg came against his. He held her breasts in his hands. Oddly, he thought, the lower one might be larger.

At age ten the madam put the child in a cage with a bear trained to couple with young girls so the girls would be frigid and not fall in love with their patrons. They fed her through the bars and aroused the bear with a stick when it seemed to lose interest. . . . "Is there feeling?" a bucktoothed man asked. "At least on the first night, after a bear?"

At length he walked around to the deer's head and, reaching into his pants, struggled for a moment and then pulled out his penis. He began to piss in the snow just in front of the deer's nostrils. . . . He asked if they should fuck the deer. [*Note: As we learn later, the answer is yes, they should.*]

Meet the Author: Senator Barbara Boxer (D-CA)
Novel: *A Time to Run*

Barbara Boxer writes about what she knows, i.e., politics, but this book is not about her, she insists. "I'm 15 years older than her," says Boxer of her protagonist Ellen Fischer. "I never sat down to write about me." This may be fortunate: *Radar* magazine in 2006 placed her at number five on its list of "America's Dumbest Congressmen," calling her "a limousine liberal running a few gallons short of a full tank." They may have a point: Boxer is the woman who once observed, "Those who survived the San Francisco earthquake said, 'Thank God I'm still alive.' But of course those who died, their lives will never be the same again." Ana Marie Cox in *The New York Times* said of Boxer's book: "Conservatives like to charge that liberals have no new ideas. Unfortunately, 'A Time to Run' seems to prove them right."

Our Favorite Sex Scenes

A ton of finely tuned muscle, hide glistening, the crest of his mane risen in full sexual display, and his neck curved in an exaggerated arch that reminded Greg of a horse he'd seen in an old tapestry in some castle in Europe Jane had dragged him to. The stallion approached, nostrils flared, hooves lifting with delicate precision, the wranglers hanging on grimly. . . . The stallion rubbed his nose against the mare's neck and nuzzled her withers. She promptly bit him on the shoulder and, when he attempted to mount, instantly became a plunging devil of teeth and hooves. . . . Greg clutched the rails with white knuckles, wondering, as these two fierce animals were coerced into the majestic coupling by at least six people, how foals ever got born in the wild. [*Note: One of the best horse sex scenes we've ever read.*]

Her skirt was very short, and Josh found himself mesmerized by her perfectly shaped, silken legs with kneecaps that reminded him of golden apples—he couldn't remember having been captivated by knees before—and her lustrous thighs. He tore his eyes away from Bianca's legs with the utmost difficulty. [*Note: Umm . . . kneecaps? Apples?*]

Meet the Author: Speaker of the House Newt Gingrich (R-GA)
Novel: *1945*
The former Speaker of the House has been married three times; during one marriage a campaign worker admitted administering oral sex to him, which evokes memories of another politician from another political party. Unfortu-

nately for the sexually minded, most of Gingrich's book is centered on the dull interiors of government offices and not the bedroom, even figuratively. A reviewer notes that the famous sexual "subplot" (as in the scenes excerpted below) "is somewhat unnecessary, at least in this volume, and appears only once more, and then briefly, making the whole thing appear like a crash publicity stunt to gain attention for the book."

Our Favorite Sex Scenes

Suddenly the pouting sex kitten gave way to Diana the Huntress. She rolled onto him and somehow was sitting athwart his chest, her knees pinning his shoulders. "Tell me, or I will make you do terrible things," she hissed.

Even though it had been only minutes since their last lovemaking, John Mayhew was as ever overwhelmed by the sight of her, the shameless pleasure she took in her own body and its effect on him. Since he wasn't sure what to say, he made a production out of lighting up and enjoying that first, luxurious after-bout inhalation.

Meet the Author: Senator James Webb (D-VA)
Novel: *Lost Soldiers*

There is something of a literary feud going on between the senator and Second Lady Cheney; she accused him of writing lurid sex scenes, and he accused her and the Republican establishment of smearing him for political gain. No matter, he won his election and his books have generally received critical and popular acclaim, despite the unfortunate scene below:

Our Favorite Sex Scene

She romped on top of Simolzak's huge frame, strad-
dling him with her hands on his chest, her back arched
and her breasts flailing wildly in the air. Her back was
to him and her long hair swung from side to side as if
accentuating the abandonment of her screams.

Meet the Author: President Jimmy Carter
Novel: *The Hornet's Nest: A Novel of the Revolutionary War*

Jimmy Carter? The name does not seem particularly connected to sex, although he did marry, father children, and
"lust in his heart," in his own words. He also lusted in print,
as this somewhat stilted and old-fashioned (should we say
biblical?) excerpt shows.

Our Favorite Sex Scene

She was overwhelmed with a desire to nurture her
husband. She soon bared her breast and held him
close against it, and he responded eagerly to this un-
precedented intimacy.

Meet the Author: Political pundit Bill O'Reilly
Novel: *Those Who Trespass: A Novel of Television and
Murder*

Another nonpolitician very closely connected with politics, Bill O'Reilly describes himself in a recent book as a "tra-
ditionalist." His book excerpted below is a racy traditional
thriller about a newsman serial killer who some say resem-
bles O'Reilly himself, as does the cop hero. Both compete for
the heart of Ashley Van Buren, a blond, sexy aristocrat turned
journalist, sort of the basic ideal woman for your prototypi-
cal adolescent. Interesting tidbit: The bathroom sex scene is
said by some to quite closely resemble the graphic sex dia-

logue alleged to have been expressed by O'Reilly to a woman who later sued him for sexual harrassment (settled out of court). O'Reilly has written a number of books, among them *The O'Reilly Factor for Kids: A Survival Guide for America's Families,* which advises the youth of America on drugs, growing up, and sex . . .

Favorite Sex Scenes

Okay, Shannon Michaels, off with those pants!

Ashley was now wearing only brief white panties. She had signaled her desire by removing her shirt and skirt, and by leaning back on the couch. She closed her eyes, concentrating on nothing but Shannon's tongue and lips. He gently teased her by licking the areas around her most sensitive erogenous zone. Then he slipped her panties down her legs and, within seconds, his tongue was inside her, moving rapidly.

Out of confusion and chaos, Ashley Van Buren had found clarity and happiness. And, as she wrapped her slender arms around Tommy's thick neck, she hoped those new feelings would deepen and last forever. . . . [Meanwhile, O'Malley] was naked and at attention.

And now, for a slightly *different* sexually related novel . . .

Meet the Author: Lynne Cheney
Novel: Sisters
Although not a politician per se, Lynne Cheney is married to the most powerful man on this and possibly other planets or realms. Dick Cheney. Interestingly, many scenes in her book seem somewhat ambiguous where sexuality is concerned. In other words, sex with men = BAD, woman-love =

GOOD. This may prompt the neutral observer to wonder about Mrs. Cheney's own inclinations. Does she enjoy sex with women? We don't know. But she sure writes about it that way. One then wonders if this attitude makes for a somewhat tepid heterosexual love life with the vice president. Which in turn prompts us to wonder, Could *sexual frustration* be at the bottom of Dick Cheney's love affair with the Iraq War, shooting friends, and making such bizarre statements on Iraq as "It's a great success" in 2006?

Mrs. Cheney vehemently defends her work and warns us not to make too much of the sex in her novels. Wolf Blitzer of CNN confronted Mrs. Cheney about the lesbianism and sex in her books:

> BLITZER: "Here's what the Democratic Party put out today, the Democratic Congressional-Senatorial Campaign Committee: 'Lynne Cheney's book featured brothels and attempted rape. In 1981, Vice President Dick Cheney's wife, Lynne, wrote a book called "Sisters," which featured a lesbian love affair, brothels and attempted rapes. . . . In 1988, Lynne Cheney wrote about a Republican vice president who dies of a heart attack while having sex with his mistress.' Is that true?"
>
> CHENEY: "Nothing explicit."
>
> BLITZER: "There's nothing in there about rape and brothels?"
>
> CHENEY: "Well, Wolf, could we talk about a children's book for a minute?"

Our Favorite Sex Scenes

The women who embraced in the wagon were Adam and Eve crossing a dark cathedral stage—no, Eve and Eve, loving one another as they would not be able to once they ate of the fruit and knew themselves as they truly were.

He kissed her, forced her lips open with his mouth. She could taste the whiskey he had been drinking, feel his whiskers and the scab on his face. A wave of revulsion swept over her, and she pushed him away.

"It's not pleasure for women. That's only how men would like it to be." She paused, then leaned forward and continued, "And it is my perfect right to be as I am, to be as God meant me to be. Why should I demean myself by pretending I find so much pleasure in the act that I would seek it as an end in itself? And that's what the devices do. They don't emancipate. They reduce a woman to the level of a prostitute."

"There are women then who enjoy—"

"Degraded women dragged down by men."

SOME EXAMPLES FROM OLDER POLITICAL SEX NOVELS

Back in 1988, *Spy* magazine excerpted a few sexual tidbits from an earlier crop of Washington insiders. Speechwriter William Safire: "[She] finally came to him in the bed and shouted 'Arragghrrorwr!' in his ear, bit his neck, plunged her head between his legs and devoured him"; pundit William Buckley: "I'd rather do this with you than play cards"; Watergate figure G. Gordon Liddy: "Tsa Li froze, her lips still enclosing Rand's glans"; and Nixon White House staffer John Ehrlichman: "It felt like a little tongue." Did they know how to write or what?!

THREE

POLITICAL SKILLS AND TALENTS

BEING A SUCCESSFUL POLITICIAN HAS ALWAYS REQUIRED specially honed skills and talents—like good public speaking, charisma, the ability to think on one's feet.

But nowadays, there's more.

Modern politicians have to be skilled at wiggling out of a sex or corruption scandal. They have to know how to pass the buck deftly when justly accused of incompetence. They have to know how to pander to every obscure special interest group under the sun.

HAIRSPLITTING

Possibly one of the most vital of political talents, hairsplitting can make or break a politician. Hairsplitting is, of course, the fine art of making extremely ridiculous distinctions to prove a point—or, more often, to get someone off your back.

Does it work? Read the examples below and be the judge. (The correct answer is *No.*)

THE "IT'S ALL IN THE TIMING" HAIRSPLIT

Representative Charles Taylor (R-NC) lunched with several lobbyists from Greenberg Traurig, of Jack Abramoff fame. A few days later, Taylor's campaign received eight checks—including one for $2,000 from Abramoff himself, and one for $1,000 from Abramoff's client, the Saginaw Chippewa tribe of Michigan. (A little bit later, Taylor "spontaneously" decided to help the Saginaws get a school construction grant from the Department of the Interior, but that's neither here nor there.)

The Associated Press termed the lunch a fund-raiser.

Nuh-unh, said Taylor. Yes, he *did* meet with a least six Abramoff-connected lobbyists on that date. But it sure wasn't a fund-raiser . . . because, as he said, he "received no checks there."

He got them later.

(Oh, he also said he doesn't remember why he met with the lobbyists in the first place, but he is sure it was "not to raise money or discuss the tribe." Funny how both of those things happened after the fact!)

THE "TEENY-TINY DIFFERENCE" HAIRSPLIT

Florida governor Jeb Bush was being harassed by anti-Republican protesters in Pittsburgh while on the way to a fund-raising event for Senator Rick Santorum (R-PA).

Media reports said that to avoid the crowd, he hid in a closet. More specifically, "a subway station supply closet."

Bush vehemently denied he hid in a closet.

It was actually a boiler room.

THE "BEING EXTREMELY SPECIFIC" HAIRSPLIT

When White House press secretary Tony Snow appeared on CNN's *Reliable Sources,* host Howard Kurtz asked him about the Iraq Study Group report, which was critical of the Bush administration's handling of the Iraq War.

> KURTZ: "They [the Iraq Study Group] also said the policy is not working."
>
> SNOW: "No, what they said is that you need a new policy."

Umm . . . okay. So they said that a new policy was needed because the old policy was working? Makes perfect sense.

THE "INNOCENT ON A TECHNICALITY" HAIRSPLIT

While running for reelection, Representative William Jefferson (D-LA) brazenly ran an ad stating, "I have never taken a bribe from anyone."

This was in response to an FBI investigation for taking bribes, in which agents videotaped Jefferson accepting a briefcase stuffed with $100,000 in cash.

But Jefferson didn't take a bribe. No sir. The money was intended for the vice president of Nigeria, not him, morons. (Of course, even though he told an informant he had indeed passed the cash to the VP, the FBI found $90,000 of it hidden in his freezer . . . but it's not a BRIBE. He's really just stealing someone else's bribe for the VP of Nigeria. Get it?

THE "IF WE DO IT, IT'S DIFFERENT" HAIRSPLIT

Representative John Boehner (R-OH) says Democrats shouldn't show pictures of flag-draped coffins from the Iraq War in political ads. It's exploitative. But Republicans CAN show pictures of flag-draped coffins from the 9/11 attacks in their ads. It's different.

Asked one reporter, What's the difference?

> BOEHNER: "You want me to describe the difference between men and women of the military out there

defending the American people, and victims—victims—of terrorist activities?"

REPORTER: "They were both killed by opponents, right? Terrorists or Islamic insurgents?"

BOEHNER: "The World Trade Center victims were victims of a terrorist act here on our shore and I think all Americans were appalled that this did in fact happen. But I think the differences, in terms of the images, are as clear as night and day."

Mmm-hmmm.

THE "I'M MORE EDUCATED THAN YOU ARE" HAIRSPLIT

National Review editor Jonah Goldberg snarkily weighed in on Democratic hypocrisy and media hype about the Representative Mark Foley (R-FL) page sex scandal—and pointed out an extremely important distinction that had heretofore been unnoticed: *Mark Foley was not a pedophile.*

As Goldberg sagely reported: "Foley may or may not be a predator, but pedophiles don't dig post-pubescent teens; ephebophiles do."

Thanks, Jonah!

THE "FRANTICALLY TRYING TO PUT A GOOD FACE ON A PITIFUL FAILURE" HAIRSPLIT

It's really not a big deal that Osama bin Laden hasn't been caught or killed, despite Bush administration vows to do so after the 9/11 attacks. The White House surely hasn't failed to do the job. Let White House homeland security and counterterrorism adviser Frances Frago Townsend explain.

CNN WHITE HOUSE CORRESPONDENT ED HENRY: "You know, going back to September 2001, the president said, dead or alive, we're going to get him. Still don't have him. I know you are saying there's successes on the war on terror, and there have been. That's a failure."

TOWNSEND: "Well, I'm not sure—it's a success that hasn't occurred yet. I don't know that I view that as a failure."

THE "IT'S ALL IN A WORD" UNSUCCESSFUL HAIRSPLIT

Senator George Allen (R-VA) had a noose hanging in his office from 1998 to 2000. When repeatedly asked about this potentially offensive knickknack, Allen explained that it was "more of a lasso" and "it has nothing to do with lynching." Finally, in 2006, he came clean and said, well, okay, it *was* a noose . . . but it was just a "little old noose."

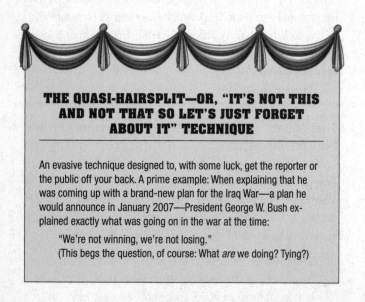

THE QUASI-HAIRSPLIT—OR, "IT'S NOT THIS AND NOT THAT SO LET'S JUST FORGET ABOUT IT" TECHNIQUE

An evasive technique designed to, with some luck, get the reporter or the public off your back. A prime example: When explaining that he was coming up with a brand-new plan for the Iraq War—a plan he would announce in January 2007—President George W. Bush explained exactly what was going on in the war at the time:

"We're not winning, we're not losing."
(This begs the question, of course: What *are* we doing? Tying?)

THE ARCANE ART OF NOT ANSWERING:
NON SEQUITURS, OBFUSCATION, AND PLAIN OLD AVOIDANCE

What do you do if you're asked a tough or embarrassing question? Or what if you're asked a question that you can't answer?

If you're a skilled politician, you don't answer it at all. Who says the public has a right to know? Instead of answering, you duck the question. Here are a number of clever and not-so-clever techniques used by our favorite politicians, their time-tested favorite ways of non-answering a question.

THE NONSENSICAL NON-ANSWER TECHNIQUE
. . . as demonstrated by Senator Joe Lieberman ("D"-CT)

> REPORTER: "Are the midterm elections a referendum on the Bush administration?"
> LIEBERMAN: "Look, I'm the only person in America who has run against the president twice, or tried to a second time. But you know, there are many things that are on people's minds."

THE "CRYPTIC, ENIGMATIC ZEN-LIKE SAY SOMETHING ELSE" NON-ANSWER TECHNIQUE
. . . as demonstrated by Senator Jim Talent (R-MO)

> REPORTER: "Are you running away from him [President Bush]?"
> TALENT: "I'm running on my record."

THE "HUMAN SHIELD NON-ANSWER—OR, 'I DARE YOU TO ASK A TOUGH QUESTION NOW' " TECHNIQUE
. . . *as demonstrated by Representative Tom Reynolds (R-NY)*

> REPORTER: "Mr. Congressman, do you mind asking the children to leave the room so we can have a private discussion on this because it's an adult topic? It just doesn't seem appropriate to me." (The reporter was referring to the Tom Foley pederasty scandal.)
>
> REYNOLDS: "Well, I'll take your questions. . . . I'm not going to ask any of my supporters to leave."

THE "THAT'S A GOOD QUESTION, BUT I'LL ANSWER AN EASIER, UNASKED QUESTION INSTEAD" TECHNIQUE
. . . *as demonstrated by Secretary of Labor Elaine Chao and a question from Representative Benjamin Cardin (D-MD) of the House Ways and Means Committee*

> CARDIN: "In the second half of 2003 the administration said that we would create 1.9 million jobs, and you fell 1.8 million short. Now, I don't remember anything extraordinary happening in the second half of 2003, but do you have a justification as to why we fell so short in the second half of 2003?"
>
> CHAO: "Let me go back to your question about the two surveys."
>
> CARDIN: "But I didn't ask a question about the two surveys, and I really—"
>
> CHAO: "Let me make a comment anyway, then. There are two surveys that the Bureau of Labor Statistics . . ."

THE "I SURE AS HELL DON'T KNOW WHAT I'M TALKING ABOUT" NON-ANSWER TECHNIQUE
. . . as demonstrated by Secretary of State Colin Powell

> REPORTER: "Where does the president stand on that?"
> POWELL: "It's not where some people say where the president is, or people who are not even in the government who claim to know where the president is. The president hasn't decided yet where he is. So I think we've been able to put it into perspective."

THE "ENIGMATIC FUCK YOU" NON-ANSWER TECHNIQUE
. . . as demonstrated by President Bill Clinton

> REPORTER: "If you had it to do over again, would you put on the nation's uniform?"
> CLINTON: "If I had to do it over again, I might answer the questions a little better. You know, I've been in public life a long time, and no one had ever questioned my role."

THE "SO I LIED BUT I DID IT ONLY BECAUSE IT WAS NECESSARY" NON-ANSWER TECHNIQUE
. . . as demonstrated by President George W. Bush

> REPORTER: "Last week you told us that Secretary Rumsfeld will be staying on. Why is the timing right now for this, and how much does it have to do with the election results?"
> BUSH: "No, you and [reporters Terrence] Hunt and [Richard] Keil came in the Oval Office, and Hunt asked me the question one week before the campaign, and basically it was, Are you going to do something about Rumsfeld and the vice president? And my an-

swer was, They're going to stay on. And the reason why is I didn't want to inject a major decision about this war in the final days of a campaign. And so the only way to answer that question and to get you on to another question was to give you that answer."

THE "COVER ALL BASES" NON-ANSWER TECHNIQUE
. . . as demonstrated by health and human services secretary Richard Schweiker

REPORTER: "Will the Consumer Price Index be revised?"
SCHWEIKER: "Let me be explicit. This administration may be looking at across-the-board revision, or non-revision, of the index."

THE "I'M JUST GOING TO KEEP ON TALKING ABOUT WHAT I'M TALKING ABOUT AND NOT EVEN LISTEN TO OR ANSWER YOUR QUESTION, YOU DIPLOMATIC DILDO" TECHNIQUE
. . . as demonstrated by Secretary of State Condoleezza Rice

FORMER AMBASSADOR PETER GALBRAITH: "How do you reconcile your supposed Kurdish commitment to Iraq with the fact that 1.7 million Kurds—80% of Kurdistan's adults—had recently signed a petition asking for a vote on independence?"
RICE: "Such referenda on independence have taken place in lots of places, including, for instance, Canada to our north. And so what I have found interesting and I think important is the degree to which the leaders of the Shia and Kurdish and Sunni communities have continually expressed their desire to have a unified Iraq."

THE "I SUPPORT THE TROOPS SO SHUT UP" TECHNIQUE
. . . *as demonstrated by Representative Eric Cantor (R-VA)*

FOX NEWS HOST NEIL CAVUTO (ABOUT REPRESEN-
TATIVE JOHN MURTHA'S PROPOSAL ON U.S. TROOPS
IN IRAQ): "Let's break down what the congressman
wants to do, sir. A lot of people even within your
party are saying some of this isn't so crazy. When he
talks about voting on the resolution, he also talks
about the idea that you certify [that] the troops who
do come are fully combat ready. That the deployments shouldn't be extended beyond one year. The
troops have to have at least one year at home between
deployments. The stop-loss program where soldiers
are to extend their enlistment period is prohibited.
What do you make of that?"

CANTOR: "Neil, let's remember, we're at war right
now. We have real lives, men and women on the bat-
tlefield, in the arena in Baghdad as we speak. First of
all, what kind of message is that to them? We have to
give them everything they need right now to fight and
win this war."

THAT WAS THEN, THIS IS NOW—
OR, "I NEVER SAID THAT . . ."

It's a woman's prerogative to change her mind, as the old
saying goes. Substitute "politician" and you're on to something.

Indeed, politicians have an enviable knack for not only
changing their minds, but also blithely pretending that they
never said what they initially said in the first place. A few recent examples of this truly necessary political skill:

PRESIDENT GEORGE W. BUSH

Then: We have to get our hands on Osama.

"The most important thing is for us to find Osama bin Laden. It is our number one priority and we will not rest until we find him." (September 13, 2001)

Then, a Little Later: Osama? *So* not important.

"I don't know where bin Laden is. I have no idea and really don't care. It's not that important. It's not our priority. . . . I am truly not that concerned about him." (March 13, 2002)

Now: Yup, we have to get our hands on Osama all right.

"Bin Laden and his terrorist allies have made their intentions as clear as Lenin and Hitler before them. The question is: Will we listen? Will we pay attention to what these evil men say? America and our coalition partners have made our choice. We're taking the words of the enemy seriously. We're on the offensive, and we will not rest, we will not retreat, and we will not withdraw from the fight, until this threat to civilization has been removed." (September 5, 2006)

Interesting (possibly coincidental) event that happened in the meantime: Didn't get Osama, couldn't get Osama, voters want me to get Osama. (Or else he's already dead. . . .)

PRESIDENT GEORGE W. BUSH

Then: The key thing is to stay the course in Iraq.
In his own (repeated) words:

"We will stay the course until the job is done. . . . And the temptation is to try to get the president or somebody to put a timetable on the definition of getting the job done. We're just going to stay the course." (December 15, 2003)

"And so we've got tough action in Iraq. But we will stay the course." (April 5, 2004)

"And my message today to those in Iraq is: We'll stay the course." (April 13, 2004)

"And that's why we're going to stay the course in Iraq. And that's why when we say something in Iraq, we're going to do it." (April 16, 2004)

"We will stay the course, we will complete the job in Iraq." (August 4, 2005)

"We will stay the course." (August 30, 2006)

Now: **Stay the course? Never felt that way.**

In Bush's own words to news analyst George Stephanopoulos in 2006: "Well, hey, listen, we've never been 'stay the course,' George."

Interesting (possibly coincidental) event that happened in the meantime: Mission not accomplished after all. "Stay the course" now political dud.

VICE PRESIDENT DICK CHENEY

Then: **Getting Saddam not worth American lives.**

After the Persian Gulf War in 1992, Cheney explained:

"And the question in my mind is how many additional American casualties is Saddam worth? And the answer is not very damned many. So I think we got it right, both when we decided to expel him from Kuwait, but also when the president made the decision that we'd achieved our objectives and we were not going to go get bogged down in the problems of trying to take over and govern Iraq."

Now: **Getting Saddam worth a *lot* of American lives.**
In the midst of the Iraq War in 2007, Cheney reexplained:

"It is the kind of conflict that's going to drive our policy and our government for the next 20 or 30 or 40 years. We have to prevail and we have to have the stomach for the fight long term. . . . The pressure is from some quarters to get out of Iraq. If we were to do that, we would simply validate the terrorists' strategy that says the Americans will not stay to complete the task, that we don't have the stomach for the fight."

Interesting (possibly coincidental) event that happened in the meantime: Became vice president. Started new and improved, Halliburton-friendly war.

Mayor Rudy Giuliani

Then: **I'm against a ban on partial-birth abortions—and that won't change.**

When getting set to run for Senate against Hillary Clinton in 1999, New York mayor Giuliani was asked whether he supported a ban on partial-birth abortions. The answer (several times)? Absolutely not! "I have not supported that, and I don't see my position on that changing" (February 1999). He expounded upon this in a 2000 interview with journalist George Will:

WILL: "Is your support of partial-birth abortion firm?"
GIULIANI: "All of my positions are firm. I have strong viewpoints. I express them. And I—I do not think that it makes sense to be changing your position. . . ."

Now: I'm FOR a ban on partial-birth abortions—and THAT won't change.

In a 2007 Fox News interview, Giuliani held forth on his theoretically unchanged position:

> GIULIANI: "Partial-birth abortion? I think that's going to be upheld. I think that ban's gonna be upheld. I think it should be. I think as long as there's a provision for the life of the mother then that's something that should be done."
>
> SEAN HANNITY: "There's a misconception that you support a partial-birth abortion."
>
> GIULIANI: "Well, if it doesn't have provision for the mother then I wouldn't support the legislation. If it has provision for the life of the mother then I would support. And I do."

Interesting (possibly coincidental) event that happened in the meantime: Realized he has to sound like a conservative as he runs for president

SENATOR JOE LIEBERMAN ("D"-CT)

Then: I demand that the Bush administration hand over all documents relating to the handling of Hurricane Katrina in New Orleans.

Outraged Joe "I Care" Lieberman criticized the Bush administration for its handling of Hurrican Katrina—and its refusal to release pertinent documents. Said the senator and senatorial candidate sternly: "[There are] too many important questions that cannot be answered. [The panel] did not receive information or documents showing what actually was going on in the White House."

Now: Documents, shmocuments. It's not necessary at all.

Not-outraged Joe "I Won the Election Now" Lieberman decided that the Hurricane Katrina info wasn't that important after all. As chair of the Senate Homeland Security and Governmental Affairs Committee, he decided not to pursue the matter. His spokeswoman, Leslie Phillips, explained: "The senator now intends to focus his attention on the future security of the American people and other matters and does not expect to revisit the White House's role in Katrina."

Interesting (possibly coincidental) event that happened in the meantime: Switched from being a Democrat to a "Democrat" after losing the Democratic primary in Connecticut—that is, got major backing from Republicans, supports Bush on the Iraq War, and said he probably will vote Republican on certain issues.

Senator John McCain (R-AZ)

Then: **Defense Secretary Donald Rumsfeld is one heckuva guy whom all should respect.**

In 2006, when Rumsfeld resigned, McCain stated that "while Secretary Rumsfeld and I have had our differences, he deserves Americans' respect and gratitude for his many years of public service."

Now: **Donald Rumsfeld was one of the worst defense secretaries EVER.**

In 2007, while making a speech at a retirement community, McCain sounded a little less than respectful or grateful: "I think that Donald Rumsfeld will go down in history as one of the worst secretaries of defense in history."

Interesting (possibly coincidental) event that happened in the meantime: Decided to run for president . . . and realized that most of the public wasn't that nuts about Rummy.

SENATOR JOHN MCCAIN (R-AZ)

Then: These two businessmen (Sam and Charley Wyly) are bad and they are using "dirty money" to pay for TV ads.

Back in 2000, McCain got very miffed ("ballistic" might be the better term) when the Wylys paid for pro-Bush TV ads that cast a bad light on McCain's record. The senator said this was "dirty money" and didn't belong in politics.

Now: I'll take some of that "dirty money," thanks.

In 2006, McCain allowed the Wylys to host a fund-raiser for him AND took a $20,000 donation from them . . . which he had to return since Sam and Charley are reportedly under federal investigation.

Interesting (possibly coincidental) event that happened in the meantime: Well, it costs a lot to run for president, you know. . . .

SENATOR JOHN MCCAIN (R-AZ)

Then: I deplore negative campaign ads, like the Swift Boat ads against John Kerry.

In 2004, when Kerry was being hammered by the non-official Swift Boat ads, McCain was swift (sorry!) to decry them and say it was a perfect example of reprehensible negative-attack politics.

Now: The guy behind the Swift Boat ads is one of my fave advisers!

When rounding up people to fill important campaign spots, McCain picked Terry Nelson as one of his top advisers. Nelson happened to be a consultant for one of the main Swift Boat people . . . and produced a highly provocative (read: People got pissed off) ad for the Tennessee Senate race that "implied" that African-American Democratic candidate

Harold Ford fooled around with white women. Not that it was racist or negative or anything . . .

Interesting (possibly coincidental) event that happened in the meantime: Can you say "presidential campaign"?

GOVERNOR MITT ROMNEY

Then: **Gay and lesbian rights are important. I love those gay folks!**

In 1994, the gay folks' pal Mitt (R), then running for U.S. Senate, sent a letter to the Log Cabin Club of Massachusetts (the gay Republican group), saying he'd be a better gay advocate than Senator Edward Kennedy. While he was against same-sex marriages, Romney was pretty chummy with the gay community. For example, while running for governor in 2002, he handed out pink flyers at a gay pride parade, wishing attendees "a great Pride weekend." In his words, "[The gay and lesbian community] needs more support from the Republican Party." "We must make equality for gays and lesbians a mainstream concern."

Now: **Gay folks? What gay folks?**

In 2006 and 2007 (when his term as Massachusetts governor ended), the straight folks' pal Mitt stopped talking about the need to protect gays from discrimination and instead started talking traditional (read: man-woman and no variations on that theme) marriage with his very vocal support of a constitutional amendment banning same-sex marriage: "I agree with 3,000 years of recorded history. I believe marriage is a sacred institution between a man and a woman and I have been rock solid in my support of traditional marriage. Marriage is first and foremost about nurturing and developing children. It's unfortunate that those who choose to defend the institution of marriage are often demonized."

Interesting (possibly coincidental) event that happened in the meantime: Decided to run for president.

GOVERNOR MITT ROMNEY

Then: **Abortion should remain legal.**

Romney said in 1994, "I believe that abortion should be safe and legal in this country. I have since the time that my mom took that position when she ran in 1970 as a U.S. Senate candidate."

Now: **Abortions are not good things.**

While still governor, Romney said he would sign a bill outlawing abortion, even in cases of rape or incest. In 2006 he explained that his philosophy had "evolved and deepened. . . . My political philosophy is pro-life."

Interesting (possibly coincidental) event that happened in the meantime: Did we mention he had decided to run for president?

SENATOR FRED THOMPSON

Then: **Abortion is a right and I support that constitutional right.**

When ol' Fred was running for a Tennessee U.S. Senate seat back in 1993, he stated in an interview with the Memphis *Commercial Appeal* that he "supports the Supreme Court's *Roe v. Wade* decision that established a constitutional right to abortion." *The Washington Post* also reported that Thompson supported a woman's constitutional right to abortion. In fact, Thompson checked a box on a campaign form stating: "Abortion should be legal in all circumstances for the first three months."

Now: **Doesn't remember checking the box saying that abortion should be legal.**

In an interview with Sean Hannity on Fox News in 2007, Thompson decided that he "always" thought the *Roe v. Wade* decision was "wrong"—a matter better left to the states, not the Feds. Like, duh!

Interesting (possibly coincidental) event that happened in the meantime: Running for office as a red-state conservative.

SENATOR JAMES WEBB (D-VA)

Then: Bill Clinton was a really, really bad guy.

In 2000, the Republican Webb, while endorsing fellow Republican George F. Allen for Senate, said the Clinton administration was "the most corrupt administration in modern memory."

Now: Bill Clinton is a really, really great guy.

In 2006, the *Democrat* Webb had Bill Clinton headline a fund-raiser for him.

Interesting (possibly coincidental) event that happened in the meantime: Just a wild guess, but could switching parties have something to do with this?

GOOD WAYS TO GET OUT OF TROUBLE, PART 1:
CREATIVE POLITICAL EXCUSES

Inevitably, politicians get into trouble. Maybe they get caught with their hands too deep in the till, maybe a little sex scandal or scatological perversion gets out, maybe a lie or two gets the attention of the Fibbies. Problems are inevitable—but the good politician knows how to wiggle out of virtually anything. The key is the *creative excuse*—an excuse that deftly shifts the blame, gets the public or the feds off your back, and puts you squarely where you belong: blamelessly taking money from voters.

Below we've highlighted the best or most common political excuses, along with examples from some of their practitioners.

The "Scientific Theoretical Memory-Recall Problematics" Method

Description: Uses memory experts to explain in dull scientific jargon that it's really impossible to remember *anything* correctly, so you'd better not trust what you hear, except for what the defense lawyers say.

Example in Action: I. Lewis "Scooter" Libby, former chief of staff to Dick Cheney (who had been accused of revealing CIA officer Valerie Plame's identity), was charged with five felony counts (and ultimately convicted of four), including lying to a grand jury and lying to FBI investigators.

The initial keystone to Libby's defense: a very bad memory. His lawyers said memory expert Dr. Robert Bjork would show how any false statements Scoot made could have been the result of "flaws in memory." They added that Bjork might also show how the three main witnesses for the prosecution, all of whom remember Scoot saying something he now says he never said, could all have flawed memories, too! In short, everyone has flawed memories, except for the lawyers! It all has something to do with how brains work. In the old days this sort of thing was called "having a convenient memory" and "lying"; we now realize it has something to do with neurochemicals. Not surprisingly, the judge denied this type of creative defense, which pundit Richard Cohen once cleverly termed "Acquired Amnesia Syndrome."

The "Incomplete Recollection, but at Least I Checked" Method

Description: A variation on the scientific method, but do-it-yourself. The key idea is the same: Memories fade, or at least the *details* fade. People forget the minor details, such as anniversary dates, their grades in chem class, their first names.

Example in Action: City Councilwoman Yvette Clarke (D), running in New York's 11th District in 2006, claimed on her website that she graduated from prestigious Oberlin College in Ohio. Problem is, she hadn't. So did she lie?

No! She just *forgot* she never graduated from college. It simply slipped her mind!

> "I spent much of the day today in contact with Oberlin College and Medgar Evers College to retrieve my academic records from two decades ago, convinced of my recollection that I had fulfilled the requirements for a bachelor's degree. Contrary to that recollection, I have now discovered that I remain two classes short of the requirements for my degree. This is an embarrassing moment for me, but I feel it is important to set the record straight."

This is one of the most believable and convincing excuses we've ever heard.

THE GRAMMATICAL METHOD

Description: Another creatively scientific method, this one focuses on the fascinating philological and grammatical ambiguity of words. It is best used by politicians caught with their pants down.

Examples in Action:

Example #1: President Bill Clinton immediately comes to mind—with his trendsetting questions, "What is sex?" and "What is 'is'?"

As he posited, is a blow job really sex? Or is it just a blow job? Fascinating stuff, that. As for the "is" matter, Clinton observed the ambiguity of "is"—i.e., "is" is *temporal,* it refers to "now," so when Mr. Clinton was not being serviced by Ms. Lewinsky, the relationship was not happening, and hence wasn't real. In other words, in his case, "is" "wasn't."

Example #2: President George Bush's pants were hitched up, but his brain was in a different place when, on October 25, 2006, he clearly asserted "absolutely, we're winning" the war in Iraq. When reporters questioned whether this assertion was really correct (it sure looked like "losing" to everyone else), White House press secretary Tony Snow took up the grammatical defense in a deft way that would have done Clinton proud. Snow questioned the meaning of the offending word (not "blow job" but "winning"). Then he tossed out a mini-essay on English grammar: "It's one of those things where you end up . . . trying to summarize a complex situation with a single word or gerund, and—or even a participle." Snow also helpfully tossed in the future tense of the verb "win," saying "we will win and we have to win."

The "Blame It on the Other Guy" Method

Description: Banal, yes, mundane, of course—but a method anyone with a sibling knows all to well: Throw the blame onto your sister or little brother. Or the dog. Or cat. Or the opposing candidate.

Example in Action: In late October 2006, a liberal blogger, attending a rally for conservative Republican senator George Allen at a Charlottesville, Virginia, hotel, was held in a choke hold and then slammed to the floor by Allen staffers, with the senator in attendance. This sort of thing does not usually happen at your better political rallies, and it tends to look bad to the voters. Unfortunately for candidate Senator George Allen, it was all caught on videotape, so the "it never even happened" convenient excuse couldn't be used.

So Allen did the next best thing—he blamed his opponent, Democrat James Webb. "It was typical of the Webb campaign, wanting to provoke an incident," Allen said. No matter that he didn't enlighten anyone as to how he knew Webb had done it, nor did he say how the incident was "provoked" in the first place, nor did he provide any evidence that the blogger even worked for the Webb campaign at all. As anyone who used this technique as a child is aware, there is the fatal flaw in this method—it usually doesn't work because everyone else has tried it, too, and knows the routine. Interestingly enough, the somewhat immature Allen lost the election.

THE "I'M NOT DRUNK, I TOOK AMBIEN AND HAD TO VOTE AT MIDNIGHT" METHOD

Description: There are many variations on this theme. Use of Ambien is optional; Xanax or any other prescription drug is perfectly acceptable.

Example in Action: This was tried by the well-described "tow-headed son of the ruddy senior senator from Massachusetts," namely Representative Patrick Kennedy (D-RI), who happened to inopportunely slam his Mustang into an antiterrorism barrier at the U.S. Capitol in Washington, D.C., in the very early hours of the morning. His car lights were off even though it was dark, which provided officers with a clue that this was not a man in perfect control of himself or his car. Kennedy informed the probably skeptical police officers that he was merely in a hurry for a special 3 A.M. vote at the House of Representatives. This sounded a little bizarre (since when does Congress meet at 3 A.M.?), so then Kennedy threw out the helpful fact that he had taken Ambien, a sleeping pill. Of course, he hadn't been *drinking.*

This method didn't work well, which led to Kennedy's use of another excuse (see below).

THE "LEARN FROM ME, A BRAVE RECOVERING ADDICT, CAN'T TALK NOW I'M OFF TO REHAB BUT LET'S TALK LATER" METHOD

Description: When all else fails, get public sympathy and start talking "healing" and "helping," then run off to some (preferably southwest) rehab center. If religious, mention God or variants thereof.

Example in Action: Our aforementioned "tow-headed son of the ruddy senior senator," namely Patrick Kennedy, quickly saw that his Ambien excuse for plowing his car into a Capitol roadblock wasn't playing well in Peoria. So when the story hit the media, he started talking depression, drug and alcohol addiction and then masterfully threw in an empathetic little bit about what a helpful caring guy he was—in effect, he crashed his car into that barrier for us all, so that he could talk about it and help us. Jesus comes to mind. As he [Kennedy, not Jesus] said, "I hope my openness today and in the past, and my acknowledgment that I need help, will give others the courage to get help, if they need it."

THE "I JUST DISCOVERED I'M JEWISH AND IT'S A HOLY DAY" METHOD

Description: Helpful in getting out of obligations.

Example in Action: Senator George Allen of Virginia scheduled a hearing of the Senate Small Business and Entrepreneurship Committee on a Monday when he was supposed to be campaigning. So he peremptorialy rescheduled it for Tuesday. Why? A spokesperson explained: "He's Jewish and Monday is Yom Kippur."

A touching incident, actually: Allen, who hadn't even

known he was Jewish until it had been revealed by his mother a few weeks earlier (he had been raised Episcopalian and claimed he often ate pork), suddenly discovering the joys and *advantages* of the Jewish faith.

THE "EVIL TEENAGERS *FORCING* GULLIBLE POLITICIANS TO ENGAGE IN ILLICIT/ILLEGAL SEX—AND BESIDES, IT'S THE PARENTS' FAULT ANYWAYS" METHOD

Description: Those teens! It's their fault, not the good politicians (as long as he's from your political party).

Example in Action: Representative Mark Foley (R-FL), caught text-messaging rather lurid and sexually explicit messages to underage teenage congressional pages, seemed about as guilty of pederasty as they come. But no, he wasn't.

Loyal Republican representative Chris Cannon (R-UT) trotted out his "evil Teenager excuse" to explain how poor Representative Foley was actually tricked by a group of egregiously mischievous teens. "These kids are actually precocious kids," Cannon told KSL Radio's *Nightside*. "It looks like, uh, maybe this one e-mail is a prank where you had a bunch of kids sitting [around] egging this guy on."

In other words, they *tricked* Foley into writing "Do I make you horny?"

And what about Speaker of the House Dennis Hastert? Shouldn't he have been handling the crisis better—getting rid of Foley and protecting the pages? Our loyal Republican representative Cannon explains that it wasn't Hastert's responsibility, either. "Frankly, this is the responsibility of the parents," Cannon said. "If you get online you may find people who are creepy. There are creepy people out there who will do and say creepy things. Avoid them. That's what you have to . . ."

Not that Foley was being creepy, of course.

GOOD WAYS TO GET OUT OF TROUBLE, PART 2:

TIME-HONORED "IT WASN'T MY FAULTS"

While some politicians get creative when it comes to making excuses, some are traditionalists. They prefer to hew to the tried-and-true methods that, while sometimes a little *tired*, still do the trick. (Kind of.)

Well, at least the politicians should get an "A" for effort.

Here are a few of the most commonly used explanations that are supposed to make a digression oh-so-understandable.

THE "I WASSH REALLY DRUNK" EXCUSE

A very popular excuse in D.C., much more popular than the related "I was really high" (which, come to think of it, actually hasn't been used that often other than by former D.C. mayor Marion Barry), since drugs are illegal and alcohol isn't.

Example in Action:

The excuser: Representative Bob Ney (R-OH)

What he was making an excuse about: Helping out clients of now-convicted uber-lobbyist Jack Abramoff—in return for trips, campaign contributions, high-priced meals at Jack's restaurant, and free fund-raising events

His explanation: "I have gone through a great deal of soul searching recently, and I have come to recognize that a dependence on alcohol has been a problem for me. I am not making any excuses, and I take full responsibility for my actions."

Translation: "I know I'm saying I'm not making any excuses, but I am, since it really wasn't my fault since I was bombed so much of the time."

Extra credit for: Entering rehab—which is designed to prove 1) he really *is* an alcoholic, and 2) he wants to change. (Also a nice move to garner a bit of sympathy.)

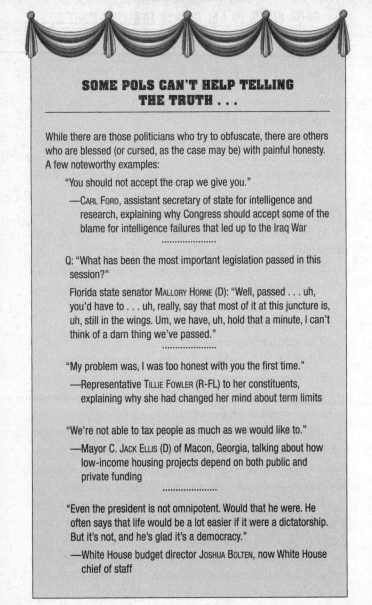

SOME POLS CAN'T HELP TELLING THE TRUTH . . .

While there are those politicians who try to obfuscate, there are others who are blessed (or cursed, as the case may be) with painful honesty. A few noteworthy examples:

"You should not accept the crap we give you."

—CARL FORD, assistant secretary of state for intelligence and research, explaining why Congress should accept some of the blame for intelligence failures that led up to the Iraq War

. . . .

Q: "What has been the most important legislation passed in this session?"

Florida state senator MALLORY HORNE (D): "Well, passed . . . uh, you'd have to . . . uh, really, say that most of it at this juncture is, uh, still in the wings. Um, we have, uh, hold that a minute, I can't think of a darn thing we've passed."

. . . .

"My problem was, I was too honest with you the first time."

—Representative TILLIE FOWLER (R-FL) to her constituents, explaining why she had changed her mind about term limits

"We're not able to tax people as much as we would like to."

—Mayor C. JACK ELLIS (D) of Macon, Georgia, talking about how low-income housing projects depend on both public and private funding

. . . .

"Even the president is not omnipotent. Would that he were. He often says that life would be a lot easier if it were a dictatorship. But it's not, and he's glad it's a democracy."

—White House budget director JOSHUA BOLTEN, now White House chief of staff

"I've had just about all of this good government stuff I can stand."

—Louisiana state senator CHARLES JONES (D), during a debate in the Louisiana Legislature

....

"My colleagues and I are upset by this blatant attempt to replace diversity with fairness."

—JOSEPH DORIA, Democratic leader in the New Jersey Assembly, on a bill repealing racial and gender preferences; as quoted in the *New Jersey Law Journal*. (Not surprisingly, he later denied saying this.)

THE "I WAS DRUNK AND ABUSED" EXCUSE

A variation on the above—not as commonly used, but packs a nice double whammy of "please forgive me for I couldn't help myself." Consider this pretty much a "throw it all at the wall to see if something sticks" excuse.

Example in Action:
The excuser: Representative Mark Foley (R-FL)
What he was making an excuse about: Racy and explicit instant messages with an underage male page
His explanation: Actually, Foley offered no public statement other than to say he was checking into rehab for alcoholism and "other behavioral issues." His lawyer also let the public know that Foley said he was gay . . . and he had

been abused by a clergyman when he was 13, but added that he didn't blame his troubles on "the trauma he sustained as a young adolescent" and that "he reiterates unequivocally that he has never had sexual conduct with a minor."

Translation: "The fact that I'm not saying it wasn't my fault makes me look like a better guy. Oh, and did I mention I was abused?"

Extra credit for: Resigning. Plus he gets points for finally admitting he is gay. (Only a few months after the public knew about it and several years after D.C. insiders first knew.)

THE "I HAD WAAY TOO MUCH WORK" EXCUSE

A great way of not only passing the buck but making it seem like you're truly on the ball doing all sorts of great stuff for the American public in general.

Example in Action:

The excuser: Speaker of the House Dennis Hastert (R-IL)

What he was making an excuse about: Not acting quickly enough about accusations of racy and explicit behavior on the part of Representative Mark Foley toward underage male pages

His explanation: "I don't recall [Representative Tom] Reynolds talking to me about that. If he did, he brought it in with a whole stack of things, and I think if he would have had that discussion, he would have said it was also resolved, because my understanding now is that it was resolved at that point. The family had gotten what it wanted to get."

Translation: "I didn't do anything about it because I didn't want to make waves."

The "It Was Just One of Those Inadvertent Mistakes" Excuse (aka "I accidentally overlooked it," "I didn't notice anything wrong at the time," and so forth)

One of the lamest tried-and-true excuses; essentially involves admitting there was an error made, but, hey, it was a simple oversight, no harm meant.

Example in Action:

The excuser: Representative Alan Mollohan (D-WV)

What he was making an excuse about: Misstatements about a dozen transactions (primarily involving real estate) on his financial disclosure forms

His explanation: "[I discovered] a limited number of inadvertent errors. . . . [I have amended the forms] to correct any inaccurate impressions about my finances."

Translation: "Damn. Busted."

Extra credit for: Throwing "limited" in there to modify "inadvertent errors." Sounds ever so much more plausible.

The "I Was Misunderstood" Excuse

Handy because it puts the onus on the listeners, the press, and so forth, but rather clumsy. Unless perfectly executed, the user of the "I was misunderstood" runs the risk of having his excuse become more analyzed than his transgression.

Example in Action:

The excuser: Senator George Allen (R-VA)

What he was making an excuse about: Calling an Indian-American cameraman—part of his opponent's campaign team—"Macaca," which was taken to be a racist comment. "This fellow here, over here with the yellow shirt, Macaca, or whatever his name is. He's with my opponent. . . . Let's give a welcome to Macaca here. Welcome to America and the real world of Virginia."

His explanation: "I'm concerned that my comments at Breaks Interstate Park on August 11th have been greatly misunderstood by members of the media. In singling out the Webb campaign's cameraman, I was trying to make the point that Jim Webb had never been to that part of Virginia—and I encouraged him to bring the tape back to Jim and welcome him to the real world of Virginia and America, outside the Beltway, where he has rarely visited. I also made up a nickname for the cameraman, which was in no way intended to be racially derogatory. Any insinuations to the contrary are completely false."

Translation: "Okay, so it was a racist comment, but let's just forget about it, okay? I mean, I'm campaigning here."

Extra credit for: Truly flogging a dead horse with his endless attempts at explanation/excuses and trying desperately to turn them into a nice stump speech: "Yesterday I apologized to anyone who may have been offended by the misinterpretation of my remarks. That was certainly not my intent. On every stop on my Listening Tour, I have talked about one of my missions for this country—to make it a land of opportunity for all. I have worked very hard in the Senate to reach out to all Americans—regardless of their race, religion, ethnicity, or gender. And I look forward to continuing to advocate this important mission for America's future."

THE "YOU GUYS JUST DIDN'T GET IT" EXCUSE

A variation of the above, used when a joke falls flat.

Example in Action:
The excuser: Senator John Kerry (D-MA)
What he was making an excuse about: Trying to bash Bush and the Iraq War with a joke: "Education—if you make

the most of it and you study hard and you do your home-work, and you make an effort to be smart, you can do well. If you don't, you get stuck in Iraq."

His explanation: Statement number one? It was a "botched joke." See, he wasn't dissing the soldiers, but "the president who got us stuck there." He even produced his notes to prove this. The joke *was* different on them, but for some reason he apparently felt compelled to improvise.

Translation: "Well, I thought it was really funny . . . until everyone got all upset about it."

Extra credit for: Totally capitulating when statement number one didn't win over the hearts and minds of the American public *or* press. He issued statement number two, a full-out apology—"I sincerely regret that my words were misinterpreted to wrongly imply anything negative about those in uniform and I personally apologize to any service member, family member, or American who was offended"—that still kept the "You didn't get it" flag waving.

THE "IT'S A CONSPIRACY, I TELL YOU!" EXCUSE

Favored by those who are either slightly paranoid or those who are trying to pin the blame for his or her woes on political enemies. Most prominently used by Hillary Clinton—à la "vast right wing conspiracy"—to explain why she and her hub were being beleaguered by allegations ranging from Whitewater to Monica's blow job. In her words: "The great story here for anybody willing to find it and write about it and explain it is this vast right-wing con-spiracy that has been conspiring against my husband since the day he announced for president." (Note: She never quite explained how the right-wingers must have gotten Monica to flash her thong at Bill. Lucianne Goldberg, maybe . . . ?)

Example in Action:

The excuser: Representative Curt Weldon (R-PA)

What he was making an excuse about: Allegedly trading political favors for lobbying and consulting contracts for his daughter—which led to a Justice Department investigation

His explanation: It was a "liberal conspiracy" led by the Democrats. He singled out Citizens for Responsibility and Ethics in Washington (CREW) as the main culprit.

Translation: "So maybe I did it, but that's not the point. The point is that the Democrats want me to look bad by telling people about it."

Extra credit for: Really running with the ball by later adding *more* members to the conspiracy, including President Bill Clinton; former CIA official Mary McCarthy; former senior Justice Department official and 9/11 Commission panelist Jamie Gorelick; former national security adviser Sandy Berger; and the Democratic Congressional Campaign Committee.

"I'M SHOCKED, SHOCKED TO HEAR THERE'S GAMBLING GOING ON IN HERE"—

OR, HOW TO (POORLY) BLOW OFF ACCUSATIONS WHEN YOUR HAND IS CAUGHT IN THE COOKIE JAR

The title alludes, of course, to *Casablanca*—and Captain Renault (Claude Rains) expostulating about how shocked he was that there was gambling going on in Rick's Place and using it as a pretext for closing it . . . even as the croupier hands him the money he has won.

In U.S. politics, life imitates art. Many politicians are shocked, SHOCKED to learn that they're being accused of some form of corruption . . . even as they pocket the swag.

We're sure you will be equally shocked to learn that some politicians get involved in allegedly shady goings-on. You probably wouldn't be shocked, however, to learn that these same politicians do their damnedest to explain that they certainly were totally, completely, and utterly blameless. They are, of course, pure as a newborn babe—or so they try to make it seem.

In some cases, the politicians themselves try to wiggle their way out of the problem. In other cases, they let their silver-tongued spokespeople deal with the mess. In *all* cases, their sincerity is most definitely on par with Captain Renault's.

And now, without further ado . . . your winnings, sir.

Shocked Politician: Illinois governor Rod Blagojevich (D)

Shocking Revelation: In one year (2006) Blagojevich's wife earned over $113,000 in commissions from four real estate deals (the only ones she made the entire year)—all through one client, Anita K. Mahajan, who held a long-standing no-bid state contract worth over $700,000 a year and whose banker husband is a big-time Blagojevich donor.

Terribly Sincere Explanation: Courtesy of Blagojevich's spokeswoman Abby Ottenhoff: "It's unfair and completely ridiculous to suggest she should be expected to keep track of every client she does business with to see if they have contracts with the state." Why were these the only transactions she managed to make? "Some years are better than others."

Captain Renault Sincerity Analysis: Of course, it is ridiculous for someone to keep track of every client one does business with—even if she has only *one* client. Besides, Mahajan said she had no idea who Patricia Blagojevich was—you know, Blagojevich being such a common name and all.

Shocked Politician: Nevada governor Jim Gibbons (R)

Shocking Revelation: Allegedly accepted illegal gifts and payments for himself and his wife from software exec Warren Trepp, who is now under investigation. Particularly problematic for the good gov is the following e-mail exchange published in *The Wall Street Journal* between Trepp's wife and Trepp just before they went on a Caribbean cruise with Gibbons and his family.

> WIFE'S E-MAIL: "Please don't forget to bring the money you promised Jim and Dawn [Gibbons]."
> TREPP'S E-MAIL REPLY: "Don't you ever send this kind of message to me! Erase this message from your computer right now!"

Terribly Sincere Explanation: As *The New York Times* put it, Gibbons claimed the "e-mail messages quoted by The Journal were probably references to campaign contributions, which he said were lawful and reported in accordance with campaign finance laws."

Captain Renault Sincerity Analysis: Yup. We too would tell someone to erase e-mails concerning contributions that were lawful and reported in accordance blah blah blah. But we don't know that we could announce it to the press with a straight face.

Shocked Politician: Representative John Murtha (D-PA)

Shocking Revelation: Back in 1980, Murtha was caught in the FBI's undercover ABSCAM sting operation in which agents posing as representatives of the faux "Sheik Abdul" offered different D.C. legislators $50,000 in return for legislative favors.

Terribly Sincere Explanation: Over 20 years later, Murtha addressed the allegations: "I am disconcerted that some are making headlines by resorting to unfounded allegations that occurred 26 years ago. I thought we were above [that] type of Swift-boating attack." And, on John McLaughlin's *One on One:* "They pulled a drawer out and they had $50,000 there and I said, 'I'm not interested.' I said, 'I'm interested in investment in my district, period.' "

Captain Renault Sincerity Analysis: Hmm . . . May we contrast that with the verbatim exchange from the undercover tapes after he was told about the money: "I want to deal with you guys awhile before I make any transactions at all, period. . . . After we've done some business, well, then I might change my mind." Call us silly, but "I want to deal with you guys awhile" doesn't *quite* sound like "I'm not interested" to us.

Shocked Politician: Arizona governor Janet Napolitano (D)

Shocking Revelation: Gave newly formed corporation the power to oversee state-authorized, low-interest student loans. The corporation just HAPPENED to be headed by two political buddies—one the former head of the firefighters union and the other the current head of the firefighters union. Also vetoed legislation that would have allowed competition for the contract.

Terribly Sincere Explanation: Napolitano claims she never ever knew that the two men were affiliated with the group until after she'd given them the contract and vetoed competition. "Not only did I not know there were firefighters involved at the time, to me the issue is were they qualified? Yes." Spokeswoman Jeanine L'Ecuyer added, "Everything that happened is completely legal. [Napolitano] is confident in how it was handled. Does it look funny? Sure."

Captain Renault Sincerity Analysis: Well, she *did* say it looks funny . . .

Shocked Politician: Senate Majority Leader Harry Reid (D-NV)

Shocking Revelation: Received $1.1 million on a Las Vegas land sale—land he had sold three years earlier to a friend's company for a financial stake in that company. Oh, and he "forgot" to report that earlier sale of the land, but kept it on his financial records as a personal asset.

Terribly Sincere Explanation: Hung up the phone when an AP reporter called him for comments about the land deal.

Captain Renault Sincerity Analysis: Silence is golden?

Shocked Politician: Representative Alan Mollohan (D-WV)

Shocking Revelation: Value of real estate holdings increased 6,566%—and he "forgot" to include this small chunk of change in his financial disclosure reports. Said reports were found to contain over 200 errors or omissions. Oh, and the real estate holdings were all through a D.C. condo company, Remington Inc., in which he had a 50% stake. The co-owner of Remington "happened" to get some mighty nice contracts from . . . Alan Mollohan.

Terribly Sincere Explanation: It was all "easily explained." The amazing windfall was "substantially due to the surge in real estate values in recent years, particularly in the District of Columbia."

Captain Renault Sincerity Analysis: Would that we could all do so well in real estate. . . .

Shocked Politician: Ohio Secretary of State J. Kenneth Blackwell

Shocking Revelation: Wanted to award no-bid contracts to the Diebold voting machine company—the company that supplied the voting machines for Ohio's 2004 election, many of which malfunctioned, causing some to say the election was stolen—and owned Diebold stock as well.

Terribly Sincere Explanation: He didn't even *know* he owned the stock since his multimillion-dollar portfolio is handled "by a financial manager without his advice and review." So, boy, was he "surprised," as he put it, when he found out that there was Diebold stock in there.

Captain Renault Sincerity Analysis: He *did* sell the stock . . . after he was caught, ahem, we mean after the stock was "discovered" in his portfolio.

CAN WE ALL GAG NOW?:
PANDERING POLS

Political pandering is the art of effectively sucking up to the appropriate minority or majority group.

The thing is to try to show that you're one of "them"— whoever they are, as long as they're voters—even though you're not the least bit like them. You're a politician. You're richer (almost always), whiter (usually), and you (more often than not) really don't give a shit. Well, except for those votes . . .

SPECIAL CHUTZPAH AWARDS

We proudly present this award to two worthy recipients:

New York state comptroller Alan Hevesi, who, after admitting that he improperly used a state employee to chauffeur his wife around, paid back the state . . . on a modified, limited layaway plan. First Hevesi "reimbursed" the state in full—$83,000 for the employee's services. A little later, the state discovered Hevesi had allegedly "inadvertently" underpaid . . . by $90,000. Then it was another $33,605—since, oops, Hevesi used FOUR government employees for personal use, not just one.

Representative William "Dollar Bill" Jefferson (D-LA), who, after being accused of taking $90,000 in bribes, had the balls and sheer unadulterated audacity to send a letter to fellow House Democrats (on his official stationery) asking them to contribute money to help him wipe out his campaign debt.

We do not know how much money he collected—and do not know if it's in the freezer or the fridge this time.

Some of our favorite examples of truly gagworthy pandering:

CHUCK SCHUMER IS OUTRAGED, YES OUTRAGED, THAT JUNE HAS NOT BEEN DECLARED NATIONAL CARIBBEAN-AMERICAN HERITAGE MONTH.

Just say the name "Senator Chuck Schumer" and you automatically think "Caribbean-American Heritage awareness."

Which is why we're absolutely sure it wasn't pandering when New York Democratic Senator Chuck shot out a very toughly worded news release angrily accusing the White

House of "stonewalling" his attempt to designate June as National Caribbean-American Heritage Month and to officially recognize Caribbean-Americans' extensive contributions to the United States . . . and to the New York state voting rolls.

We're also *sure* that the House sponsor, Barbara Lee (D-CA), didn't even think about the fact that her own state of California also has a large Caribbean-American population. It's the *principle* of the thing.

"RASTA NED" LAMONT APPEALS TO THE JAMAICAN-AMERICAN VOTING BASE.

Ned Lamont, running against Joe Lieberman to be the Democratic senatorial candidate for Connecticut in 2006, knows you gotta "get down" with those minority voters. You gotta connect, mon.

So when he walked into a Jamaican restaurant during his campaign, connect he did. He praised the scent of the beef patties on display, then trotted out his knowledge of all things Jamaican—which seems to essentially consist of one thing. Said Ned to the Jamaican-American men behind the counter: "So, do you guys like Bob Marley?"

HILLARY SHOWS HOW SHE JES' REALLY UNNERSTANS DEM BLACK FOLK.

Appropriately enuf (as Hillary would have written it that day), it happened on Martin Luther King Day. Hillary Clinton opined to a mostly black audience at a Harlem church that "when you look at the way the House of Representatives has been run, it has been run like a plantation, and you know what I'm talking about."

Being that the audience members were mostly from Harlem, which is in, like, a *big city,* and being that the audience members were mostly under 150 years old, which is

how old they'd have to be to even vaguely remember plantation slavery, and being that Hil is a white midwesterner, we
for one (or two) aren't sure we *do* know what she's talking
about . . . other than rather disingenuously trying to get
votes.

ON THE OTHER HAND, KILL DEM COONS—AND PASS THE BUD . . .

Delaware Senator Joe Biden—the Energizer bunny of a
Dem perennially in search of a presidential nomination—
faced down criticisms that he couldn't carry the South because he was a northeastern liberal with this brilliant
retro–Civil War attempt at winning the Old Confederacy:

> "You don't know my state. My state was a slave state.
> My state is a border state. My state has the eighth-
> largest black population in the country. My state is
> anything from a Northeast liberal state."

(Then, of course, he picked up his shotgun, got into his
pickup, and drove away. Or at least he should have.)

HILLARY CLINTON WANTS TO BE THERE FOR ALL THE PEOPLE— AND, GOSH DARNIT, PHARMACEUTICAL CEOS AND MULTIMILLIONAIRE LOBBYISTS ARE PEOPLE, TOO!

When Democratic presidential candidates John Edwards
and Barack Obama pledged that they wouldn't take money
from big-time Behind-the-Beltway lobbyists, Hillary Clinton
made her own proud pandering pledge: She would take
money from lobbyists.

Why? See, Hill is no bigot and she's proud of that fact. She
doesn't want to discriminate against any Americans—regardless of race, color, creed . . . or influential money-raising-for-
big-industry job. As she explained:

"A lot of those lobbyists, whether you like it or not, represent real Americans. They represent nurses, they represent social workers, yes, they represent corporations that employ a lot of people."

And of course, besides nurses and social workers, lobbyists also represent big pharmaceutical firms, which happen to have made Hillary their number one candidate in terms of cash payments. What a wonderful way to defend the rights of all Americans to representation: by taking money from the lobbyists. Let's give Hillary a hand for pandering where no candidate has pandered before. . . .

YOU KNOW WHAT I SAY, HANS? HOLOCAUST, SHMOLOCAUST.

Spartanburg, South Carolina, Mayor Bob Rowell (R) decided not to publicize a proclamation dedicated to Holocaust survivors in 1992. Not that Rowell had anything against the Holocaust survivors—but he did have something against the Holocaust itself, or at least all that *whining* about it. After all, it might be *offensive* and in *poor taste* to mention it publicly, at least in the presence of the grandsons and granddaughters of the people who actually organized the thing.

You see, the BMW car company (BMW stands for Bayerische Motoren Werke, which happens to be German) was deciding between Spartanburg and Omaha, Nebraska, for a new U.S. plant. Maybe because they were so touched by Rowell's sensitivity, BMW chose Spartanburg.

Pandering, shmandering!

JOE BIDEN POINTS OUT THAT INDIANS ARE *EVERYWHERE.* IN A GOOD WAY.

Senator "Slushy" Joe (D) was trying to be gracious—he was thanking a young Indian-American man for support from his Indian-American group. And he wanted to point out how Indians were the fastest-growing immigrant group in Delaware, which was *good,* particularly if they supported Joe.

As he put it: "You CANNOT go into a 7-Eleven or a Dunkin' Donuts without an Indian accent."

Of course, we take exception with Mr. Biden's statement. Indian-Americans aren't the only people in 7-Elevens. Pakistani-Americans also work there.

MITT ROMNEY JUST *LOVES* GUNS—AND GUN-TOTIN' VOTERS.

We're sure that Governor Mitt "Top Gun" Romney (R) was "on the level," as they say at the shooting range, when he showed up at the annual 2007 SHOT (Shooting, Hunting, Outdoor Trade) Show, the annual expo of America's gun industry. Mitt couldn't stop oogling all those rifles and assault weapons. Of course, back in 1994 when he was running for Senate in liberal Massachusetts, Mitt favored stuff the gun industry didn't like—like a five-day waiting period on gun sales and a ban on certain assault weapons. But that was then and this was now. With a Republican presidential primary fast approaching, Mitt just couldn't stop himself from being at the show with 1,800 of America's gun manufacturers, distributors, and dealers, along with ol' buddies like NRA Executive Vice President Wayne LaPierre. You didn't know that ol' Mitt was an NRA member? Why, sure—since August 2006. Isn't that a little recent? "I would argue not many Americans care when you join, but why you join, and I think I've made that clear," said a Romney spokesman. No, this clearly was not pandering to the gun lobby.

Oh, did we mention that Mitt's also a big-time hunter? "I've been a hunter pretty much all my life," he said in early 2007. His campaign office clarified: He had been on two whole hunting trips—once when he was 15 and the other, with GOP donors, in 2006. But Mitt set the record straight:

"I've always been a rodent and rabbit hunter. Small varmints, if you will. I began when I was 15 or so and I have hunted those kinds of varmints since then. More than two times."

But who's counting?

SENATOR HILLARY CLINTON SAVES THE FLAG FROM A FATE WORSE THAN BURNING.

We all know Senator Hillary Clinton's deep identification with the flag. We remember all those times when her husband was in office that she kept on admonishing him and the public to protect Old Glory!

So we *knew* she wasn't pandering to the right wing when she cosponsored a measure by Senator Bob Bennett (R-UT) in 2005 that called for criminalizing flag desecration.

And in the same way, we *know* she wasn't triangulating when she said that although she was against flag desecration and wanted to make those desecrators criminals, she also was opposed to a constitutional amendment banning flag attacks. Was this a counter-pander to the left? No, we're sure it wasn't.

FOUR

THE POLITICAL PERSONALITY

Politicians Acting, Being, and Doing

WHAT MAKES POLITICIANS TICK? HOW DO THEY BEHAVE? How do they joke? How do they lead? How do they act? And who really cares?

Well, we do.

THE GREAT AMERICAN POLITICAL EGO

Many politicians have large and healthy egos. This is a good thing—those egos help succor the politicians through tough times, the rigors of a campaign, the slings and arrows of the media.

But how can one scientifically assess political egotism? Politicians often give off clues as to the size of their egos (camera-hogging, overuse of the personal pronoun, fatuous expressions, etc.). The student of political egos collects these clues and measures them, obtains an aggregate number, and then compares this number to the gold standard: the large ego of Senator Chuck "I've Never Met a Camera I Didn't Center Myself in the Viewfinder Of" Schumer (D-NY).

So below we've examined the egos of several politicians who have up-and-coming Chuck Schumer–class egos. We've listed the vital clues that lead us to conclude that these individuals are worthy of ranking, along with preliminary assessments as to the absolute size of the ego in question, as measured, of course, in standard Chuck Schumer Ego Units, or "CSEUs."

First, the measuring stick by which all other egos are judged:

Politician: Senator Charles "Chuck" Schumer (D-NY)
Clues to Size of Ego:
Clue #1: Senator Jon Corzine (D-NJ) said: "Frankly, sharing a media market with Chuck Schumer is like sharing a banana with a monkey . . . take a little bit and he will throw his own feces at you."

Clue #2: Schumer's colleagues in Congress coined a new verb *Schume,* as in "getting Schumed," which was defined as what happens to them after they have worked hard on an issue without him—and then watch him take all the credit.

Clue #3: Take a look at *any* photo that shows Chuck Schumer with anyone else, anywhere, anytime. Notice how Chuck stands forward, his large head and face literally *straining* toward the camera. (And no, he's not taking a quickie dump.)

Clue #4: At the John Roberts Supreme Court confirmation hearings, Schumer made a 10-minute statement, ostensibly about Roberts and not about himself. There were 49 first-person references in the speech, or about one Chuck Schumer–oriented pronoun every 12.24 *seconds.*

Estimated Size of Ego: 1.00 CSEU. The gold standard in egos.

And now, in ascending order . . .

Government Bureaucrat: New York state health commissioner Antonia Novello

Clue to Size of Ego:

Clue #1: Ordered a $15,000 fancy oil portrait of herself to hang in state offices before leaving the administration. "This is something that is way out of line, and I'd say that if it was a Democrat or a Republican," said Assembly Health Committee chairman Dick Gottfried (D). Taxpayers agreed, but Antonia Novello did not. Her spokesperson at the Health Commission stated, "The commissioner has done a superb job for seven and a half years," he said. "It is just as appropriate for her to have a portrait as it was for her predecessors." He had no immediate information on what the earlier portraits cost but our guess is: somewhat less than $15,000. How about settling for a $15 caricature?

Estimated Size of Ego: 0.25 CSEU

Government Bureaucrat: Secretary of Labor Elaine Chao

Clues to Size of Ego:

Clue #1: Chao replaced 58 of 130 photographs of American workers in the executive offices of the Labor Department with pictures of herself instead.

Clue #2: At a recent Labor Department conference Chao ordered lanyards to be given to the participants that said "US DOL [Department of Labor]" with her name, "Secretary Elaine L. Chao." (Why didn't she include her full middle name? Modesty, undoubtedly.) Participants were also given high-quality fleece blankets embroidered with "Opportunity Conference / Asian Pacific and Hispanic Americans" and "Secretary Elaine L. Chao / U.S. Department of Labor," just in case they forgot who the secretary of labor was.

Clue #3: At a mine rescue contest (run by the department's Mine Safety and Health Administration), Chao gave attendees gold-colored half-dollar-size coins, with a bas-relief of Secretary Chao in the center looking much like a Roman empress.

Clue #4: An official Labor Department website for Chao included over 50 photos of Chao at work (versus no photos of secretaries of defense or education on their sites), complete with items announcing how "Secretary Chao" (not the "Department of Labor") awarded grants to deserving groups. Also, hers was the *only* government website (except for the Department of State) to offer personal condolences on the death of the pope, as if Chao had been personally in contact with the man.

Clue #5: The monthly department newsletter *The Labor Beacon* included seven photos of Chao in a single issue. The newsletter was six pages long.

Clue #6: Chao compared herself and her husband to another Washington power couple, the Doles, perhaps implying presidential ambitions.

Estimated Size of Ego: 0.5 CSEU

Politician: New York governor George Pataki (R)
Clues to Size of Ego:
Clue #1: Pataki spent more than $100 million in taxpayer money over 12 years on television and radio commercials starring himself as a spokesperson for state programs.

Clue #2: In his last months in office, Pataki spent uncounted thousands of dollars putting his name and face on new state publications, knowing full well they'd be outdated in a few weeks.

Clue #3: Apparently felt entitled, as Grand Master of the Universe, to take his official government office furniture with him—including a high-quality Stickley desk and credenza that according to one source were on loan to the governor's office from a prominent upstate New York family.

Estimated Size of Ego: 0.74 CSEU

Politician: Senator Ted K. Stevens (R-AK)
Clues to Size of Ego:
Clue #1: Stevens has his very own nonprofit, called, aptly enough, the Ted Stevens Foundation, whose mission is to "assist in educating and informing the public about the career of Senator Ted Stevens."

Clue #2: Citizens of Alaska, probably not spontaneously, decided to name their main airport the "Ted Stevens Anchorage International Airport."

Clue #3: The governor of Alaska, also probably not spontaneously, decided to name November 18, 2003, Stevens's 80th birthday, as "Senator Ted Stevens Appreciation Day."

Estimated Size of Ego: 0.86 CSEU

Politician: Senator Robert C. Byrd (D-WV)
Clues to Size of Ego:
Clue #1: Byrd convinced the West Virginia Legislature to fund and erect a statue of himself in the state capitol—even though state law prohibits statues of government officials until they have been dead for 50 years.

Clues #2–36: In a similar spirit, the self-effacing senator has allowed a few buildings, etc., to be named for him here and there, including:

Robert C. Byrd Drive, from Beckley to Sophia (Byrd's
     hometown)
Robert C. Byrd National Technology Transfer Center at
     Wheeling Jesuit University
Robert C. Byrd Highway

Robert C. Byrd Federal Correctional Institution
Robert C. Byrd High School
Robert C. Byrd Freeway
Robert C. Byrd Center for Hospitality and Tourism
Robert C. Byrd Science Center
Robert C. Byrd Health Sciences Center of West Virginia
Robert C. Byrd Cancer Research Center
Robert C. Byrd Technology Center at Alderson-
    Broaddus College
Robert C. Byrd Hardwood Technologies Center
Robert C. Byrd Bridge
Robert C. Byrd addition to the lodge at Oglebay Park,
    Wheeling
Robert C. Byrd Community Center
Robert C. Byrd Honors Scholarships
Robert C. Byrd Expressway (U.S. 52)
Robert C. Byrd Institute
Robert C. Byrd Institute for Advanced Flexible
    Manufacturing
Robert C. Byrd Visitors Center at Harpers Ferry
    National Historic Park
Robert C. Byrd Federal Courthouse
Robert C. Byrd Academic and Technology Center
Robert C. Byrd United Technical Center
Robert C. Byrd Federal Building (there are two)
Robert C. Byrd Hilltop Office Complex
Robert C. Byrd Library and Robert C. Byrd Learning
    Resource Center
Robert C. Byrd Rural Health Center
Robert C. Byrd addition to the veterans' hospital in
    Huntington
Robert C. Byrd Industrial Park
Robert C. Byrd Scholastic Recognition Award

Robert C. Byrd Community Center (in a naval radio
    station)
Robert C. Byrd Clinic at the West Virginia School of
    Osteopathic Medicine
Robert C. Byrd Biotechnology Science Center at
    Marshall University

Estimated Size of Ego: 0.9956 CSEU (incredibly, almost
there!)

Last but not least, here are two up-and-coming pols with
some definite Chuck Schumer mega-ego potential.

Senator Thad Cochran (R-MS)—a young senator who
already has the Thad Cochran National Warmwater Aqua-
culture Center at Mississippi State University's Stoneville
campus; the Thad Cochran Research, Technology and Economic Development Park in Starkville; and, at his alma
mater, the University of Mississippi in Oxford, the Thad
Cochran Research Center.

Representative Nick Rahall (D-WV)—whose name already graces the Nick J. Rahall II Appalachian Transportation
Institute at Marshall University.

THE BOLD POLITICIAN

American politicians have always been bold, decisive leaders,
people who aren't afraid to take a *stand* (and stay there).
    Think of Patrick Henry and his bold, stirring words:

"Is life so dear, or peace so sweet, as to be purchased at
the price of chains and slavery? Forbid it, Almighty
God! I know not what course others may take; but as
for me, give me liberty or give me death!"

And today, the spirit of Patrick Henry still lives!
Sort of.

Modern-Day Patrick Henry #1.0: Senator Hillary Clinton (D-NY)

Bold Patrick Henry–like Stance: "America should stay in Iraq—before it leaves. (But I don't know when we should leave. On second thought, let's leave before I get elected president but let's not cut off funding before that, though. Maybe later. Do you think we should leave? Let's take a poll. . . .)"

Some examples of Hillary Clinton's strong, bold, consistent, well-stated, clearly understandable stands on the Iraq War . . .

• In the Early Years, with 80% of the U.S. pro-war, 90% of Hillary pro-war:

"No, I don't regret giving the president authority because at the time it was in the context of weapons of mass destruction, grave threats to the United States, and clearly, Saddam Hussein had been a real problem for the international community for more than a decade." (April 2004)

"Democrats must make it clear to the public that we stand for winning in Iraq, not a rush for the exits." (Democratic Leadership Council statement, signed by Hillary Clinton, December 2005)

• In the Middle Years, with 50% of the U.S. pro-war, 65% of Hillary pro-war:

"I do not think it is a smart strategy, either, for the president to continue with his open-ended commitment, which I think does not put enough pressure on the new Iraqi government. Nor do I think it is smart strategy to set a date certain." (June 2006)

• In the Later Years, with less than 30% of the U.S. pro-war, less than 50% of Hillary pro-war:

"We expect him [President Bush] to extricate our country from this [Iraq] before he leaves office." (January 2007)

"If I had been president in October 2002, I would not have started this war." (February 2007)

Wow! She sounds just like she's actually *channeling* Patrick Henry. She has so moved the populace that they're saying, "What the hell is she talking about?"

Modern-Day Patrick Henry #1.1: Senator Hillary Clinton (D-NY)
Bold Patrick Henry–like Stance: "Keep tax cuts or raise taxes? That deserves a good answer. Next question."
Asked about repealing the tax cuts, Clinton cogently explained:

> "I'm not sure that that's exactly what we should do, but I think the combination of fiscal responsibility and economic growth proves to be very positive for our country."

Who can argue with that?

Modern-Day Patrick Henry #1.2: Senator Hillary "The Buck Stops Here" Clinton (D-NY)
Bold Patrick Henry–like Stance: Hillary was asked this question by a resident of New Hampshire, Roger Tilton:

> "I want to know if right here, right now, once and for all and without nuance, you can say that war authorization was a mistake. I, and I think a lot of other primary voters—until we hear you say it, we're not going to hear all the other great things you are saying."

Hillary "I Channel Harry Truman Every Day" Clinton boldly answered:

> "Well, I have said, and I will repeat it, that knowing what I know now, I would never have voted for it. But I also, and obviously you have to weigh everything as you make your decision—I have taken responsibility for my vote. The mistakes were made by this president, who misled this country and this Congress."

Someone asked, "Aren't you trying to have it both ways?" Our question: Can't you ever, Hil, just once, say, "Yes, it was" or "No, it wasn't"? That's not so hard, is it?

(Meanwhile, John Edwards said, "It was a mistake to vote for this war in 2002. I take responsibility for that mistake." Is it us, or does that sound a little bit *bolder*?)

Modern-Day Patrick Henry #2: Senator John Kerry (D-MA)

Bold Patrick Henry–like Stance: "America should have, maybe, declared war on Iraq. Perhaps."

Asked by a reporter during his campaign for president, "Would you have gone to war against Saddam Hussein if he refused to disarm?" John Kerry resolutely replied, "You bet we might have." He also famously added, referring to his stand on the Iraq War funding bill, "I actually did vote for the $87 billion before I voted against it."

Modern-Day Patrick Henry #3: Senator Bill Frist (R-TN)

Bold Patrick Henry–like Stance: "I would condemn the page-sex scandal if I knew anything about it . . . which I don't because I was overseas in Iraq, for Pete's sake, Iraq, so it's bad if it's true but I don't know if it's true so I can't really comment."

At the height of the sex scandal in which Republican congressman Mark Foley (R-FL) allegedly propositioned several young congressional pages, then Senate Majority Leader Bill Frist was stopped by reporters and asked his take on the crisis.

BARACK THE BRAVE

Barack Obama announced his candidacy and said, "What's stopped us is the failure of leadership . . . our chronic avoidance of tough decisions." So how did he vote on various issues back in the state legislature where he served? Did he make those "tough decisions"?

Well, kinda.

He voted on the tough issues. He just didn't vote *for* them. Or *against* them.

He voted "present." That's an option in the Illinois legislature. It's not a yes. Or a no.

According to the *Opinion Journal,* in 1997, Obama voted "present" on two bills (HB 382 and SB 230) that would have prohibited a procedure partial-birth abortion. In 1999, Obama voted "present" on SB 759, which called for mandatory prosecution for firing a gun on or near school grounds. He also voted "present" on HB 854, which protected the privacy of sexual-abuse victims. (Note: He was the *only* member to not support the bill.) In 2001, Obama voted "present" on two parental-notification abortion bills, and he voted "present" on a series of bills (SB 1093, 1094, 1095) that sought to protect a child if it survived a failed abortion. Then, in 2001, Obama voted "present" on SB 609, a bill prohibiting strip clubs and other adult establishments from being within 1,000 feet of schools, churches, and day care centers.

So, is Obama a bold leader—yes or no?

We say, "Present."

Bill's immortal words, so *strong and bold,* are as follows:

"I have, as you know, been in Afghanistan and in Iraq, and I don't mean to avoid your question, but really have not been briefed on the events of the last 48 hours. When I left, obviously Congressman Foley, the allegations had come out. That is to be condemned if those are true. The events of the last 48 hours I just haven't been briefed on. Obviously I have tremendous respect for [then House Speaker] Denny Hastert but have not been briefed on any of the details. . . . I can't comment on what happened in the House because I don't know. We have a strong page program in the United States Senate, though we have not had allegations like that."

Men like this should become *president.*

THE "MAN OR WOMAN OF THE PEOPLE IN THEORY ONLY" AWARDS

It's the old populist ideal: Politician emerges from log cabin or backwoods shack, takes Washington by storm, but remains the humble man of the people.

Well, we've come a long way, baby!

Why *should* a politician be like the people—living like the schlubby plumber or academic or lowly humble country corporate lawyer he or she was before being elected or appointed—when instead the pol can live like a king. Or a queen? (Depending on sex—or inclination.)

And all on the taxpayer's dollar.

It's much more modern.

And so, here we honor the best of kingly—or queenly—behavior, in our first annual "Man or Woman of the People in Theory Only" Awards.

IN THE MARIE ANTOINETTE "LET THEM EAT CAKE" CATEGORY, THE WINNER IS . . .

Queen Condoleezza "Let Them Buy Ferragamos" Rice (Secretary of State)

Condi gets our vote for her bold and unceasing insensitivity to the plight of her fellow citizens, and for keeping to her mission of supporting the Italian economy by spending several thousands of dollars on Ferragamos—while fellow people of color (as well as people of white) were being pummeled by Hurricane Katrina. Condi, in her capacity as third-highest-ranking administration official, might have thought it was her duty to go down to New Orleans to help in what was arguably the greatest natural disaster to strike the continental United States, but instead she chose to stay in New York and shop.

For shoes, specifically.

A fellow shoe shopper saw the secretary trying on some shoes at Ferragamo's on Fifth Avenue and yelled at her, "How dare you shop for shoes while thousands are dying and homeless!"

Appropriately enough, this shopper, who was exercising her First Amendment rights (but doing it so *rudely*), was thrown out of the store. Leaving Queen "Imelda" to shop on in peace.

AND THE RUNNER-UP IS . . .

Queen Condoleezza "Banish Them" Rice

Again. Congratulations, Condi!

Marie Antoinette had her own palace—so why can't Condi at least have a dining room to herself? And so, the Good Queen demanded that a hotel close down a dining room completely so that her party of three could dine in peace and comfort, far from the madding crowd of commoners.

AND IN THE "KNEEL, COMMONER, BEFORE PARFIT GENTIL KNYGHTS" CATEGORY, THE WINNER IS . . .
the recently knyghted Rudolph "Honorary-Sir Rudy" Giuliani

Sir Rudy, who was given an honorary knighthood by Queen Elizabeth, takes his honorary knighthood seriously. (Maybe he should. After all, after the ceremony he reportedly actually even *joked* and *laughed* with Her Majesty!) In 2006 he was asked to speak before the students at Oklahoma State University for an "Evening with Rudy Giuliani." In addition to a princely (and standard) $100,000 speaking fee, the gentil homme made a number of knightly demands, as mentioned in the contract, and released to the public by public-spirit-minded Oklahomans:

- First-class travel, preferably by private jet: "Please note that the private aircraft MUST BE a Gulfstream IV or bigger."
- Must be met by "one sedan and one large SUV."
- Must be booked into a hotel room with "a king-size bed, on an upper floor, with a balcony and view."
- Sir Rudy's room must be flanked by rooms for his aides—four rooms in all, all on the same floor.
- No "candid photo opportunities"—but will stand for posed photographs, as long as there is sufficient light, no direct on-camera flashbulbs.
- Rudy to speak for 45 minutes (clock to be provided to face him as he speaks), with 15 minutes (only) for answering questions.

Of course, the good Sir Rudy must also be protected from the sweaty common folk. "There must be rope and stanchions to assist with attendee control," the contract stipulates, "as well as staff appointed to push and pull."

IN THE "I'M A GENIUS, YOU'RE NOT" CATEGORY, THE
WINNER IS . . .
King Michael "What's the Frequency?" Powell (chairman, Federal Communications Commission)

Powell, chairman of the FCC from 2001 to 2005, and son of former secretary of state Colin Powell (of course he got the FCC job solely on his own merits), supported monopolistic media giants—and, indeed, let them become more giant.

When a reporter questioned the wisdom of this, King Son of Colin looked down and opined loftily: "I think to the average consumer this is too sublime a concept for a lot of them to be agitated by."

IN THE "TO HELL WITH THE COMMONERS, MY HOUSE IS
UNDERWATER!" CATEGORY, THE WINNER IS . . .
King William "L'état, C'est Moi" Jefferson (representative, D-LA)

During the Hurricane Katrina disaster in New Orleans, while people were clambering on rooftops trying to get rescued, the good and intrepid Representative Jefferson used six National Guardsmen and a half-ton military truck to take him on a "tour." Said tour allegedly got changed (on King Bill's request) to include driving to his own house in an upscale district, pulling up onto the front lawn (so he wouldn't have to walk in the water), waiting an hour (on the porch) while he "rescued" piles of personal items from his house, and then letting the guardsmen load all of his goodies onto the truck.

When the truck—laden with "rescued" items—got stuck, a rescue helicopter responded to Jefferson's party's distress signal. But Jefferson decided he'd rather wait—for another truck to take him and his personal property safely back to the Superdome.

King Bill denies the particulars. "This wasn't about me going to my house. It was about me going to my district," he said. (Luckily, his house was in his district.)

IN THE "NYAH, NYAH! WE'RE SPECIAL, WE GET OUR OWN EL-
EVATOR" CATEGORY, THE WINNER IS . . .
Their Royal Highnesses, the entire U.S. Congress

See, senators and congresspeople are too busy to travel in regular elevators. They *need* special Senate- or Congress-only elevators. With elevator operators, natch, because these important politicians are just too darn *busy* to push elevator buttons, too.

Nonsenators and nonreps—i.e., lowly people—are allowed to ride only if asked by a senator or congressperson.

Some senators, such as King Ted K. Stevens (R) of Alaska and King Robert C. Byrd (D) of West Virginia, have a reputation for glaring at or grumbling to transgressors who dare ride these elevators. King Frank Lautenberg (D-NJ) explained the problem with those noncongressional riders: "There is terrific crowding. . . . Sometimes you have to shove your way through, push people," he said.

Can you imagine the *utter angst* of being crowded in an elevator? Probably not.

Some congresspeople can get a tad testy about interlopers on their private elevators. In 2001, representative Queen Melissa Hart (R-PA) noticed a black woman (gasp) riding on a Congress-only elevator. She sternly informed the offender it was a members-only lift.

The offensive black woman then introduced herself to the white representative: She was Julia Carson (D-IN). Yes, she was a congressperson, too. Isn't democracy wonderful?

THE RUNNER-UP IS . . .

Hillary "Don't Pee on My Parade" Clinton

Kings and queens are accustomed to being treated with deference. Peeing is not deferential.

Hence, members of a wealthy East Hampton, New York, crowd should not have been surprised when after paying $1,000 a pop to listen to Bill tell everyone why Hillary was another Him, they were also informed that the bathrooms were off limits. "Security reasons." What if they *had* to go? Tough luck. "It's a basic right that you should be able to use the bathroom," grumbled one guest at the event.

Not in the presence of the Royal Clintons, you schmuck!

BOYHOOD HIJINKS

"The child is the father of the man." So wrote poet William Wordsworth. He wasn't speaking of politicians, as far as we know. But he could have been.

It's wonderful to read about the childhood hijinks of our favorite political leaders. We see in each lighthearted prank the *essence* of the man; we can see how, early on, friends and neighbors watching those boyish pranks realized: This man is destined to go far. He will become a *politician*.

CUTE GEORGIE BUSH—BLOWING UP FROGS

Before Iraq, before the National Guard, George Bush, perhaps predictably, liked playing with fireworks. According to the newsletter *Hightower Lowdown:* "W.'s family laughs that, as a boy, he used to light firecrackers and shove them down the throats of frogs just to watch them explode." How utterly cute! We *howled* when we first read this.

SMART SENATOR BILLY FRIST—ADOPTING KITTENS TO DISSECT THEM

From Senator Frist's (R-TN) autobiographical first book, *Transplant:*

> Desperate, obsessed with my work, I visited the various animal shelters in the Boston suburbs, collecting cats, taking them home, treating them as pets for a few days, then carting them off to the lab to die in the interests of science. And medicine. And health care. And treatment of disease. And my project . . . It was, of course, a heinous and dishonest thing to do, and I was totally schizoid about the entire matter. By day, I was little Billy Frist, the boy who lived on Bowling Avenue in Nashville and had decided to become a doctor because of his gentle father and a dog named Scratchy. By night, I was Dr. William Harrison Frist, future cardiothoracic surgeon, who was not going to let a few sentiments about cute, furry little creatures stand in the way of his career. In short, I was going a little crazy.

Frist also admits that when he went to animal shelters he lied to the attendants and told them he wanted their cats as pets instead of for dissecting. That tricky little tusker! He has our vote. Always.

MISCHIEVOUS SENATOR GEORGE ALLEN—THREATENING LITTLE GIRLS

Senator George Allen (R-VA, defeated in 2006 in an election squeaker but promising to return) was a very mischievous little boy. In the book *Fifth Quarter,* little sister Jennifer remembers how "George would swerve his Mach II Mustang while [brother] Gregory held the baseball bat out the window to clear the mailbox of its post." But smashing neighbors' mailboxes was small potatoes for George, at least according to Jennifer. Adds lil' sis, "Ever since my brother George held me over the railing at Niagara Falls, I've had a fear of heights."

HOW MANY POLS DOES IT TAKE TO SCREW IN A LIGHTBULB?:
FIVE MODERN HILARIOUS JOKES (WHICH JUST HAPPEN, FOR SOME REASON, TO BE ETHNIC) FROM SOME OF OUR FAVORITE POLITICIANS

How better to understand the inner workings of an individual than to examine his or her sense of humor?

Statesman Winston Churchill was well-known for his cutting ripostes and witty comebacks. But, on this side of the pond, we don't go for that dry British humor stuff. No, our politicians prefer a more *earthy* medium: the Ethnic Joke.

Of course, we all know that underneath ethnic jokes and stereotypes are *truths.* Here, a few of our favorite politicians tell their jokes—and reveal *their* truths about various ethnicities.

Hilarious Ethnic Joke: "We're on Injun time. They don't tell time by the clock."

Underlying Hilarious Truth: Indians are lazy and backward!

Political Jokester: Steve Kagen, Democratic candidate for Congress in Wisconsin, after arriving late for a campaign event at an Indian reservation

Hilarious Ethnic Joke: "They should start packing their little Palestinian terrorist bags."

Underlying Hilarious Truth: All Palestinians are terrorists!

Political Jokester: Representative Anthony Weiner (D-NY), discussing legislation that would effectively force the Palestinian U.N. delegation to leave the United States

Hilarious Ethnic Joke: We don't have the joke verbatim, but it sort of goes like this: During an immigrants rights case, a Supreme Court justice said that a Mexican man who had been deported would be unlikely to keep from drinking tequila. You know those Mexicans! (Okay, you had to be there.)

Underlying Hilarious Truth: Those crazy drunken Mexicans drink so much tequila!

Political Jokester: Supreme Court Justice Antonin Scalia

Scalia excused the statement as "an exercise in the conceivable" and added, "Nobody thinks your client is really, you know, abstaining from tequila down in Mexico because he is on supervised release in the United States."

Carlos Ortiz, former president of the Hispanic National Bar Association, was not in the audience but reacted strongly when he was told of the joke or comment: "Justice Scalia is supposed to be very smart, but anyone who is supposed to be so smart would not and should not say something that insensitive. It is a really terrible comment, and he should be called on it."

Hilarious Gay Joke: "My prostate cancer operation was just not natural, unless maybe you're Barney Frank."

Underlying Hilarious Truth: Congressman Barney Frank is gay!

Political Jokester: Representative Randy "Duke" Cunningham (R-CA), now serving time for corruption. Frank countered Cunningham's joke with the observation that Cunningham "may have suffered a little slight brain damage" during the anal surgery.

Hilarious Ethnic Joke: "You know what I'm gonna tell those Jews when I get to Israel, don't you, Herman? . . . I'm telling 'em they're all going to hell."
Underlying Hilarious Truth: Jews aren't Christians—so they don't get to go to heaven!
Political Jokester: Texas governor George W. Bush

Hilarious Ethnic Joke: "There are probably not 72 virgins in the hell he's at and if there are, they probably all look like Helen Thomas."
Underlying Hilarious Truth: He thinks that 85-year-old journalist Helen Thomas is ugly—and that's really funny!
Political Jokester: Representative Steve King (R-IA)

DO AS I SAY, NOT AS I DO:
POLITICAL HYPOCRISY IN ACTION

To paraphrase the great Mark Twain: Reader, pretend you are a hypocrite. And pretend you are a politician. But we repeat ourselves . . . once again.

REPUBLICAN NATIONAL COMMITTEE
What They Say: Rep. Harold Ford, Jr. (D-TN), is disgusting for accepting campaign contributions from porn movie producers, so don't vote for him.
What They Do: Accept political contributions from *gay* porn movie producers

Apparently there's a fine distinction here that escapes us, but the good folks at the RNC, who gleefully ran an attack ad saying that Ford took money from porn producers, regularly received contributions from the owner of Marina Pacific Distributors, producer and distributor of such fine films as *Fire in the Hole* and the ever-popular *Flesh and Boners*.

VICE PRESIDENT AL GORE (D)

What He Says: Be green like me! Live a "carbon-neutral" lifestyle!

What He Does: Serves on the board of Apple—which was cited by Greenpeace as a non-environmentally-friendly company since it uses unrecyclable toxins in its products; owns, as part of his family trust, hundreds of thousands of dollars of stock in Occidental Petroleum, a company that has done oil drilling in ecologically sensitive areas; and gets $20,000 a year in royalties for a zinc concession on his home in Carthage, Tennessee, from Pasminco Zinc, a company that has been cited by the state for polluting the nearby Caney Fork River.

Oh, and did we mention that Mr. "I'm Not Ed Begley" Gore chiefly lives in two *other* houses—a 10,000-square-foot, 20-room, 8-bathroom home in Nashville, and a 4,000-square-foot home in Arlington, Virginia? (Note: These are pretty big houses. To us, at least.) While both the Nashville and Washington, D.C., area utilities offer wind energy to customers for a few cents more per kilowatt hour, Gore still opted for traditional energy. His office, however, had a succinct explanation: The Gores were "looking into making a switch." And Gore has stated that he has purchased "carbon offsets"—which we would like to purchase, too, if we had the moolah. . . .

GOLDEN STATE FENCE COMPANY

What They Say: We're helping build a fence to keep out those pesky illegal immigrants.

What They Do: Hire those pesky illegal immigrants to help build the fence

Okay, so the Golden State Fence Company isn't a politician . . . but we couldn't resist putting this in and are stretching the point because the Golden State Fence Company is involved in a highly charged political job—building the U.S.-Mexico border fence, which is designed to stem the flow of illegal immigrants from Mexico. So there was a beautiful irony when the firm was fined $5 million and two of its execs were headed to jail, all for hiring illegal immigrants. The company's attorney tried (*tried*) to put a positive spin on it by noting that this *proved the need for a guest-worker program.*

SENATE MAJORITY LEADER HARRY REID (D-NV)

What He Says: Those damn Republicans are corrupt as hell—accepting freebies to influence their votes and all . . .

What He Does: Accepts free ringside tickets for pro boxing bouts from the Nevada Athletic Commission—when he was working on boxing-related legislation

Reid claimed this was just a way to learn how his legislation could affect such an important issue in his state. "Anyone from Nevada would say I'm glad he is there taking care of the state's No. 1 businesses." Besides, he added, he happens to love boxing.

GOVERNOR ARNOLD SCHWARZENEGGER (R)

What He Says: There are a lot of state government jobs that are a waste of taxpayer money—and should be cut.

What He Does: "Cut" his staff by reassigning 40 of them to *other* positions, over half of which paid more (some by over $30k a year)—and also gave six former staffers jobs on boards and commissions he previously had tried to get rid of

Senator Joe Lieberman ("D"-CT)

What He Says: In a convocation address to New York University Law School in 2001, Lieberman said,

> "As our public places and spaces are changed to comply with that law [the ADA], most Americans are becoming more aware of, more sensitive to—and more supportive of—both the needs and the abilities of those with disabilities, again showing the profound potential the law has to alter our views and our behavior."

What He Does: Park in handicapped spaces

Well, actually we can only report about one handicapped parking moment: During the often rancorous Democratic primary campaign for senator from Connecticut, a Ned Lamont supporter posted a photo of Lieberman's car (license plate #2) parked in a handicapped space at Fairfield University. Perhaps this isn't much of a surprise—considering that in 2006 the organization Disabled American Veterans gave Lieberman a lower voting score than any other Democrat in the Senate on disabled veterans' issues.

Governor Mitt Romney (R)

What He Says: We should curb the flood of low-skilled illegal immigrants into the U.S.

What He Does: Hired low-skilled illegal immigrants to keep his yard and shrubs looking snappy

The Boston Globe found that for a decade "the governor has used a landscaping company that relies heavily on workers like these, illegal Guatemalan immigrants, to maintain the grounds surrounding his pink Colonial house on Marsh Street in Belmont." The paper also noted that other than a casual *"buenos dias,"* Romney never really talked to the lawn guys so didn't know if they were legal or illegal. When confronted by a reporter about this issue, Romney defended himself with the explanatory statement, "Aw, geez," before walking away.

SENATOR BARBARA BOXER (D-CA)

What She Says: We must go against the Bush administration's cozying up to big oil and work to reduce our dependence on foreign oil and use alternative forms of energy.

What She Did: Set up a press event at a gas station to tout the "New Direction" the Democrats offered (so different from the oil-company-loving Republicans)—then got into a waiting gas guzzler (18 mpg) and drove away to her office . . . a whole block away

SENATOR BARACK OBAMA (D-IL)

What He Says: Why are you Detroit car companies making gas guzzlers?

What He Did: Drives a gas guzzler

Specifically a near top-of-the-line V-8 hemi-powered Chrysler 300C—which gets a cool 17 mpg in the city, 25 highway.

GOVERNOR GEORGE PATAKI (R)

What He Says: The New York Legislature spends money on ridiculous projects like "cheese museums and pro wrestling halls of fame."

What He Did: Controlled a fund that sent thousands to the so *not* ridiculous Cuba Cheese Museum in Cuba, New York

But there is a crucial distinction to be made here. Money funding the Cuba Cheese Museum should not be confused with the inane wasteful spending on the New York State Museum of Cheese in Rome, New York.

SENATOR EDWARD KENNEDY (D-MA)

What He Says: All-male clubs are sexist, so belonging to one means you shouldn't get a federal appointment.

What He Did: Belonged to the all-male Owl Club for Harvard alumni and students

He did, however, quit it SIX WHOLE MONTHS before he criticized one of President George Bush's nominees to the federal bench, Judge Samuel Alito, for belonging to an all-male dining club for Princeton alumni. (Note: Perhaps there is a difference between belonging to a plain old social club versus a dining one? Just asking . . .)

GOVERNOR JIM GIBBONS (R)

What He Says: Illegal immigrants are a scourge!

What He Does: Hired illegal immigrant nanny

According to Dawn Gibbons, wife of the Nevada governor, the woman worked only "occasionally" in their house and they thought she was here legally. According to a Democratic Party spokeswoman, the Peruvian nanny told a Las Vegas television station that "she was told to hide in the basement when people came over to the house."

SENATOR JOHN EDWARDS (D-NC)

What He Says: Poverty is a terrible moral issue facing the United States.

What He Does: Charges $55,000 for giving a speech about how poverty is a terrible moral issue facing the United States

And he gave this speech at the taxpayer-funded University of California at Davis. (One side note: Edwards has proposed an educational policy that would remove "every financial barrier" for students who want to attend college. Ironically, UC Davis is increasing its tuition by 7%—maybe to help pay for speeches?)

SPEAKER OF THE HOUSE NANCY PELOSI (D-CA)

What She Says: Corruption is bad, bad, bad—and I'm going to clean up Congress.

What She Does: Allows Congressman Alan Mollohan (D-WV), who has been under federal investigation for financial "irregularities," to chair the panel that oversees the budget of the Justice Department . . .

. . . who just happen to be the guys investigating his own financial, er, "irregularities." As Pelosi said, "Quite frankly, I think the Justice Department is looking into every member of Congress. I always say to everybody, 'You're now going to get a free review of your family tree—past, present and future, imagined and otherwise." Yes. True. Then again, Mollohan filed papers correcting SIX YEARS of prior financial disclosure reports involving millions of dollars in unreported or misreported assets—after he spent two straight months denying problems and saying any allegations against him were "entirely and demonstrably false." So . . . either every member of Congress has gone through this or . . . ??? We're confused.

FRANK FIGUEROA, HEAD OF THE DEPARTMENT OF HOMELAND SECURITY'S "OPERATION PREDATOR" PROGRAM TO CATCH CHILD SEX CRIMINALS

What He Says: We must keep our children safe from sexual predators.

What He Did: Got busted for exposing himself to a 16-year-old girl

The victim said he exposed himself to her and began masturbating in the food court of a mall in Orlando, Florida. Figueroa initially said he was not guilty, but then pleaded no contest to charges of exposure of sexual organs and, an understatement if we ever heard one, disorderly conduct.

THE ALZHEIMER'S CORNER:
POLITICAL MEMORY AT ITS (CONVENIENT) WORST

We're a little worried about many politicians and government officials. And we think we should send them some gingko or "improve your memory" books.

PUNDITS CAN BE HYPOCRITES, TOO!

"Journalist" Bill O'Reilly gets mad, mad, mad when he thinks about journalists wearing American flag lapel pins and otherwise exploiting the ol' Stars and Stripes. As he explained, "I've never worn an American flag lapel, ever . . . because I am a journalist. I am. And I don't think I should have any insignias on. . . . You know what I think. I tell you what I think. I don't need to wear a lapel. I don't need to do it. . . . And even a flag, I don't—I felt uncomfortable wearing it. I'm not a jingoist."

He might not be a jingoist, but he sure seems to be a capitalist, by gum! On his website, BillOReilly.com, "premium members" can buy a No Spin lapel pin, which is a little teeny U.S. flag with the words "No Spin" beneath it. And then there's the "No Spin Microfiber Jacket" (modeled by Bill himself on the site), which has an American flag insignia. And the fleece vest . . . and the polo shirt . . . and the wind shirt . . . and the coffee mug . . . and the magnet . . . and the baseball cap.

See, it seems that they have a little problem with their memories. Maybe it's something in the water?

ABC News *This Week* host George Stephanopou-los: "Have you ever authorized any U.S. military over-flights of Iran since you've been defense secretary?"

Defense Secretary Donald Rumsfeld: "Well, I don't—I don't think I have, but I don't know. I'd have to check. And I don't know that I'd answer it if I did find out that we had. But I don't believe we have."

Stephanopoulos: "You don't believe you have?"

Rumsfeld: "Yes, and I can't recall any."

....

Q: "Certainly if it happened, nothing remarkable would have occurred?"

President Bill Clinton: "No, nothing remarkable. I don't remember it. . . ."

Q: "When was the last time you spoke with Monica Lewinsky?"

Clinton: "I'm trying to remember. . . ."

Clinton: ". . . I remember that she came in to visit that day. I remember that she was upset. I don't recall whether I talked to her on the phone before she came in to visit, but I may well have. I'm not denying that I did. I just don't recall that. . . ."

Clinton: "I told you so before and I will say again—in the aftermath of this story breaking, and what was told about it, the next two days, the next three days are just a blur to me. I don't remember to whom I talked, when I talked to them or what I said."

Q: "So you're not declining to answer. You just don't remember."

Clinton: "I honestly don't remember—no. I'm not

saying that anybody who had a contrary memory is wrong. I do not remember."

—during Clinton's deposition about the Monica Lewinsky affair

....

Q: "And are you presently still an officer or director of [Albo Pest Control]?"

REPRESENTATIVE TOM DELAY (R-TX): "I don't think so. No."

Q: "All right, you're still an officer, are you not?"

DELAY: "I don't think I am."

Q: "Okay. Did you resign as an officer?"

DELAY: "Not written. It was sort of an agreement. . . ."

DELAY: (in testimony later the same day) "I'm not even sure I am resigned. . . ."

—testimony in a lawsuit that claimed DeLay and a partner used money from their Albo Pest Control Company to pay off campaign loans and more

....

SPECIAL COUNSEL PATRICK FITZGERALD: "Is it your testimony under oath, you don't recall [Ambassador Joseph] Wilson's wife working for the CIA—between the sixth [of July 2003] and your conversation with Russert?"

I. LEWIS "SCOOTER" LIBBY, FORMER CHIEF OF STAFF TO DICK CHENEY: "That's correct, sir, I don't recall discussing it. . . ."

FITZGERALD: "Isn't it a fact, sir, that you told Mr. [Ari] Fleischer over lunch that this was hush-hush or on the QT?"

LIBBY: "I don't recall that. . . ."

FITZGERALD: "Do you recall any conversation at any time when Secretary [Marc] Grossman told you that the former ambassador's wife worked at the CIA?"

LIBBY: "I don't recall."

FITZGERALD: "You have no memory of that whatsoever?"

LIBBY: "I'm sorry, sir, I don't."

—testimony in the Valerie Plame CIA leak perjury trial

....

REPORTER: ". . . Tom Reynolds [R-NY] said that he spoke with you about it last spring."

HOUSE SPEAKER DENNIS HASTERT (R-IL): "You know, I don't recall Reynolds talking to me about that. . . ."

REPORTER: "I mean, Congressman Reynolds put out a statement on Saturday saying that he told you in the spring. Do you think he's lying?"

HASTERT: "No, I'm not saying. I just don't recall him telling me that. If he would have told me that, he would have told me that in the context of maybe a half a dozen or a dozen other things. I don't remember that."

—CNN interview about the Mark Foley–congressional page sex scandal

....

KEN MEHLMAN, CHAIRMAN OF THE REPUBLICAN NATIONAL COMMITTEE: ". . . I also don't recall the specifics of this matter involving Mr. [Allen] Stayman. . . . But as a matter of course, and certainly the first term, I had, frequently, people come to see me with political issues they wanted talked about."

REPORTER WOLF BLITZER: "Including Jack Abramoff?"

MEHLMAN: ". . . Again, I don't recall that specific matter that he came to me for. . . ."

—CNN interview about lobbyist Jack Abramoff and efforts to oust Clinton holdover Allen Stayman from the State Department

....

SENATOR EDWARD KENNEDY (D-MA): "I'm interested in what's in your mind at this time, but what
was in your mind at that time?"

SAMUEL ALITO: "I can't specifically recall what was in
my mind at that time [in 1990, about the duration of
a pledge that as federal circuit judge he would recuse
himself from cases involving the Vanguard mutual
fund company]."

KENNEDY: "You had indicated in your '85 job applica-
tion that you were a member of the Federalist Society
for Law and Public Policy and a regular participant in
its luncheon and a member of the Concerned Alumni
at Princeton University, a conservative alumni group.
And you said yesterday that you wracked your memory about the issue and really had no specific recollection of the [alumni] organization; is that correct?"

ALITO: "I have no specific recollection of joining the
organization. . . ."

KENNEDY: "You called CAP a 'conservative alumni
group.' It also published a publication called *Prospect*,
which includes articles by CAP members about the
policies that the organization promoted. You're familiar with that?"

ALITO: "I don't recall seeing the magazine. . . . Senator, I don't believe I had any active involvement with
this group. I've wracked my memory and I can't recall
anything. . . ."

—Senate Judiciary Committee hearing on Judge Samuel
   Alito's nomination to the Supreme Court

....

SENATOR PATRICK LEAHY (D-VT): "I just want to
know, did you agree—we can spend an hour with

that answer, but frankly, it would be very simple. Did you agree with that interpretation of the torture statute back in August, 2002?"

ALBERTO GONZALES: ". . . I don't recall today whether or not I was in agreement with all of the analysis. . . ."

SENATOR EDWARD KENNEDY (D-MA): "Now, the *Post* article states you chaired several meetings of which various interrogation techniques were discussed. These techniques included the threat of live burial and 'water boarding,' whereby the detainee is strapped to a board, forcibly pushed underwater wrapped in a wet towel and made to believe he might drown. The article states that you raised no objections. Now, without consulting military and State Department experts, they were not consulted, they were not invited to important meetings, that might have been important to some, but we know of what Secretary Taft has said about his exclusion from these. Experts in laws of torture and war prove the resulting memos gave CIA interrogators the legal blessings they sought. Now was it the CIA that asked you?"

GONZALES: "Sir, I don't have a specific recollection. . . ."

—Senate Judiciary Committee hearing on Alberto Gonzales's nomination to be U.S. attorney general

....

"I don't recall a so-called emergency meeting. . . . We'll have to go back to the records to see if there was a meeting."

—SECRETARY OF STATE CONDOLEEZZA RICE, on a meeting about terrorism threats with CIA head George Tenet that, according to Bob Woodward's book *State of Denial,* took place prior to 9/11

....

"I can't pretend to know or remember every fact that may be of relevance."
—ATTORNEY GENERAL ALBERTO GONZALES, in testimony before Congress regarding the dismissal of eight U.S. attorneys

"I don't remember."
—GONZALES

"I don't remember."
—GONZALES

"I don't remember."
—GONZALES

(This phrase was repeated 119 more times—winning the world record in the "I don't remember/recall/or otherwise have any idea" sweepstakes.)

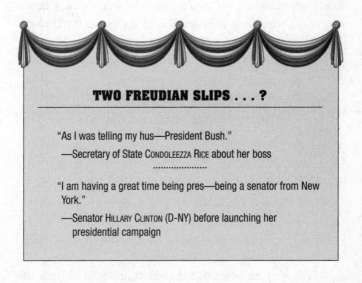

TWO FREUDIAN SLIPS . . . ?

"As I was telling my hus—President Bush."
—Secretary of State CONDOLEEZZA RICE about her boss

....

"I am having a great time being pres—being a senator from New York."
—Senator HILLARY CLINTON (D-NY) before launching her presidential campaign

FIVE

POLITICAL COMMUNICATION

Politicians have to communicate—with their constituents, with their colleagues, with the press. It's kind of crucial to their job.

Note: We didn't say they had to communicate *well*.

THE RHETORIC OF POLITICS:
STIRRING CHURCHILLIAN MOMENTS

"I have nothing to offer but blood, toil, tears, and sweat."

So said Winston Churchill. And by those few words he inspired an entire people in its darkest hour. But do such silver-tongued rhetoricians exist today? Do they inspire us as much as those great orators of old? Of course!

Following are some of the greatest orators and some of the most stirring words ever uttered by modern American statesmen and stateswomen.

SENATOR JOE LIEBERMAN ("D"-CT), IN HIS HISTORIC "IT'S JUST LIKE THE 1930S, THE SPANISH CIVIL WAR, NO I MEAN THE 1940S, YOU KNOW, PEARL HARBOR?" SPEECH

Here, Senator Joe lets loose his silver tongue in a speech at the Heritage Foundation in January 2007. He shows off his deep knowledge of 20th-century history, along with a powerful command of stray facts. Follow his argument—it shouldn't take too many rereadings. Joe warns America of the dire perils of not thinking exactly as he thinks. He compares our era to some past eras; in fact, he compares our era to quite a few past eras . . .

> "There are people who have spoken of this moment in history as if it were the '30s, and there are some parallels, I fear, there. People say the war in Iraq is comparable to the Spanish Civil War, and the war in Iraq, to the larger war against Islamist terrorism, comparable to the Spanish Civil War, to the Second World War, the late '30s and the failure to grasp the growing threat of fascism in Europe until it was almost too late. The painful irony of this moment in our history is that while in some senses it is comparable to the 1930s, it's also already 1942. Because Pearl Harbor [9/11], in this war, has already happened."

FORMER SECRETARY OF STATE AND IRAQ STUDY GROUP CO-CHAIR JAMES BAKER, IN HIS "PROMISES, WHAT PROMISES?" SPEECH

Here, Secretary Baker utilizes the rhetorical technique of numbering—letting the public clearly see what is going on in his mind, 1, 2 . . . and clearly revealing to an interested public the faults with his opponent. Of course, it is a good technique to keep in mind the *words* that follow these numbers. . . .

> "And there are the two major promises he has not been able to keep. And those are the promises to put more Americans back to work and the second promise is to—uh—what is that second promise?"

Senator Ted K. Stevens (R-AK), in His Lucid "Let Me Explain the Internet Even Though I'm Not the Fastest Chip on the Motherboard" Speech

Ours is a technical era and it is incumbent upon our leaders not only to debate technical issues, but to do so in crystal-*clear* rhetoric so all of us can understand. Here on the floor of the Senate in June 2006, Senator Stevens explains the role of the Internet in a modern technological society so simply, so cleanly, that a third-grader could understand—the words, that is, not the argument.

> "There's one company now you can sign up and you can get a movie delivered to your house daily by delivery service. Okay. And currently it comes to your house, it gets put in the mailbox when you get home and you change your order but you pay for that, right.
>
> "But this service is now going to go through the Internet and what you do is you just go to a place on the Internet and you order your movie and guess what you can order ten of them delivered to you and the delivery charge is free. Ten of them streaming across that Internet and what happens to your own personal Internet? I just the other day got, an Internet was sent by my staff at 10 o'clock in the morning on

Friday and I just got it yesterday. Why? Because it got tangled up with all these things going on the Internet commercially. So you want to talk about the consumer? Let's talk about you and me. We use this Internet to communicate and we aren't using it for commercial purposes.

"We aren't earning anything by going on that Internet. Now I'm not saying you have to or you want to discriminate against those people.

"The regulatory approach is wrong. Your approach is regulatory in the sense that it says 'No one can charge anyone for massively invading this world of the Internet.' No, I'm not finished. I want people to understand my position, I'm not going to take a lot of time.

"They want to deliver vast amounts of information over the Internet. And again, the Internet is not something you just dump something on. It's not a truck.

"It's a series of tubes."

SENATOR JOHN CHAFEE (R-RI), IN HIS "SWISH-SWISH OR IS IT ZING-ZING" EXPLANATION

The key to modern communication is use of the *vernacular,* that is, common, everyday speech. Here Chafee explains the sometimes dull topic of budgeting in a fun, *inspiring* way.

"The things they believed in for so long happening overnight—zing, zing, zing, balanced budget amendment, line-item veto—and everything swish, swish, swish . . . It isn't something where the Speaker says, 'We'll finish this tonight, zing, zing.' "

Minnesota State Senatorial Candidate Rae Hart Anderson, in Her Famous "Humpty Dumpty, God, and the Bible" Posting

Although Ms. Anderson lost her election in November 2006, we can clearly see in her words the makings of a powerfully *unique* rhetorician. And although denied a public platform in Congress, Ms. Anderson was at least able to give the public a sample of herself at her most eloquent, here in an electronic posting on a blog unfairly mocking her electoral loss.

> "Eggs are fragile creations, and a broken Humpty Dumpty hard to glue . . . but the Creator of all things takes an egg, and breaks it with superior life from the inside out . . . lets life form inside, and peck its way out and twin chicks set foot on earth with voices and purpose—with bodies and smallish minds that grasp little. Some fractured human ideas lead to more of life and more knowledge of the lack of knowledge, even in the talking heads found everywhere—that fragment into even less so easily."

President George W. Bush: A Few Examples from the Man with Churchill's Bust on His Desk

When it comes to speechmaking ability, it is hard to forget President George W. Bush. He keeps a bust of Churchill on his desk for inspiration, it is said, and if he is channeling the great orator and statesman, it is in his words where we would find the evidence. So let us see in these examples from a few of Bush's speeches if we can find a bit of "old Winnie."

> "I was proud the other day when both Republicans and Democrats stood with me in the Rose Garden to announce their support for a clear statement of purpose: 'You disarm, or we will.' "

Vice President Richard "Dick" Cheney, Our Modern Cato

Perhaps the most *Roman* of our current crop of orators is the vice president, a man of few words—terse, blunt, to the point. Sometimes, listening to him, we feel transported back to the era of the great Roman Republic, and of that great Stoic, Marcus Porcius Cato.

"Go f*** yourself."

SPONTANEOUS MOMENTS AT SPONTANEOUS PHOTO OPS

Photo ops are a crucial part of the political image-making process. The key thing is SPONTANEITY! The camera shows you, as the politician, *just the way you really are.* After all, as a politician, you don't care about the image, you care about the people! You're so dedicated, caring, concerned. So spontaneous. Just the natural, *unrehearsed* you in front of the cameras . . .

All of this unrehearsed spontaneity takes some planning, some prep work, maybe a makeup person or two, a few handlers, a fashion expert, maybe some extra lighting, some props, some hired extras, some rehearsing . . .

Spontaneous Photo Op #1:
Caring Senator Bill Frist (R-TN) Visiting Tsunami-Stricken Sri Lanka

Standing next to a pile of ocean-swept wreckage, Frist told a photographer: "Get some devastation in the back."

Spontaneous Photo Op #2:
Helpful Second Lady Tipper Gore Visiting Honduras to "Help" with the Devastation of Hurricane Mitch

"She's going to be shoveling mud. Then she'll wipe the sweat from her brow, like this. Make sure you get that shot, all right?" Thus did Nathan Naylor, Vice President Al Gore's press spokesman, brief network television crews just before Tipper Gore arrived on the scene in Honduras.

SPONTANEOUS PHOTO OP #3:
Concerned President Bush Speaking to Ordinary Workers About Taxes

Problem: When George Bush arrived in Indianapolis to push his tax cut plans, the people standing behind him were all wearing ties. *They looked too rich*—and "tax cuts for the rich" doesn't play very well with the voters. So White House

GREAT MOMENTS IN BUREAUCRATIC PHOTO OPS

Key to the photo op: photogenic humans.

Forget sacrifice, forget honor, forget reality.

Case: Sergeant David Thomas, wounded in action in Iraq and missing a leg, was a patient at Walter Reed Hospital. He wanted to watch the citizenship ceremony of a fellow amputee—who was being granted the honor by President Bush himself. A caseworker asked him what he would wear. Since it was summer, Thomas said he would wear shorts. The caseworker told him shorts weren't advisable because amputees had to be seated in the front row.

"Are you telling me that I can't go to the ceremony 'cause I'm an amputee?" Thomas asked.

"No, I'm saying you need to wear pants."

"I'm not ashamed of what I did, and y'all shouldn't be neither," answered Thomas.

But when the guest list came for the ceremony, one name was missing: David Thomas.

aides did the logical thing: They told everyone to take off their ties and look like poorer, working-class people.

SPONTANEOUS PHOTO OP #4:
Selfless FEMA Chief Michael Brown Getting Ready to Go on Television to Speak to the Nation About the Disaster of Hurricane Katrina

Michael Brown was very concerned as Hurricane Katrina approached New Orleans. He almost immediately asked his press secretary, Sharon Worthy, about his clothing: "Tie or not for tonight? Button-down blue shirt?" Later, Worthy advised Brown: "Please roll up the sleeves of your shirt, all shirts. Even the president rolled his sleeves to just below the elbow. In this [crisis] and on TV you just need to look more hardworking." On the day of the storm, Worthy told him, "You look fabulous," and Brown replied, "I got it at Nordstrom's. . . . Are you proud of me?"

Hey Brownie: All of America was . . . kind of. Not really. Sorry.

I WISH I HADN'T SAID THAT

Sadly, some politicians lose their gift of gab from time to time. (Well, sad for them but not for those of us who enjoy a laugh at a politician's expense.)

Here then, are some "Ohmigod, I wish I hadn't said that" statements—most of which spawned agonized mea culpas from the culprits.

I WISH I HADN'T SAID THAT TO . . . *an audience of black union leaders.*

"Nigger labor organizations . . ."
—LIEUTENANT GOVERNOR CRUZ BUSTAMANTE (D) of California in a speech about the black union movement

I WISH I HADN'T SAID THAT TO . . . *an African-American Senate candidate.*

"[He has] a career of slavishly supporting the Republican Party."
—REPRESENTATIVE STENY H. HOYER (D-MD) about African-American Republican Senate candidate, Lieutenant Governor Michael Steele. Bloggers called this "Macaca: The Sequel."

I WISH I HADN'T SAID THAT TO . . . *a decorated Marine.*

"I have a message for Congressman Murtha: Cowards cut and run, Marines never do."
—REPRESENTATIVE JEAN SCHMIDT (R-OH) referring to Representative John Murtha's (D-PA) "withdraw the troops from Iraq" policies. Murtha served as a Marine in Vietnam, and received the Bronze Star with Valor, two Purple Hearts, the Vietnamese Cross of Gallantry, and the Navy Distinguished Service Medal.

I WISH I HADN'T SAID THAT ABOUT . . . *someone who was accused of being a lesbian by political opponents.*

JON STEWART: "So your plan is to find Franklin Delano Roosevelt, exhume him, reanimate him—"
REPRESENTATIVE (AND FORMER CLINTON ADVISER) RAHM EMANUEL (D-IL): "Well, Hillary's already helping us with the Eleanor part—"
STEWART: "Settle down . . ."

I WISH I HADN'T SAID THAT TO . . . *a blind man.*
Scene: Rose Garden press conference
Characters: President George W. Bush, reporters (one of whom, Peter Wallsten, is wearing dark glasses and is legally blind)

Wallsten asks question. Bush answers with his own question:

BUSH: "Are you going to ask that question with shades on?"
WALLSTEN: "I can take them off."
BUSH: "I'm interested in the shade look. Seriously."
WALLSTEN: "All right, I'll keep it, then."
BUSH: "For the viewers, there's no sun."
WALLSTEN: "I guess it depends on your perspective."
BUSH: "Touché."

Bush was later informed that Wallsten needed the glasses to protect his eyes.

I WISH I HADN'T SAID THAT TO . . . *a paraplegic.*

"[Members] cannot be recognized on the floor to debate unless they are standing, and I don't believe he is standing."
—MISSOURI STATE REPRESENTATIVE CYNTHIA DAVIS (R), citing the state House rule book and referring to Representative Chuck Graham (D), who was speaking without standing (mainly because he is wheelchair-bound and has been for 21 years)

BAD METAPHOR DEPARTMENT:
WHEN POLITICIANS TRY TO GET CREATIVE IN A SPEECH

In their quest to be quotable, many politicians opt for metaphors or similes. They use, of course, your basic sports metaphors—one of the more popular ways of making a point. But some metaphors are a bit more, well, let's just say *creative*. To the nth degree.

THE "THE IRAQ WAR IS A FOOTBALL GAME" METAPHOR

"Go Big. Go Long. Go Home."
—Pentagon insiders' terms for the three options in Iraq: to
send in more troops, pull out some troops but stay longer,
or pull out

THE "YES, THE IRAQ WAR IS DEFINITELY A FOOTBALL GAME" METAPHOR

"Some commentators have compared the Bush plan to
a 'Hail Mary' pass in football—a desperate heave deep
down the field by a losing team at the end of the
game. Actually, a far better analogy for the Bush plan
is a draw play on third down with 20 yards to go in
the first quarter. The play does have a chance of working if everything goes perfectly, but it is more likely to
gain a few yards and set up a punt on the next down,
after which the game can be continued under more
favorable circumstances."
—SENATOR RICHARD LUGAR (R-IN)

THE "NO, THE IRAQ WAR IS A POKER GAME, WELL, A COUNTRY SONG *ABOUT* A POKER GAME" METAPHOR

"This one [the Iraq War] is for all the marbles. [Iraqis
should heed] Kenny Rogers's old song: 'You got to
know when to hold 'em and know when to fold 'em.'
It's time for them to deliver on the hand that they've
dealt."
—SENATOR JOHNNY ISAKSON (R-GA)

THE "NO, NO, THE IRAQ WAR IS LIKE FRODO AND SAM IN THE LORD OF THE RINGS" METAPHOR

"As the hobbits are going up Mount Doom, the Eye of
Mordor is being drawn somewhere else. It's being

drawn to Iraq and it's not being drawn to the U.S. You know what? I want to keep it on Iraq. I don't want the Eye to come back here to the United States."
—Senator Rick Santorum (R-PA)

The "No, No, No, the Iraq War Is an *Egg*" Metaphor

Journalist Jim Lehrer: "Is there a little bit of a broken egg problem here, Mr. President, that there is instability and there is violence in Iraq—sectarian violence, Iraqis killing other Iraqis, and now the United States helped create the broken egg and now says, 'Okay, Iraqis, it's your problem. You put the egg back together, and if you don't do it quickly and you don't do it well, then we'll get the hell out.'"

President George W. Bush: "Yeah, you know, that's an interesting question. I don't quite view it as the broken egg; I view it as the cracked egg—"

Lehrer: "Cracked egg?"

Bush: "—that—where we still have a chance to move beyond the broken egg. And I thought long and hard about the decision, Jim. Obviously it's a big decision for this theater in the war on terror, and you know, if I didn't believe we could keep the egg from fully cracking I wouldn't ask 21,000 kids—additional kids to go into Iraq to reinforce those troops that are there."

As for non-war-related metaphors:

The "White House Staffers Are *Star Trek* Vulcans, No, Klingons, Wait, Make That FAUX Klingons" Metaphor

"This president has listened to some people, the so-called Vulcans in the White House, the ideologues.

But you know, unlike the Vulcans of *Star Trek* who made the decisions based on logic and fact, these guys make it on ideology. These aren't Vulcans. There are Klingons in the White House. But unlike the real Klingons of *Star Trek,* these Klingons have never fought a battle of their own. Don't let faux Klingons send real Americans to war."
—REPRESENTATIVE DAVID WU (D-OR)

THE "THE U.S. IS A BABY, OR THE CONGRESS IS AN OB/GYN, OR BOTH, KINDA" METAPHOR

"When you're delivering a baby and the baby's getting in trouble, and you can see the baby's heartbeat, which is normally about 130 or 140 beats per minute, going down to 50 or 60, and you're standing there watching it go down, you know you've got about three minutes to make a decision. You can use a pair of forceps and try to pull it out, you can use a vacuum extractor, or you can leave labor and delivery, put her on the table, put her to sleep, cut a hole in her belly, and take it out with a C-section—but you've got to do something, and you've got to do it now. That baby's life depends on what you do in those three minutes. And that's exactly where we are in our country today. We are in those critical three minutes. If we wait to act, it's going to be too late. We're going to lose the baby."
—SENATOR TOM COBURN (R-OK), on the federal budget and the need to cut pork

INCREDIBLE STRETCHES TO MAKE YOUR POINT

Some politicians have a gift for making a pithy statement that sums up a key and complex political point and lets us dumb voters really *understand* a meaty and complex issue.

JANET ROWLAND, COLORADO CANDIDATE FOR LIEUTENANT GOVERNOR

Gay marriage isn't far from bestiality. "Do we allow a man to marry a sheep?"

This statement from unsuccessful 2006 Colorado Republican lieutenant gubernatorial candidate Janet Rowland really, really *clarifies* the entire gay rights issue for us. *Gayness is a lot like having sex with animals.*

On the Rocky Mountain PBS show *Colorado State of Mind*, Rowland, who was also serving as the Mesa County commissioner, said that while she has gay friends, and a lot of respect for gay people, there were, well . . . *problems.* She explained:

> "I believe marriage is between a man and a woman. Homosexuality is an alternative lifestyle. That doesn't make it a marriage. Some people have group sex. Should we allow two men and three women to marry? Should we allow polygamy with one man and five wives? For some people, the alternative lifestyle is bestiality. Do we allow a man to marry a sheep? I mean at some point you have to draw the line."

After something of an uproar over these statements, and after a lot of people called her "intolerant," "over the top," and "bigoted," Rowland (predictably) explained that she had been "taken out of context." She added that maybe she had "stepped over the line by referring to bestiality."

John Marshall, campaign manager for her gubernatorial running mate, Bob Beauprez, conceded that Rowland had made a "regrettable statement." He added, "In the real world, people make mistakes. She's an unbelievably good candidate."

REPRESENTATIVE STEVE KING

My wife "is at far greater risk being a civilian in D.C. than an average civilian in Iraq."

Representative Steve King (R-IA), an unsung genius-expert on the Iraq War, knows a truth that all those Iraqis and American soldiers don't know: *Iraq isn't dangerous at all!*

We thought it was, but now we know that all those deaths and stuff are *propaganda.* We hadn't heard King's speech on the House floor in 2004, explaining this for all of us stupidos. King explained:

> "27.51 Iraqis per 100,000 die a violent death on an annual basis. 27.51. Now what does that mean? To me, it really doesn't mean a lot until I compare it to people that I know or have a feel for the rhythm of this place. Well I by now have a feel for the rhythm of this place called Washington, D.C., and my wife lives here with me, and I can tell you, Mr. Speaker, she's at far greater risk being a civilian in Washington, D.C., than an average civilian in Iraq. Forty-five out of every 100,000 Washington, D.C., regular residents die a violent death on an annual basis."

We say—let's send Mrs. King to Iraq, now! For her own safety.

REPRESENTATIVE PETER KING

Baghdad is just like Manhattan!

Here's another amazingly comforting take on Iraq from another self-appointed real-life-in-Iraq expert—Congressman Peter King (R-NY). He says that not only is the Iraqi capital, Baghdad, just like Manhattan—the restaurants are cheaper! *So we'll tell you again: Iraq isn't dangerous at all—and there's lots to do!*

Here's the astute congressman, with his laser-like ability to see things as they truly are, describing Baghdad:

> "Conditions on the ground are different than what you see on television. As we go through the city of Baghdad, it was like being in Manhattan. I'm talking about bumper-to-bumper traffic. Talking about shopping centers, talking about restaurants, talking about video stores, talking about guys on the street corner, talking about major hotels. And so, at that moment, people must be amazingly resilient and you would never know that there was a war going on."

We're canceling our trip to Paris. Baghdad, here we come.

SENATOR JOHN MCCAIN
Baghdad is a GREAT place for a relaxed stroll!

Senator McCain (R-AZ) says that Americans aren't "getting the full picture" on Iraq, claiming that there "are neighborhoods in Baghdad where you and I could walk through those neighborhoods, today." And, to prove his point, went for a short stroll in a Baghdad shopping district.

Never mind that with him he had 100 American soldiers, 3 Blackhawk helicopters, and 2 Apache gunships overhead. Hey, they might have been there to help carry his purchases home!

DEPUTY ASSISTANT SECRETARY OF STATE COLLEEN GRAFFY
Guantanamo prison suicides were a "good PR move to draw attention."

Colleen Graffy of the State Department explained that three detainees who committed suicide in 2006 at Guantanamo (and at least one of them had been found innocent by a military tribunal and was due to be released) hadn't killed themselves out of despair but rather for *public rela-*

tions. In short, they weren't despairing prisoners but instead were PR geniuses. Rear Admiral Harry Harris, camp commander, agreed. He called the suicides "an act of asymmetrical warfare waged against us." Both said that the three dead detainees had valued neither their lives nor the lives of those around them. *In other words, the Guantanamo prisoners killed themselves to spite the United States and specifically didn't kill any Americans, to look even better.*

We want to ask a question: If *all* the Guantanamo detainees killed themselves, would that be an even bigger PR victory for the terrorists?

Newt Gingrich

People who criticize Bush are like those people who enabled Hitler.

On Fox News's *Hannity & Colmes* in September 2006, Newt Gingrich, the former House Speaker, commentator, and ever-potential presidential candidate, said he agreed with a statement by then secretary of defense Donald Rumsfeld that critics of Bush's Iraq War strategies were like Nazi appeasers. Gingrich said this "was not an insulting comment." *So if you've got any doubts about the Iraq War, remember, you're helping Hitler.*

We didn't realize so many people were Nazi appeasers, including hundreds of U.S. Army brass, thousands of soldiers, and about 65% of the population. Watch out, Poland.

Senator James Inhofe

Speaking of Hitler, did you know that environmentalists are Nazi Gestapo fascists? Just asking.

Senator James Inhofe (R-OK), who also happens to have absolutely no homosexuals in his family, teaches us that *environmentalists are just like the Nazis.*

Inhofe (not a climate scientist, but a highly qualified former real estate developer and insurance company exec) realizes that all of the scientific evidence on global warming is fake—and that the environmentalists talking about it

> "kind of reminds . . . I could use the Third Reich, the Big Lie. . . . You say something over and over and over and over again, and people will believe it, and that's their [the environmentalists'] strategy. . . . A hot summer has nothing to do with global warming. Let's keep in mind it was just three weeks ago that people were saying, 'Wait a minute; it is unusually cool. . . .'"

Appropriately, Inhofe also once compared the Environmental Protection Agency to the Gestapo.

REPRESENTATIVE RANDY KUHL
The federal government did a wonderful job helping out during Hurricane Katrina.

You know, we were surprised. We watched the response to Hurricane Katrina on TV and it looked like a *mess.* But Congressman Randy Kuhl (R-NY), who hails from his state's 29th district, which is a little far from New Orleans, but not too far for someone smart to know the truth, knows better. *The government did a great job of helping out all those poor people during the hurricane.*

The smart congressman explained (with a straight face, and no, he wasn't kidding): "You can see that when, in fact, this government needs to react, like it did with Katrina with immediate appropriations to help out people who were dying." At first this didn't make sense to us, but then we thought about former first lady Barbara Bush's realization that for many of those New Orleanians, the whole thing was like a vacation.

REPRESENTATIVE PHIL GINGREY

An anti-gay, pro-marriage vote is "perhaps the best message we can give to the Middle East and all the trouble they're having over there right now."

We wouldn't have thought of it. We would have thought that other issues were more important, but now we know. *The best way to help the Middle East is to ban gay marriage in America.*

Unfortunately for the Middle East, Representative Phil Gingrey (R-GA) and his anti-gay-marriage compatriots failed to pass an amendment banning same-sex marriage in July 2006. The vote was 237 to 187 (and one member voting "present"), which means that 188 members of Congress are, for some sad reason, *against* peace in the Middle East.

POLITICAL PLAGIARISM OR COSMIC COINCIDENCE?—
OR, HAVEN'T WE HEARD THAT BEFORE?

The temptations for a politician to plagiarize are obvious— why go to all the bother of writing a speech (or hiring someone to write a speech) if someone else has already done it for you?

And if someone notices that the words sound awfully familiar, you as a politician can chalk it up to the wondrous nature of the universe, where cosmic coincidences occur and reoccur.

We're sure you know the old idea: If a monkey spent hours typing at random, eventually it would produce the complete works of Shakespeare. However, the amount of time a monkey would have to spend is debatable and apparently approaches infinity. In 2003 researchers left a computer keyboard with six Sulawesi crested macaques at a zoo in Devon, England, for a month. Unfortunately, the monkeys only typed out five pages, mostly consisting of the letter *S*, and attacked the keyboard with a stone and urinated and defecated on it as well. But sooner or later, some think, the monkeys might have produced a speech by, say, Joe Lieberman.

And now, in this section, and in the spirit of democracy, which may be somewhat unfamiliar to us here in the 21st century, we will let you, the reader, decide if the following politicians (or speechwriters) were being plagiarists or were merely victims of a great and wondrous cosmic coincidence.

ADJUTANT GENERAL MARTHA RAINVILLE (R-VT)

"I strongly believe that our present system of energy is weakening our national security, hurting our pocketbooks, and threatening our children's future."
(September 2006)

STRANGELY SIMILAR SPEECH SOMEONE ELSE MADE EARLIER

"Our present system of energy is weakening our national security, hurting our pocketbooks, violating our common values, and threatening our children's future."
—SENATOR HILLARY CLINTON (D-NY) (May 2006)

REPRESENTATIVE JIM GIBBONS (R-NV)

"I say we tell those liberal, tree-hugging, Birkenstock-wearing, hippie, tie-dyed liberals to go make their movies and their music and whine somewhere else."
(February 2005)

STRANGELY SIMILAR SPEECH SOMEONE ELSE MADE EARLIER

"Tell the liberal, tree-hugging, hippie, tie-dyed liberals to go make their movies and music and whine somewhere else."
—ALABAMA STATE AUDITOR BETH CHAPMAN (March 2003)

Representative Jean Schmidt (R-OH)

"Two and a half years ago, Republicans delivered on a promise we made to the American people by passing sweeping Medicare reform, including a comprehensive Medicare prescription drug benefit to give America's seniors access to affordable prescription drugs. Now that the program is off the ground, the evidence is in and we have much to celebrate: The Medicare prescription drug benefit is working, and seniors are saving money." (August 2006)

Strangely Similar Speech Someone Else Made Earlier

"Two and a half years ago, Congress delivered on a promise we made to the American people by passing sweeping Medicare reform, including a comprehensive Medicare prescription drug benefit to, for the first time, give America's seniors access to affordable prescription drugs. As we have now passed the May 15th deadline, the evidence is in and we have much to celebrate: The Medicare prescription drug benefit is working, and seniors are saving money."

—Representative Deborah Pryce (R-OH) (July 2006)

Senator Joe Biden (D-DE)

"I started thinking as I was coming over here, why is it that Joe Biden is the first in his family ever to go to a university? Why is it that my wife who is sitting out there in the audience is the first in her family to ever go to college? Is it because our fathers and mothers were not bright? . . . No, it's not because they weren't as smart. It's not because they didn't work as hard. It's because they didn't have a platform upon which to stand." (August 1988)

STRANGELY SIMILAR SPEECH SOMEONE ELSE MADE EARLIER

"Why am I the first Kinnock in a thousand generations to be able to get to university? Why is Glenys the first woman in her family in a thousand generations to be able to get to university? Was it because our predecessors were thick? Does anybody really think that they didn't get what we had because they didn't have the talent or the strength or the endurance or the commitment? Of course not. It was because there was no platform upon which they could stand."

—BRITISH LABOR PARTY LEADER NEAL KINNOCK (June 1987)

REPRESENTATIVE STEVE PEARCE (R-NM)

"I have received numerous constituent complaints about high gasoline prices and the summer driving season has not yet started. While government policies are not the sole reason for these high prices, they do contribute to regional and seasonal price fluctuations that increase costs and reduce flexibility to meet consumer demand." (April 2005)

STRANGELY SIMILAR SPEECH SOMEONE ELSE MADE EARLIER

"Members of Congress have already received complaints from their constituents about high gasoline prices and the summer driving season—with its increased demand—has not even started. . . . While government policies are not the sole reason for these high prices, they do contribute to regional and seasonal price fluctuations that increase costs and reduce flexibility to meet consumer demand."

—WRITER CHARLI COON on Heritage.org (May 2004)

FORMER PRESIDENT BILL CLINTON (D)

"They [the Bush administration] believe that in large measure people make or break their own lives, and you're on your own." (2006)

STRANGELY SIMILAR SPEECH SOMEONE ELSE MADE EARLIER

"The [Bush administration] message can be summed up in three words: On your own."
—SENATOR HILLARY CLINTON (D-NY) (2006)

SENATOR HILLARY CLINTON (D-NY)

"How do you get tough on your banker?" (2006)

STRANGELY SIMILAR SPEECH SOMEONE ELSE MADE EARLIER

"When's the last time you got tough on your banker?"
—FORMER PRESIDENT BILL CLINTON (2006)

SIX

POLITICAL CAMPAIGNS

IN AN IDEAL WORLD, NO POLITICIAN WOULD HAVE TO GO through the hassle and expense of a campaign. But this world is far from ideal. And, sadly, many campaigns are far from ideal. . . .

THE "HOW I BOTCHED MY CAMPAIGN" AWARDS

Let us give credit where credit is due to those awe-inspiring candidates who made the wrong, the ridiculous, and, indeed, the truly stupid, mistakes—that cost them elections.

THE "SILVER-TONGUED RHETORIC" AWARD GOES TO . . .
New York Republican U.S. Senate hopeful Jeanine Pirro
. . . for her gripping and catchy announcement speech in 2005:

> "I support making President Bush's tax cuts perma-
> nent. But I also support the right of a woman to
> choose. . . . I believe in immigration. . . . But I also be-

lieve in the Patriot Act. . . . Hillary Clinton has short-changed New York. . . . Hillary Clinton hasn't delivered. But I am not Hillary Clinton. [*Pause for optimal effect.*] You will know where I stand on the issues. Hillary Clinton— [*Pause. Much shuffling of pages. Silence for 32 seconds.*]"

Then the gutsy "I Can Think on My Feet" Jeanine picks it right up . . . with the stirring: "Do you have page 10?"

THE "TIMING IS EVERYTHING" AWARD GOES TO . . .
Will Cobb, Democratic hopeful in Ward 6, Washington, D.C.
. . . for tirelessly going door-to-door and collecting 560 petition signatures—then forgetting to hand them in on time.

When a reporter from a local paper called Cobb for an interview and asked him how he felt filing those petitions, Cobb was taken by surprise. "Holy cow, I got them sitting at my house right now!" His campaign manager sped to the D.C. Board of Elections and Ethics (yup, that's what it's called, and we aren't sure why . . .) to hand in the petitions—and arrived there at 5:45, or 45 minutes after the deadline. Cobb was unable to run.

THE "A PICTURE SAYS A THOUSAND WORDS" PHOTO-OP AWARD GOES TO . . .
Senator Joe "Democrat" Lieberman ("D"-CT), then in the middle of his failed attempt to get the Democratic senatorial nod
. . . for picking picture-perfect photo-op places and people.

Scene: The parking lot of Mickey's Oceanic Grill in East Hartford, Connecticut

The press watches as Joe approaches the amassed throng there to meet him. Said "amassed throng" consists of two people: a supporter (who shakes Lieberman's hand and assures him of his vote) and a man in a dirty tan trench coat accessorized by a fleck of food at the left corner of wearer's mouth. Joe, always quick to seize the moment and desperate for *some* support, greets the Man in the Raincoat.

MITR (leaning in very closely toward Joe): "What color are your eyes?"

JOE: "Ha ha ha!"

Lieberman quickly walks away. Perhaps toward the other man, er, half of the throng? We are not sure.

RUNNER-UP:

Joe "Dem" Lieberman again

. . . for pursuing said photo ops to the nth degree.

Scene: Interior of Mickey's Oceanic Grill

The press watches as Joe walks through the tables of people eating lobster rolls and other Oceanic Grill–type comestibles. Most continue eating.

NICE SYMPATHETIC MAN (patting Joe on back): "It's gonna be okay."

FERVENT SUPPORTER WHO HAD BEEN FOLLOWING HIM AROUND ALL DAY: "You gotta give them hell, Joe."

OTHER PEOPLE IN RESTAURANT: "Chew, chew. Chomp. Swallow."

They do not look up from their Oceanic food to acknowledge our intrepid candidate.

Joe leaves.

Total time of campaign stop (including parking lot): 10 minutes. Planned time of stop: 35 minutes.

THE "HOW TO COURT THE IRISH VOTE, BAD CHOICES DIVISION" AWARD GOES TO . . .

Senator Joe "Dem" Lieberman (yes, it's a trifecta for Joe!)

. . . for campaigning at an Irish pub quite early on a Monday morning. On a day that wasn't St. Patrick's Day.

Apparently someone in the "Democrat's" crack primary campaign team figured there would be tons of people bellying up to the bar at 9 A.M. (Note to Joe: Perhaps you should rid yourself of those anti-Irish stereotypes, okay?)

So Joe wound up at the bar with a mass of newspeople, a couple of supporters . . . and almost no bar patrons. (We do not know if he got the vote of those few drinkers.)

THE "DISASTROUS NEWS CONFERENCE" AWARD GOES TO . . .

Los Angeles mayoral hopeful Tom Houston (D)

. . . for innovatively scheduling a news conference 60 feet underwater in Santa Monica Bay.

Houston was hoping to publicize his environmental initiatives by coming up with this boffo news conference concept. Unfortunately, only one reporter showed up (and he got seasick); the campaign banner was virtually invisible because of the cloudy water; some of the candidate's divers got lost in the less-than-crystal-clear water and freaked out; and the candidate himself had to be rescued after he developed breathing trouble at a depth of 10 feet.

THE "DON'T BELIEVE EVERYTHING YOU READ" AWARD GOES TO . . .

Katherine Harris (R) in her campaign for a U.S. Senate seat from Florida

. . . for creatively including fiction in her ostensibly nonfiction campaign mailer.

More specifically, Harris—or staffers, as she later claimed—sent out a campaign flyer titled "Campaign 2006: Fact and Fiction," in which she listed endorsements from Florida governor Jeb Bush and Florida Republican Party chairwoman Carole Jean Jordan. It also cited a poll showing Harris trailing Senator Bill Nelson (D-FL) by less than 4%.

But the *fact* was that neither Bush nor Jordan had endorsed her. In fact, Jordan had asked Harris to drop out of the race. As for the poll numbers—well, they *had* been fact ten months before. At the time of the mailing, though, she trailed by 30, not 3.9, points.

WHAT *NOT* TO DO WHILE RUNNING FOR OFFICE

No, political candidates don't have it easy. They have to go through day after day of pressing the ol' flesh, giving stump speeches, kissing babies, all while maintaining that high level of moral rectitude we Americans *expect* from our illustrious candidates.

(Yes, we said moral rectitude. Please stop laughing.)

And sometimes these candidates do something a little stupid—something that they don't think will affect their campaign, something, say, involving attempted murder . . . or body paint. You know, silly little things like that, that could kind of ruin all their intensive electioneering, for some odd reason . . .

Bad Move	Who Was Involved	Attempt to Get Around It	Fallout
Throttling mistress	**Rep. Don Sherwood (R-PA)** and his then mistress (a former Capitol Hill intern—what a shock!)	Claimed it was just one of those innocent "vigorous back rubs"	Political opponents used the "throttling" incident in ads. Sherwood lost his reelection bid. (He also had to shell out big bucks (about $500,000) to settle a lawsuit the ex brought against him.
Knocking wife around—or, more specifically (to paraphrase the wife), grabbing wife by the neck and pushing her around the house	**Rep. John Sweeney (R-NY)** and his wife	Since the state police wouldn't release their copy of the incident report (but didn't dispute that the report being circulated was real), Sweeney's spokesperson got the chance to say it was just part of a nasty Democratic smear campaign. (Just like the questionable car accident several years before and the reported drunkenness at a college frat party in 2006? We're just asking . . .)	Sweeney lost. He is, however, still married.

Bad Move	Who Was Involved	Attempt to Get Around It	Fallout
Allegedly attacking woman in parking garage, after playing unwanted footsie with her in a restaurant (Woman also alleged that "he pushed me against a wall" near a stairway and an elevator and added that he said, "You have two choices. You can leave, or you can do the other choice.")	Gubernatorial candidate Rep. **Jim Gibbons (R-NV)** and cocktail waitress Chrissy Mazzeo	Gibbons said he was just walking her to the garage when she slipped; he grabbed her arm to stop her from falling, and that was that. No sexual advances, no nothing. (Well, actually at first Gibbons never mentioned a garage, saying the so-called incident happened outside a restaurant. An oversight, obviously . . .) Mazzeo didn't press charges at first, but later did—saying she'd been threatened to keep her mouth shut. Garage surveillance tapes showed nothing. We're sure that the fact that Gibbons was well connected and that the sheriff had already endorsed him is merely a coincidence. . . .	Gibbons won. Ultimately, no charges were filed.

Bad Move	Who Was Involved	Attempt to Get Around It	Fallout
Saying hardworking firemen did a lousy job	Sen. **Conrad Burns (R-MT)** and firefighters working on containing a 92,000-acre blaze near Billings	When he said that the firefighters had "done a piss-poor job" and "should have listened to the ranchers," and when he pointed to one Virginia firefighter and said, "See that guy over there? He hasn't done a Goddamned thing. They sit around," he meant it as helpful and *constructive*. Gol-durn it if it sounded wrong: "In retrospect, I wish I had chosen my words more carefully."	Burns lost.

Bad Move	Who Was Involved	Attempt to Get Around It	Fallout
Getting photographed nude. With body paint. And at least two other men (nude).	West Virginia state senator **Randy White (D)** and those other nude guys. Also a large balloon glass of red wine.	Said he was "shocked" and "horribly embarrassed" after the pictures ran on the news. Explained that "the pictures were taken approximately two years ago in private and were stolen from my personal computer, I am not sure why they were given to the media, but I must assume for obvious political reasons." (The married father of three offered no explanation of the body paint or just what he was doing nude two years ago with those other nude guys.)	White kept his seat—but won by a much closer margin than expected.
Pushing wife to ground three times	Minnesota state representative **Mark Olson (R)** and his wife	Said he actually just grabbed wife by the shoulders and *placed* her on the ground. Then (after his first court appearance on charges of domestic assault) asked his wife, the public, and, of course, God for forgiveness. (He also, in a very nice touch, clutched a Bible.)	Ha ha! Olson was the smart one in this group as he didn't allegedly assault his wife until five days AFTER Election Day! So he had already won his seat! Way to plan things, Mark!

BAD WAYS TO WIN VOTERS

Some people, such as the late Ronald Reagan or the still-living Bill Clinton, have a knack for winning over voters: They say the right thing (even if it doesn't mean anything at all), they smile the right way, they avoid all the pitfalls and mistakes that make for a disaster. In short, they are good vote-getters.

But what if you want to turn off voters? Here some creative politicians explore the other, darker side of vote-getting: *vote-deflecting.*

Politician: Representative Steve King (R-IA)

Voter Deflection Technique: Comparing illegal immigrants to stray cats who kill mice, then have kittens

King's somewhat bizarre metaphorical comments were made at a Republican fund-raiser in the Boulders Conference Center in Denison, Iowa. He compared illegal immigrants to stray cats that wind up on people's porches. King said that at first stray cats help by chasing mice, so people feed them. The stray cats then have kittens, which are liked for their cuteness, but eventually the strays, fed by the people, end up getting lazy, just like illegal immigrants, King said. King refused later to discuss his comments; he let the words stand for themselves.

Voters Deflected: Brilliant but weird technique turned off not only relatives of illegal immigrants, but many Hispanic and immigrant groups in general; Americans who tend to think that fellow humans, even if they are illegal immigrants, are not animals; and people looking for sanity in their leaders.

Politician: Senator James Inhofe (R-OK)

Voter Deflection Technique: Suggesting that not many government employees were victims of the early morning bombing of the Alfred P. Murrah Federal Building in Oklahoma City in 1995 because federal employees wouldn't have been at work—they were probably out having coffee somewhere

Voters Deflected: Apparently not many, since Inhofe remains a senator from Oklahoma, which says something about Oklahoma voters' attitudes about federal employees, or the general intellectual level of the Oklahoma electorate. (No, seriously, we're sure they're *very* bright.)

Politician: Representative J. D. Hayworth (R-AZ)

Voter Deflection Technique: Hiring loudmouthed criminal as personal representative and then sending him to insult a Jewish group

In 2006, incumbent congressman J. D. Hayworth claimed he didn't know that a campaign spokesman he hired, one Jonathan Tratt, had a criminal record for having coordinated betting for a criminal gambling ring. Tratt had pled guilty to racketeering in 2001. But this was minor compared with Tratt's real ability—insulting ethnic groups.

Tratt was filling in for the Christian congressman at a debate in Phoenix at Temple Beth Israel, where he informed the congregants that Hayworth was a "more observant Jew" than some members in the audience. Since the overwhelming majority of members of the audience were Jewish and Hayworth was not, some of these members felt a bit slighted and told Tratt so. At that point Tratt's wife reportedly said, "No wonder there are anti-Semites."

Voters Deflected: Just a guess, but possibly most members of Temple Beth Israel, and their friends, didn't pull the lever for good ol' Hayworth. And although Tratt himself was Jewish, Hayworth already had been criticized for supporting the ideas of "Americanization" as championed by Henry

Ford, who was known not to be overly fond of Jews, observant or otherwise. Amazingly, Hayworth lost in 2006.

Politician: Senator Wyche Fowler (D-GA)

Voter Deflection Technique: Insulting children of constituents

Not the most brilliant idea if you want to win over voters, but in the opposite case it works wonders. Specifically, when asked questions by student volunteers who were campaigning for deficit reductions in 1992, Fowler reportedly said: "Students don't vote. Do you expect me to come here and kiss your ass?"

Fowler, in evident damage control mode, later denied he said that, but the student volunteers insisted he had. Fowler, who had won five congressional terms and one Senate term, lost his final bid for Senate and was rewarded with the ambassadorship to the desert kingdom of Saudi Arabia.

Voters Deflected: Parents—i.e., students don't vote, but their parents do.

Politician: Lieutenant Governor Michael Steele, Republican candidate for U.S. Senate in Maryland

Voter Deflection Technique: Bad-mouthing party and leader, making dubious ethnic comments

Steele bad-mouthed President Bush and the Republican Party, which would have been fine had he been a Democrat, but as a Republican this was not appreciated by fellow members of his party; then he referred to Bush as his "home-boy"—in somewhat dubious taste even if Steele himself is black, because of its ghetto (and dated '70s) connotations. Then came the pièce de résistance: Steele compared stem-cell research to the Holocaust—deliberately, in front of an audience of Jewish civic leaders in Boston. Most apparently thought it was in quite dubious taste.

Voters Deflected: Republicans, non-ghetto whites and blacks, hip people, Jews. Predictably, Steele is now referred to as a *former* candidate and former lieutenant governor.

Politician: Tramm Hudson, Republican congressional candidate in Florida

Voter Deflection Technique: Making blanket assessment of racial group natatorial abilities

An unusual technique, but effective. Candidate Hudson (who happens to be a Caucasian) threw out the following rather broad observation on the swimming abilities of African Americans: "Blacks are not the greatest swimmers or may not even know how to swim," for which he was roundly ridiculed on television and on blogs. The saying "any publicity is good publicity" seems not to have applied except as regards to turning away potential supporters.

Voters Deflected: Blacks, people without senses of humor, people with senses of humor. Predictably, Hudson lost his primary.

Politician: Hugh Foskett, Republican candidate for state representative in Washington state

Voter Deflection Technique: Publicly stated strong belief in "very conservative" All-American values—then posted homoerotic pictures of self grabbing friends' balls and self in sailor suit

Ah, the Internet, which allows for the "other side" to come out. Foskett, we must add, is apparently quite heterosexual. In fact, the conservative college sophomore also posted statements on his Facebook page stating "*Interested In:* Women" and "*Looking For:* Whatever I can get," as well as photos showing him with beer frothing from his mouth (a probable indicator of high-testosterone heterosexuality).

Voters Deflected: "Family values" voters, people with taste, i.e., people who admire people who don't vomit on floor.

WHEN POLS TRY TO ACT COOL

There comes a time in most politicians' lives—particularly during campaign season—when they feel the need to present themselves as the epitome of coolness, hipness, thugness, edginess, dopeness, or whatever the term du jour is.

Or perhaps they're *told* to present themselves as the e of c, h, t, e, d, etc.

Whatev. What matters is that by trying hard to act cool, they wind up looking like dorks, feebs, and wusses. Or whatever the term du jour is.

Remember Democratic presidential candidate Michael Dukakis in the tank? We personally cannot wipe that image out of our minds. (It burns. It BURNS!)

But there are more recent examples—and, because these otherwise ostensibly intelligent (perhaps) men and women felt compelled to share their hipnitude with the masses, we feel equally compelled.

Herewith, a few of those brave souls who tried to be the coolest of the cool.

And failed.

CHRISTOPHER "I'M DOWN WITH THE TUNES, MAN" DODD
Street Cred: Senator (D-CT) running for president
Cool Attempt: Has links on his website to Facebook, My-Space, and Flickr
Truly Cringeworthy "Cool" Touch: Website also includes a playlist of music that Dodd listens to. (His playlists are heavy on '70s soft rock—à la Jackson Browne—but he helpfully includes a form so supporters can suggest new music to him.) The worst part? The playlist is coyly called the "DoddPod."

JACKIE "GITTIN' MY VOTES FROM THE HOMEYS IN THE HOOD" WAGSTAFF

Street Cred: Former Durham, North Carolina, City Council member who ran for mayor

Cool Attempt: Wore bright-orange Chuck Taylor Converse sneakers and large gold earrings to announce her "hip-hop agenda" for City Hall

Truly Cringeworthy "Cool" Touch: Called herself "J-Dub"

MICHAEL "BUSTIN' A MOVE" STEELE

Street Cred: Republican candidate for U.S. Senate in Maryland

Cool Attempt: Set up Facebook page

Truly Cringeworthy "Cool" Touch: Wrote the following on his Facebook page: "*About Me:* I'm hip hoppin my way to the United States Senate!"

GEORGE W. "SHUFFLE OFF TO BUFFALO" BUSH

Street Cred: President of the United States

Cool Attempt: Proudly showed off his new iPod to reporters in the Oval Office

Truly Cringeworthy "Cool" Touch: Tried to explain how the iPod worked by saying, "I get the shuffle and then I shuffle the shuffle." Also said among the artists he had stored were the Archies. And "Dan [sic] McLean"—as in "American Pie."

THE DEMOCRATIC "WE DA BOMB" SENATORIAL CAMPAIGN COMMITTEE

Street Cred: Coordinate the campaigns of Dems running for the Senate

Cool Attempt: Set up hip website

Truly Cringeworthy "Cool" Touch: Website was based on the supposed-to-be-totally-cool-but-wound-up-bombing film *Snakes on a Plane* and had the snappy domain name www.snakesonasenate.com, and included heads of prominent Republican senators on cartoon snake bodies

BIZARRO CAMPAIGN WEBSITES—
OR, JUST BECAUSE IT'S ONLINE
DOESN'T MEAN IT WORKS

Nowadays, any politician worth his or her salt puts up a website. It's a great way to reach potential voters, keep constituents informed, and otherwise keep the campaign rolling.

So let's recognize those politicians who have harnessed the Web and made it a fascinating factor in their run for office.

For good or for ill.

THE "AT LEAST WE'LL GET THE MASTURBATOR VOTE!" AWARD GOES TO . . .
New York state assemblyman Gary Finch (R)
. . . for not realizing that his domain name had been taken over by someone else. Someone else who changed it into a hardcore porn site. Anyone typing in the domain for Finch (garyfinch.com) didn't get the typical government information and news releases. They got a release of a different kind (if they so desired), i.e., super-raunchy, very graphic porn. Finch wound up becoming a master of his domain by getting a new address—and the new site is definitely G-rated.

THE "BAGHDAD, ISTANBUL, WHAT'S THE DIFF?" AWARD GOES TO . . .
California Republican congressional candidate Howard Kaloogian
. . . for refuting the "liberal media's" biased coverage of the Iraq War by posting a picture of the oh-so-peaceful Baghdad

that the press never showed the public. The photo, showing a street corner, happy pedestrians, and busy shops, was captioned: "Iraq (including Baghdad) is much more calm and stable than what many people believe it to be. But each day, the news media finds any violence occurring in the country and screams and shouts about it—in part because many journalists are opposed to the U.S. effort to fight terrorism."

But it wasn't Baghdad. It was a suburb of Istanbul. Which is in Turkey. Which is a country we haven't invaded. (At least as of this writing . . .) Kaloogian claimed that photos got mixed up and pulled it from the site . . . after bloggers posted about it.

THE "I'VE GOT A WEBSITE, NOW WHAT DO I DO?" AWARD GOES TO . . .
Representative Stephen F. Lynch (D-MA)
. . . for having a website that had NOTHING on it for months. And it had nothing on it even when the election was only one week away. Yes, on October 30, 2006, the only thing on the site was "This site is currently down for reconstruction. Please visit again soon. Thank you! Paid for and Authorized by the Stephen F. Lynch for Congress Committee."

Lynch was an incumbent. And he did win.

THE "OUR EYES ARE BOTHERING US" AWARD GOES TO . . .
Ohio Democratic congressional hopeful Bill Conner
. . . for being terribly, terribly fond of the "blink" function on web pages. The menu links at the top and bottom of his site never stop blinking. And, to add a special little zazz, the term "Family Values" blinks over and over again—at the end of a long, impassioned screed against Republican family values. We have a feeling he lost the migraineurs' vote with this site.

The **"Let's Put the Party Back in 'Grand Old Party'"**
Award goes to . . .
Representative Kay Granger (R-TX)
. . . who posted her "Killer Margarita" recipe on her campaign website. (Said recipe included beer. This is one odd margarita recipe.)

The **"Maybe I Shouldn't Have Had That Killer Margarita Before I Proofed My Website"** Award goes to . . .
Speaker of the House Dennis Hastert (R-IL)
. . . for proudly posting an endorsement from the *Northwest Herald* that said "We ednorse Hastert's re-election."

The **"So Cute We Could Puke"** Award goes to . . .
Virginia congressional candidate Shawn O'Donnell (D)
. . . for including an incredibly cloying blog on his campaign website—ostensibly written by his dog, Josie. An example:

> "Nine days and counting until Election Day. . . . I feel like running around and chasing birds. (I'm a springer spaniel and our instinct is to flush birds.) . . . I don't see Dad very often except late at night when he gets home from the last event or meeting of the day and he often has to leave the house early. I'm so happy when I see him! With the weather changing, the bursitis in my right elbow bothers me sometimes, so Dad (or Mom) only takes me campaigning to places that aren't too far away and for just one or two appearances. Someone brings me home after that because five, six or more events a day are just too much for me. I need my naps! . . . I keep telling Dad he's got a great radio/TV voice, but he just looks at me and laughs. He really does, though. . . . Dad met another Democratic dog at

a campaign event last week, she's a collie named Molly . . . hey, that rhymes! After Dad wins, I think I'll ask if I can throw a party and invite all my new canine friends, the collie, the golden retriever, and the Portuguese water spaniel. We'll have a wonderful time."

GOD, THE ULTIMATE POLITICAL ENDORSEMENT—
OR, "WITH GOD ON MY SIDE, WHY DO I NEED DIEBOLD?"

Forget movie stars. The best endorsement, the ultimate endorsement, comes from God. But does God really take sides in political contests?

Yes.

Let's examine theologically the implications of God's role. The presence of God in U.S. politics raises a lot of questions. *Should* God take sides at all? Is God a Republican? How can we know who God is voting for? How does God reveal His political picks without appearing on *Meet the Press*?

GOD APPARENTLY MAKES CELL PHONE CALL TO ARKANSAS GOVERNOR (AND PRESIDENTIAL CANDIDATE) MIKE HUCKABEE (R)

Apparently God called Huckabee on the latter's cell while he was introducing President Bush at the Republican governors' meeting. Huckabee answered his cell phone, and the conversation, as overheard by Keith Olbermann, who was nearby, went as follows. And Huckabee said unto the Caller:

> "We know you don't take sides in the election. But if you did, we kind of think you'd hang in there with us, Lord, we really do. Yes, sir. We'll pass those good words on. I see. You talked to the president, and he talks to you anyway."

Theological Implications: Here God, as a nonvoter and a non–U.S. citizen, seems to understand that His real role is to *encourage,* not to endorse.

GOD STRONGLY ENDORSES MICHELE BACHMANN FOR CONGRESS

At the Living Word Christian Center in Brooklyn Park, Minnesota, Michele Bachmann (R-MN) revealed what God told her, after she fasted and prayed . . .

> "God then called me to run for Congress. . . . In the midst of him making this calling sure, what's occurred in this particular race is that this congressional seat—one of 435 in the country—has become one of the top five races in the country and in the last week has become one of the top three races in the country and you may have seen now God has in his own will and in his own plan has focused like a laser beam after this scandal that came up about a week or so ago he has focused like a laser beam with his reasoning on this race."

Theological Implications: God endorsed Bachmann, and Bachmann won the election. Having Him focused "like a laser beam" on one's election probably helps. Frankly, we were surprised that God would stoop so low, but we surmise that because He's infinite, God can easily spread His political endorsements globally, even extending down to relatively minor Minnesota congressional seats. But another question arises. Is God then a Republican? See below . . .

GOD OFFERS ONLY TEPID ENDORSEMENT OF KATHERINE HARRIS FOR SENATE

Harris, the controversial former representative from the 13th Congressional District in Florida, ran for the U.S. Senate as the Republican candidate in 2006. She seemed an unlikely choice for God; as unlikely as Michele Bachmann. And God seemed to have some second thoughts as well. His endorsements were indirect, subtle, not out in the open . . . tepid.

In her 2002 book, *Center of the Storm,* Harris compares herself to the biblical Esther, and mentions Esther's uncle Mordecai's famous words to his niece ("And who knows but that you have come to royal position for a time such as this?"). Harris appears to see these words as directed at her; as a sort of backhanded godly endorsement for her own political ambitions. But she seems to be stretching a little. And God didn't seem very forthcoming later. Harris recounted to the *Tampa Tribune* in 2002 that she had originally expected her controversial role as Florida secretary of state in the Gore/Bush Florida election recount would end her political career. Instead, she said, she "*stumbled* into [her] own destiny," and realized that running for office was "fulfilling the role God has put [her] on this Earth to accomplish" (italics ours).

But this was not a *clear* endorsement: God didn't specifically say: "Harris for Senate." In fact, Harris *denied* reports that she had said privately that God had endorsed her Senate run. "That would be presumptuous," she explained.

In other words, God, who works in mysterious ways, never wholeheartedly and *openly* endorsed Harris for Senate as He apparently did with Bachmann for Congress—even though Harris openly and enthusiastically endorsed Him. Apparently, no quid pro quos with God. Nevertheless, Harris explained the necessity of the Christian God in politics:

"If you are not electing Christians, tried and true, under public scrutiny and pressure, if you're not electing Christians then in essence you are going to legislate sin. They can legislate sin. They can say that abortion is alright. They can vote to sustain gay marriage . . . we have to have the faithful in government and over time, that lie we have been told, the separation of church and state, people have internalized, thinking that they needed to avoid politics and that is so wrong because God is the one who chooses our rulers. And if we are the ones not actively involved in electing those godly men and women and if people aren't involved in helping godly men in getting elected then we're going to have a nation of secular laws. That's not what our founding fathers intended and that certainly isn't what God intended."

Theological Implications: Harris lost by a landslide. Either God chose her and lost, which is impossible if we believe in divine omnipotence, or, by Harris's own logic, He *wanted* her to lose. We thus can see that God not only endorsed her opponent, Democrat Bill Nelson, He punched a lot of chads for the man. *Is God, then, a secularist, gay-loving Democratic deity?* A good question.

GOD *DECREES* THAT INCUMBENT JEWISH DEMOCRAT ED RENDELL BE ELECTED FOR ANOTHER TERM AS GOVERNOR

Much better than an endorsement—announcing a decree. You can't lose with a Heavenly decree.

And that's what God did with Pennsylvania governor Ed Rendell, according to the Reverend Carl Vining, pastor of the nondenominational House of Judah Ministries—and chaplain-on-call for the Pennsylvania Senate. During a voter awareness event at the Capitol rotunda, the Reverend Vining, a registered Republican, introduced the Democratic governor Rendell to the large audience and told them that "the God of Israel" recently sent word through him on the outcome of this year's gubernatorial election. "The God of Israel said, 'One more term.'"

Most interesting, Rendell's opponent was a conservative Christian Republican.

Theological Implications: From a Christian perspective, if God chose a Jew to be His only Son, why can't He choose a Jew to be His only Pennsylvania governor? But again, is God going liberal? "God has his own reasoning. It's the will of our Father in Heaven," the Reverend Vining answered enigmatically.

GOD ENDORSES YET ANOTHER GOVERNOR: FLORIDA REPUBLICAN CHARLIE CRIST

The year 2006 seemed to be the year of God speaking through ministers about his choices for upcoming gubernatorial campaigns. According to the political blog *Wonkette,* the Reverend O'Neal Dozier's Worldwide Christian Center in Pompano Beach, Florida, announced to a waiting world that the Lord had come to him in a dream two years earlier: "The Lord Jesus spoke to me and he said, 'There's something I want you to know. Charlie Crist will be the next governor of the state of Florida.'" The Reverend Dozier said that before his dream, he had not known of Crist, and that Crist had not announced his plans to run for governor.

Theological Implications: Crist won the election. Why did God choose Crist for Florida governor? A Floridian *Wonkette* reader offers a fascinating insight: "Maybe it's because their names are so similar." Interestingly, the third public event on the new governor's calendar, after an inaugural breakfast in Miami's Parrot Jungle theme park, was an official inaugural *Prayer* Breakfast. Coincidence?

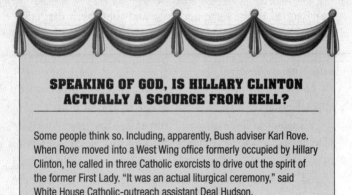

SPEAKING OF GOD, IS HILLARY CLINTON ACTUALLY A SCOURGE FROM HELL?

Some people think so. Including, apparently, Bush adviser Karl Rove. When Rove moved into a West Wing office formerly occupied by Hillary Clinton, he called in three Catholic exorcists to drive out the spirit of the former First Lady. "It was an actual liturgical ceremony," said White House Catholic-outreach assistant Deal Hudson.

CLASSY CAMPAIGN MOVES

The basic idea behind a good campaign is letting the voters understand your positions on important issues. But what if the issues aren't that compelling? What if the voters are idiots? What if the voters prefer the other candidate to you?

Then it's time for a better, smarter, *dirtier* campaign. Did we say dirtier? We meant much more *truthful* and *informational*. The key: *educate* the voters as to the true background, viewpoints, sexual proclivities, and deviancies of your opponent. And who cares if it's true as long as it's salacious?

Herewith, some of the best—and most educational campaigns—of recent years.

Classy Political Candidate: Vernon Robinson, 2006 Republican challenger for a U.S. House seat in North Carolina

Educational Campaign Tactic: Helpfully informing voters in numerous ads that his incumbent opponent, Democrat Brad Miller, was childless and hence gay, was anti–U.S.

Army and wanted to import homosexuals to the United States and supported teenage girls watching pornography

- "Brad Miller spent your money to study the masturbation habits of old men."
- "If Miller had his way, America would be nothing but one big fiesta for illegal aliens and homosexuals."
- "What kind of congressman would try to deny our soldiers the body armor they need to save their lives? The answer is your congressman, Brad Miller."
- "Brad Miller even spent your tax dollars to pay teenage girls to watch pornographic movies with probes connected to their genitalia. Brad Miller pays for sex, but not for body armor for our troops."
- "[Miller voted to spend money] to study the sex lives of Vietnamese prostitutes in San Francisco."

"Those are San Francisco values, not North Carolina values," concluded Robinson accusingly. And he implied that Miller, who had married late and didn't have children, might be gay—ignoring the fact that Miller's wife had had a hysterectomy and couldn't have children.

Unfortunately for Robinson, all of his valiant efforts to educate the voters came to naught—he didn't win a seat and vowed never to run for office again. We say, for God's sake, *why not*?

Classy Political Candidates: Republican Maryland governor Robert Ehrlich and Republican lieutenant governor Michael Steele

Educational Campaign Tactic: Sending out fake flyers supposedly from local Democratic leaders who wanted to tell voters they supported the two Republicans

These guys win the chutzpah award, Maryland division, for sheer audacity. Just before the election, Ehrlich and Steele sent out a glossy flyer, in African red, black, and green, with pictures of Prince George's County Executive Jack B. Johnson; his predecessor, Wayne K. Curry; and past NAACP president and former U.S. Senate candidate Kweisi Mfume—and these words: "Ehrlich-Steele Democrats" . . . "These are OUR Choices."

Of course, the fact that the three hadn't endorsed the two was a moot point. And an Ehrlich aide reportedly said that no one inside the campaign expected a strong reaction.

Classy Political Candidate: Republican Pennsylvania state representative Jeffrey Habay

Educational Campaign Tactic: Informing voters of "derogatory" information on a campaign-audit petitioner by putting materials under voters' windshield wipers; also informing voters that a letter sent to Habay contained a mysterious white powder

Once considered a rising young star, Habay was elected at age 28 to the Pennsylvania Legislature in 1994. During his 2004 campaign (unopposed), he allegedly decided to safeguard his star potential by the aforementioned derogatory informational campaign on a political foe—and not content to stop there, he also allegedly made threatening phone calls to the same man. He also allegedly sent out his legislative staffers to do original research—i.e., to collect dirt on the constituent and his family. Later, when he was sent a request for an audit of his campaign finances, Habay claimed that the letter contained a white powder—leaving it up to the creativity of his audience to decide if it was supposed to be cocaine, plutonium, or anthrax. (We voted anthrax.)

Unfortunately, the legal system did not appreciate Habay's admirable if somewhat aggressive campaign creativity—and sentenced him to jail for campaign violations.

Classy Political Candidate: Caryn Garber, staffer for Representative Mark Kirk (R-IL) (member of the House Foreign Aid Appropriations subcommittee)

Educational Campaign Tactic: Urging the head of Tel Aviv University's American fund-raising arm to pressure a prominent donor and supporter of Democratic challenger Dan Seals to back away from the Democrat—or else the university might suffer

Some people might call this blackmail—we prefer to call it *targeted informational campaigning.*

Garber told the president of Tel Aviv University's American Council that National Chairman Robert Schrayer's support for Democrat Dan Seals could "have a very bad effect on the university"—obviously she was trying to alert the president to possible bad developments, much as a weather forecaster does. She helpfully followed that threat—we mean, statement—with another: "Revenge is a dish best served cold."

To our knowledge, Garber still works for Congressman Kirk.

Classy Political Candidate: Senator Orrin Hatch (R-UT)

Educational Campaign Tactic: Informing voters that if Democrats win, terrorists will strike

In an effort to educate the public before the November 2006 congressional elections, Senator Hatch thoughtfully let voters know that Middle Eastern terrorists were "waiting for the Democrats here to take control, let things cool off and then strike again." He also added, in a helpful clarification, that people who favor withdrawal of troops from Iraq are merely "terrorist appeasers." He also helpfully noted that opponents of Samuel Alito's Supreme Court nomination were anti-Italian, and opponents of Arkansas attorney general Bill Pryor's judicial nomination were anti-Catholic.

Earlier, he told voters that a vote for John Kerry in 2004 would be a vote for terrorists—in fact, the bad guys supported the Democratic contender. Hatch said that terrorists would "throw everything they can between now and the election to try and elect Kerry."

It's wonderful having such informative senators in Congress. We've learned a lot from Orrin Hatch.

Classy Political Candidate: Maryland comptroller William Donald Schaefer
Educational Campaign Tactic: Informing voters that his opponent is old, fat, prissy, and submissive

Schaefer considerately told voters about various crucial alleged shortcomings of his opponent, Janet S. Owens, namely that she was a "prissy little miss" who wears "long dresses, looks like Mother Hubbard—it's sort of like she was a man." He later added, "She's got these long clothes on and an old-fashioned hairdo. You know it sort of makes you real mad." After Owens complained, Schaefer pointed out, "I can't help how she looks." He finally did air an ad apologizing . . . but shortly thereafter tossed out the observations that Owens was "getting fat" and that "her husband rules her."

Classy Political Candidate: David Mills, 2006 Republican hopeful for Florida House
Educational Campaign Tactic: Saying that opponent (female) in primary was a former pole dancer

Based on absolutely no evidence, an eager Mills allegedly let leak out that his Republican primary opponent, Sarasota School Board member Laura Benson, had been married five times and was a former pole dancer. Benson was not amused. She also was not a serial-marrying former pole dancer.

LOSING GRACEFULLY

If you're a politician who loses an election or post, you'll have to acknowledge your loss. Experts say the best way to handle losing is to be humble, tough, and *gracious*.

Key point: Take this opportunity to show the *real you*. . . . Be a good sport. Concede graciously. Be classy. Here are some of the best examples of good political losers, people so classy, such good sports, we're absolutely *horrified* and *crushed* that they lost.

Good-Sport Politician: Representative Alcee Hastings (D-FL), after losing the bid to become the House Intelligence Committee chairman

Classy Concession Speech Line: "Sorry, haters, God's not finished with me yet."

Comments: "Haters" of course, refers to those *evil* ones who didn't support Representative Hastings.

Good-Sport Politician: Rae Hart Anderson, after losing a Minnesota state Senate race to a heathenish non-Christian Hindu, incumbent senator Satveer Chaudhary

Classy Losing Conduct: Writing a letter to the non-Christian Hindu winner of the election implying that even though he may have won the election, he was still a loser—unless he converted to Christianity. Some excerpts from Anderson's charming letter to Chaudhary:

I've enjoyed much of this race, especially the people I've met . . . even you! I see your deficits—not all of them, and your potential—but not all of it. Only your Creator knows the real potential He's put in you. Get to know Him and know yourself. . . . You'll be more interesting even to you!

The race of your life is more important than this one—and it is my sincere wish that you'll get to know Jesus Christ as Lord and Savior. . . . Pay attention . . . this is very important, Satveer. Have you noticed Jesus for yourself . . . at some moment in time, yet??? . . . Become His family and know the love of God that passes knowledge. See Isaiah and the Gospel of John . . . good reading while waiting for fishes to bite. . . . God waits to be gracious to each person that knows they need to be forgiven. Do you? I think you do. Just ask. Christ won eternal life for you and said so. Take Him at His Word. Take some time to get acquainted with God. . . . There's nothing like belonging to Christ . . . not winning, not money, not degrees . . . it's the best. Good wishes and better wishes . . . until you wish for the best!

Rae Hart Anderson

Comments: Perhaps not all that surprisingly, Chaudhary had won in a landslide, beating Ms. Anderson with 63% of the vote.

Good-Sport Politician: Former Texas Republican state representative Rick Green four years after losing an election to Democrat Patrick Rose

Classy Losing Conduct: Allegedly shoving and punching the long-ago winner, Representative Patrick Rose. The alleged punching and shoving occurred outside a polling place at Sunset Canyon Baptist Church, east of Dripping Springs, Texas, on November 7, 2006, as Rose was campaigning against Republican Jim Neuhaus for a third term. According to a witness, during the assault Rose tried to get away from the punching and shoving Green; finally a group of men pulled former representative Green off. But Green "continued trying to go after him and kept shouting 'You need to stop lying' [a Rose flyer had portrayed Neuhaus as a Green pawn] and 'Let him defend himself, the big baby.' "

Comments: Although the witness claims she saw Green punching Rose in the face, Rose claims Green didn't actually land a punch. Both men were treated for minor injuries, and Green turned himself in that afternoon at the county sheriff's office and was charged with assault with bodily injury. (Green received deferred adjudication on a Class C misdemeanor.)

Good-Sport Politician: Incumbent senator Joe Lieberman ("D"-CT), after losing the Democratic primary (and before [somehow] winning the general election as an independent)

Classy Concession Speech Line: "For the sake of our state, our country, and my party, I cannot and will not let that result stand."

Comments: A perfect "Let the voters speak" moment. Note that this is the same Lieberman who during the campaign (also quite classily) implied that maybe his opponent Ned Lamont was a Nazi-sympathizer, a terrorist supporter, and . . . well, a jerk. Some quotes:

"If we just pick up [in Iraq] like Ned Lamont wants us to do, get out by a date certain, it will be taken as a tremendous victory by the same people who wanted to blow up these planes in this plot hatched in England. It will strengthen them and they will strike again."

"It's like the voters of this great state would've let the Nazis win. I am counting on your support."

WOMAN IN A NAIL SALON: "You know what I'm going to do? I'm going to write in my husband. I don't like any of them. Ned Lamont is the biggest jerk in the world."

CANDIDATE LIEBERMAN (WITH A CHUCKLE): "Well, we agree on that. So if you've got a choice between a jerk . . ."

Senator Joe, he saved Connecticut from Nazism!

GRACEFUL WINNERS

Losing is one thing; winning is something else. We mean, if you've won, why rub salt into the wound? And so, we must say that Steve Kagen (D-WI), who won a tough campaign against his Republican opponent, which included visits from Bush adviser Karl Rove, is not our choice for poster boy for the future politicians of America as "gracious winning behavior."

According to some reports, when Kagen met Rove in a White House bathroom in December 2006, he held the door closed and told Rove: "You're in the White House and think you're safe, huh? You recognize me? My name's Dr. Multimillionaire and I kicked your ass." For what it's worth, he also reportedly called Laura Bush, "Barbara."

SEVEN

POLITICAL FAMILIES

POLITICIANS JUST LOVE FAMILIES. THINK ABOUT IT: EVERYONE has a family. (Except for unmarried orphans. And that's only one vote.)

So politicians are family-friendly. They support families, they have families, they talk a lot about families. And they give their families money. Taxpayer money.

POLITICIANS WHO REALLY LOVE THEIR FAMILIES (AND THEIR FRIENDS, TOO!)

Many politicians are true family people. They really really *really* love their families. And they're not afraid to show it—to the tune of some mighty nice cash.

Warms the cockles of your heart, doesn't it?

The Loving Politician: Representative Maxine Waters (D-CA)

How Much She Loves Her Family: Over $1 million worth

Proof of Maternal Love:
- Hired Progressive Connections (owned by daughter Karen) to work on local ballot mailings in district.
  Value: $450,000
- Hired son Edward to work on local ballot mailings.
  Value: $115,000
- Introduced politicians to hubby, Sidney, who works as part-time consultant to bond underwriters. Sid, in turn, introduced pols to his clients—who got big-bucks government-related biz.
  Value: $500,000
- Endorsed county supervisor who was in charge of deciding who got to run county-owned golf course. Coincidentally, Edward and Sid were chosen to run said golf course!
  Value: Somewhere between $140,000 and $400,000

The Politician Clears Things Up: "[My family members] do their business, and I do mine."

The Loving Politician: Representative Richard W. Pombo (R-CA)

How Much He Loves His Wife and Brother: At least $357,625 worth, but possibly millions in the offing

Proof of Spousal and Filial Affection:
- Paid wife and brother for campaign "bookkeeping, fund-raising, and consulting." (We're sure they were truly excellent bookkeepers, fund-raisers, and consultants since that sum represents 25% of the total campaign funds Pombo had raised.)
  Value: $357,625
- Arranged for federal funds for a study of two proposed freeway projects in his district

. . . coincidentally, right around where the Pombo family owns over 1,500 acres!

Value: Potentially many many millions

The Politician Clears Things Up: Well, actually Pombo didn't clear things up. But his spokesman, Brian Kennedy, tried: "Each of the charges is baseless." The accusations came from "a Democratic attack group, and all of their charges should be taken with a grain of salt."

The Loving Politician: Representative Curt Weldon (R-PA)

How Much He Loves His Family and Friends: Over $1,000,000 (but over several years)

Proof of Paternal Love and Friendly Affection:

- Three companies linked to "Sugar Daddy" Curt also happen to be the entire client list of daughter Karen's consulting/lobbying firm, Solutions North America (SNA).
  Value: At least $500,000
- Recommended Russian energy company ITERA International as a "great source" to partner with U.S. energy firms—and a short time later, ITERA signed on to a $500,000-a-year contract with daughter Karen's SNA.
  Value: $500,000
- Also became fascinated with Russian aviation firm Saratov's drone airplane; expressed interest and visited the plant . . . and shortly thereafter, the firm contracted with Karen's lobbying firm.
- Before the above lobbying job, Karen worked for Boeing (which happened to be one of the congressman's major campaign donors).

- Other daughter Kim got a job with helicopter manufacturer AgustaWestland, which happened to have won a major contract (beating out front-runner United Technologies) and is a subsidiary of Italian company and Weldon personal fave Finmeccanica.
- Son (and budding race car driver) Andrew is sponsored by Schaffer Motorsports, owned by a senior Boeing employee.
- Curt Weldon's real estate agent pal became a lobbyist for several small defense firms, including Oto Melara—another subsidiary of Finmeccanica.

The Loving Politician's Daughter Karen Clears Things Up: "Because of who he [Weldon] is, people have questioned me all my life about whether I'm qualified and if I can do the job. I have nothing to hide. I haven't done anything inappropriate."

The Loving Politician: Representative William Jefferson (D-LA)

How Much He Loves His Family: $7 million—plus a $30,000 pickup truck

Proof of Paternal and Brotherly Love:

- Funneled earmarks worth $7 million to four charities that happen to be connected with his sister, his daughter, his brother, and a former aide.
- Brother Mose Jefferson received use of a $30,000 pickup truck that had been donated by DaimlerChrysler to the city of New Orleans after Hurricane Katrina—and that was, in turn, donated to Mose's charity.

The Politician Clears Things Up: Actually, he didn't clear things up. He was too busy claiming that he never accepted a bribe and hid money in his freezer to comment about the charities. But we're sure he *would* have cleared things up if he'd had the time.

The Loving Politician: Representative Jerry Lewis (R-CA)
How Much He Loves His Pals: About $5,000,000 worth
Proof of Friendly Affection:
- Oversaw nearly $900 billion a year in federal spending—and made it clear that anyone wanting a slice of that money pie had to hire his best friend, lobbyist Bill Lowery. Miraculously, Lowery's firm tripled its revenue!
  Value: About $5 million in revenue for Lowery's firm

The Politician Clears Things Up: "If you don't want to make the contributions, you will get left behind."

The Loving Politician: Representative John T. Doolittle (R-CA)
How Much He Loves His Wife: $140,000 worth
Proof of Spousal Love:
- Paid increasing commissions to wife Julie's one-person fund-raising company, totaling 15% of all contributions to his campaign and political action committees.
  Value: $77,947 in 2003–2004; $82,127 in 2005–2006
- Also spent thousands on gifts from Saks Fifth Avenue and Tiffany—as well as a Ritz-Carlton day spa.
  Value: About $40,000

The Politician's Spokesperson Clears Things Up: Explained spokesman Richard Robinson, "Having family members paid for such work is both legal and ethical."

The Politician Clears Things Up, Too (Sort Of): Doolittle said he was severing his campaign's and PACs' relationships with his wife; then he said that she dropped the campaign as a client—but she would still be doing fundraising for his PACs. We are sure this had nothing to do with all the flak he had received about his "love" for his wife.

The Loving Politician: Senate Majority Leader Harry Reid (D-NV)

How Much He Loves His Family: Hundreds of thousands of dollars' worth

Proof of Familial Love:

- All four sons and his son-in-law have been or are lawyers or lobbyists for special interests that have dealings with Washington.
- Has given breaks to companies that, in turn, steer business to sons' and son-in-law's firms. For example, the son-in-law's "tiny" law firm got $300,000 in fees from the Howard Hughes Corporation.
- Introduced legislation opening federal land for private development by sons' employers. As the *Los Angeles Times* put it, the bill would provide "a cavalcade of benefits to real estate developers, corporations and local institutions that were paying hundreds of thousands of dollars in lobbying fees to his sons' and son-in-law's firms."

The Politician Clears Things Up: Reid claims they don't talk about business, except perhaps casually. "Have they said something? I am sure they have. I don't have meetings with my children to go over business things."

YOU CAN'T CHOOSE YOUR FAMILY:

POTENTIAL POLITICAL PROBLEMS FROM POLITICAL FAMILY MEMBERS

Sometimes politicians' families are a bit of a problem.

Who can forget Billy Carter, Roger Clinton, and other bad boy and girl siblings, spouses, children, and other nefarious relatives? That they're embarrassing to the dignified politician is bad enough—but worse yet, they threaten the voter base! Ohmigod.

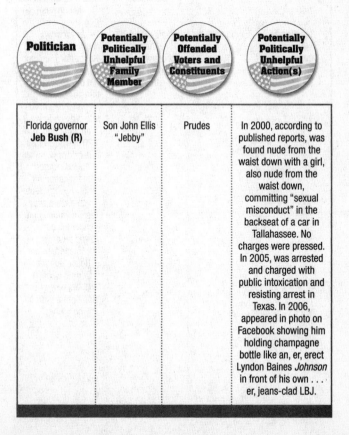

Politician	Potentially Politically Unhelpful Family Member	Potentially Offended Voters and Constituents	Potentially Politically Unhelpful Action(s)
Florida governor **Jeb Bush (R)**	Son John Ellis "Jebby"	Prudes	In 2000, according to published reports, was found nude from the waist down with a girl, also nude from the waist down, committing "sexual misconduct" in the backseat of a car in Tallahassee. No charges were pressed. In 2005, was arrested and charged with public intoxication and resisting arrest in Texas. In 2006, appeared in photo on Facebook showing him holding champagne bottle like an, er, erect Lyndon Baines *Johnson* in front of his own . . . er, jeans-clad LBJ.

Politician	Potentially Politically Unhelpful Family Member	Potentially Offended Voters and Constituents	Potentially Politically Unhelpful Action(s)
Senate candidate **Bob Corker** (R-TN)	Daughter Julia	Anyone who liked his "family values" stance and isn't keen on same-sex dalliances	On her Facebook page, posted photo of herself kissing (on the mouth, natch) a blond girl and dancing in her undies
Rep. **Randy "Duke" Cunningham** (R-CA)	Estranged wife Nancy	People who don't like their pols accepting bribes; clean underwear freaks	In exclusive interview with Kitty Kelley (for *The New Republic*), dished the dirt on Duke, saying that he had dumped a duffel bag filled with dirty underwear and $32,000 in $20 and $100 bills in her driveway after he was under investigation for bribe-taking; slept with a knife and, later, a loaded gun under his pillow; and physically threatened former House Speaker **Dennis Hastert (R-IL)** when he didn't get a position he wanted.

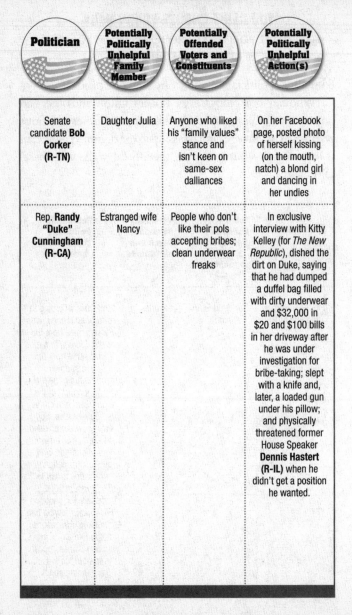

Politician	Potentially Politically Unhelpful Family Member	Potentially Offended Voters and Constituents	Potentially Politically Unhelpful Action(s)
Senate Majority Leader **Bill Frist (R-TN)**	Son Jonathan	Nonwhites, Jews, teetotallers	On his Facebook page, wrote that he was a member of the "Jonathan Frist appreciation for 'Waking Up White People' Group," and also made reference to belonging to a group where there were "No Jews allowed. Just kidding. No seriously." Also was in a photo with six cans of beer strapped to his belt.
Senate Majority Leader **Bill Frist (R-TN)**	Son Bryan	Pacifists, moderates, reasonable people, humans	In his online profile, wrote, "I was born an American by God's amazing grace. Let's bomb some people."
San Francisco mayor **Gavin Newsom (D)**	Wife Kimberly	Gays; people who are offended by imitations of oral sex in the middle of speeches	During speech at gay rights dinner said, "I know that many of you wanted to see my husband and some of you had questions out there. Is he hot? Yeah. Is he hung? Yeah. Is he—[waves hand, apparently to denote bisexuality]? Not unless you can give a better [pretends she is eating, er, a banana] than me."

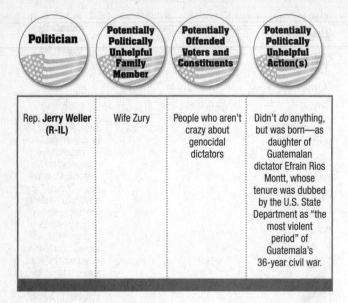

Politician	Potentially Politically Unhelpful Family Member	Potentially Offended Voters and Constituents	Potentially Politically Unhelpful Action(s)
Rep. **Jerry Weller** (R-IL)	Wife Zury	People who aren't crazy about genocidal dictators	Didn't *do* anything, but was born—as daughter of Guatemalan dictator Efrain Rios Montt, whose tenure was dubbed by the U.S. State Department as "the most violent period" of Guatemala's 36-year civil war.

BREAKING UP ISN'T HARD TO DO (FOR POLS, THAT IS)

The old Neil Sedaka song says that breaking up is hard to do. Bushwa, say certain prominent politicians. They know it can be easy—and they'll tell you how!

EASY BREAK-UP TIP #1: *Don't do it face-to-face. Announce it in a press conference!*

Former New York City mayor Rudy Giuliani (R) told his second wife, Donna Hanover, that he wanted a separation—during a press conference. Not that Rudy's a churl or anything . . . It's just that there was a whole media hoo-hah when he marched in the city's St. Patrick's Day parade with his then mistress (and now wife #3), Judith Nathan. (*Daily News* columnist Jim Dwyer termed the duo's parade appearance akin to "groping in the window at Macy's.") So where else to turn but to the media when it was time to tell Donna that things were officially over?

Easy Break-up Tip #2: *Make sure the soon-to-be-ex is somewhere where she has to sign the divorce papers. Like, say, a hospital bed where she's being treated for cancer!*

There was no way former Speaker of the House Newt Gingrich (R) was going to let wife #1 wiggle out of a divorce. This is why he came up with the clever (if not terribly PR-astute) move of cornering her when she was in the hospital undergoing her third surgery for cancer. And (extra points here) he even got his two daughters to unwittingly help. Ac-

CASE OF THE MISSING KIDS
(AND EX-WIVES, FOR THAT MATTER . . .)

Presidential wannabe and former New York City mayor Rudolph Giuliani seems to have a bit of a mental block where certain family members are concerned.

More specifically, on the bio page of his website, Rudy goes into a lot of detail about his career. Fair enough. And he goes into a bit of detail about his current wife. Still fair. But it's what he *doesn't* talk about that is interesting. As of April 2007, there's no mention—not one teeny-weeny peep—about his two children. Said kids happened to be the spawn of his second marriage (not the one to his second cousin, which was annulled and isn't mentioned, either), but the one that he was still in when he started seeing his current wife.

Hmm . . . could that be why someone "forgot" to mention his kids in the bio? Or, wait, is it just that it's so darn easy to forget you have a 21-year-old son and a 17-year-old daughter? That must be it.

cording to his wife, "the two girls came to see me, and said, 'Daddy is downstairs. Could he come up?' When he got there, he wanted to discuss the terms of the divorce while I was recovering from my surgery." Now that's using the ol' casaba, Newt! No WAY your wife was gonna get away from you there!

EASY BREAK-UP TIP #3: *Or just use the phone to say, "Sorry, baby, I'm moving on!"*

Another Newt method and simple to follow. When leaving wife #2 (the one he left his cancer-coping first wife for), he just picked up the phone. Wife #2 was at her mom's for Mom's birthday—so Newt first sweetly and compassionately wished his soon-to-be-ex-mother-in-law a happy 84th, then asked to speak with his wife. When wife #2 got on the phone, he told her he wanted a divorce. He politely added that he was having an affair with a congressional aide.

POLITICAL FAMILY VALUES:
SOME INTERESTING TWISTS ON REAL FAMILY GUYS

Many politicians present themselves as the protectors of the family, the defenders of morality, and, essentially, as the people who stand for Truth, Justice, and the American Way (which means gays bad; marriage between man and woman good; sex okay but only clean, honest, matrimonial sex, of course).

But—believe it or not—these paragons of family values sometimes AREN'T AS CLEAN-CUT AS YOU MIGHT THINK.

Yes, we too are stunned.

A few notable standouts:

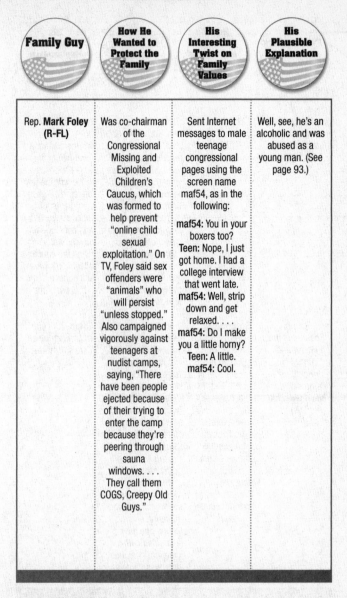

Family Guy	How He Wanted to Protect the Family	His Interesting Twist on Family Values	His Plausible Explanation
Rep. **Mark Foley** (R-FL)	Was co-chairman of the Congressional Missing and Exploited Children's Caucus, which was formed to help prevent "online child sexual exploitation." On TV, Foley said sex offenders were "animals" who will persist "unless stopped." Also campaigned vigorously against teenagers at nudist camps, saying, "There have been people ejected because of their trying to enter the camp because they're peering through sauna windows. . . . They call them COGS, Creepy Old Guys."	Sent Internet messages to male teenage congressional pages using the screen name maf54, as in the following: maf54: You in your boxers too? Teen: Nope, I just got home. I had a college interview that went late. maf54: Well, strip down and get relaxed. . . . maf54: Do I make you a little horny? Teen: A little. maf54: Cool.	Well, see, he's an alcoholic and was abused as a young man. (See page 93.)

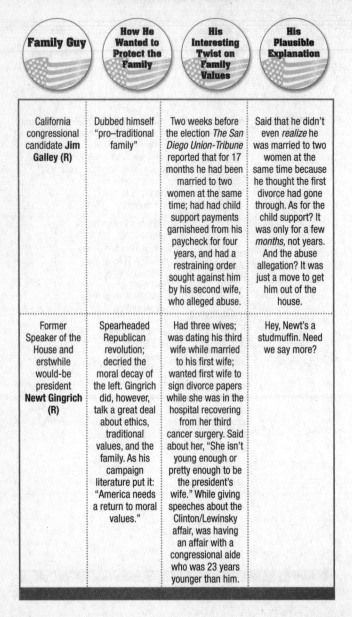

Family Guy	How He Wanted to Protect the Family	His Interesting Twist on Family Values	His Plausible Explanation
California congressional candidate **Jim Galley (R)**	Dubbed himself "pro–traditional family"	Two weeks before the election *The San Diego Union-Tribune* reported that for 17 months he had been married to two women at the same time; had had child support payments garnisheed from his paycheck for four years, and had a restraining order sought against him by his second wife, who alleged abuse.	Said that he didn't even *realize* he was married to two women at the same time because he thought the first divorce had gone through. As for the child support? It was only for a few *months,* not years. And the abuse allegation? It was just a move to get him out of the house.
Former Speaker of the House and erstwhile would-be president **Newt Gingrich (R)**	Spearheaded Republican revolution; decried the moral decay of the left. Gingrich did, however, talk a great deal about ethics, traditional values, and the family. As his campaign literature put it: "America needs a return to moral values."	Had three wives; was dating his third wife while married to his first wife; wanted first wife to sign divorce papers while she was in the hospital recovering from her third cancer surgery. Said about her, "She isn't young enough or pretty enough to be the president's wife." While giving speeches about the Clinton/Lewinsky affair, was having an affair with a congressional aide who was 23 years younger than him.	Hey, Newt's a studmuffin. Need we say more?

Family Guy

How He Wanted to Protect the Family

His Interesting Twist on Family Values

His Plausible Explanation

Family Guy	How He Wanted to Protect the Family	His Interesting Twist on Family Values	His Plausible Explanation
Pundit **Bill O'Reilly**	Defends traditional family values by writing books, including *The O'Reilly Factor for Kids: A Survival Guide for America's Families*	Was accused of sexual harassment by Fox News producer Andrea Mackris, who quoted parts of his phone sex calls to her as follows: "You would basically be in the shower and then I would come in . . . and I would take that little loofa thing and kinda soap up your back . . . and then with my other hand I would start to massage your boobs, get your nipples really hard . . . 'cuz I like that and you have really spectacular boobs. . . . So anyway I'd be rubbing your big boobs and getting your nipples really hard, kinda kissing your neck from behind . . . and then I would take the other hand with the falafel thing and I'd put it on your pussy but you'd have to do it really light, just kind of a tease business." The complaint goes on to say: "During the course of Defendant Bill O'Reilly's sexual rant, it became clear that he was using a vibrator upon himself, and that he ejaculated. Plaintiff was repulsed."	Said there was "no wrongdoing in the case whatsoever by anyone" and added, "Please do not believe everything you hear and read"—but settled out of court with his repulsed accuser.

Family Guy	How He Wanted to Protect the Family	His Interesting Twist on Family Values	His Plausible Explanation
Illinois Senate candidate **Jack Ryan (R)**	Said his priorities were God, family, country, in that order, and that when he was on the road, he was perpetually on the lookout for a church so he could pray. "As we drive through rural areas of Illinois, I say, 'Can't we stop at a church here? Isn't there a church around here somewhere?' "	Wife, actress Jeri Ryan, claimed he insisted she go to sex clubs with him. "They were long weekends, supposed 'romantic' getaways. . . . One club I refused to go in. It had mattresses in cubicles. The other club he insisted I go to . . . was a bizarre club with cages, whips and other apparatus hanging from the ceiling. Respondent wanted me to have sex with him there, with another couple watching. I refused. Respondent asked me to perform a sexual activity upon him, and he specifically asked other people to watch. I was very upset. . . . Respondent apologized, said that I was right and that he would never insist I go to a club again. He promised it was out of his system. Then during a trip to Paris, he took me to a sex club in Paris, without telling me where we were going. . . . People were having sex everywhere. I cried, I was physically ill. Respondent became very upset with me, and said it was not a 'turn on' for me to cry."	"I did arrange romantic getaways for us, but that did not include the type of activity she described. We did go to one avant-garde nightclub in Paris. . . ."

Family Guy	How He Wanted to Protect the Family	His Interesting Twist on Family Values	His Plausible Explanation
Spokane, Washington, mayor **Jim West** (R)	According to the *Seattle Post-Intelligencer*, West initiated legislation to outlaw sexual contact between consenting teenagers; supported a bill that would have barred gays and lesbians from working for schools, day care centers, and some state agencies; voted to define marriage as a union between a man and a woman; and, as state senate majority leader, allowed a bill that would ban discrimination against gays and lesbians to die in committee without a hearing.	Accused of child molestation by two felons who said he fondled them and forced them to perform sexual acts when they were Boy Scouts. Offered gifts, favors, and a City Hall internship during Internet chats with a man he believed was 18—but who was actually a computer expert working for *The Spokesman-Review* of Spokane, which was investigating the molestation allegations.	Sent an e-mail to staffers saying he wanted to apologize. "I stumbled and let you down." Went on to categorically deny the molestation allegations, and added, "The newspaper also reported that I have visited a gay chat line on the Internet and had relations with adult men. I don't deny that." But "I wouldn't characterize me as 'gay.' "

EIGHT

BUREAUCRACY

THE BACKBONE OF OUR POLITICAL SYSTEM ISN'T TRUTH, freedom, justice, or any of those other high-falutin concepts.

It's bureaucracy.

Good old-fashioned, paper-pushing, memo-making bureaucracy.

Does the U.S. bureaucracy work for we the people? Who ya kiddin'?

THE SEVEN COMMANDMENTS OF BUREAUCRACY—
OR, "WE WOULD HAVE HAD TEN BUT WE'RE TOO BUSY COLLECTING OUR BENEFITS"

Political bureaucracies are a lot like religions: They follow certain rules whether or not logic dictates. After all, in the case of religion, it's all about faith. In the case of bureaucracy, it's all about making things tough on everyone else but not on yourself. Which is kind of like faith if you think about it. (Well, okay, it's not . . .)

The First Commandment of Bureaucracy:
Always tell yourself: "It's not my problem, it's theirs."

A good bureaucrat understands that he or she should *always* shift work—even work he or she is hired to do—over onto someone else. Why do the work when someone else can do it?

Case in Point: A dead and decaying cow caught on a tree branch at a dam near West Milford, West Virginia

Obvious solution: Take the dead cow away. And it is at this point that bureaucracy sets in—in all its obtuseness. *Who* should take the dead cow away?

The West Milford town government said not them—the dead cow was outside the town line.

The state Division of Natural Resources said not them, either—the dead cow was not a wild animal; they only handle wild animals.

The state Department of Environmental Protection refused responsibility—the dead cow posed no immediate environmental hazard.

The state Department of Agriculture said no—the dead cow was a local, not a state, issue.

The Clarksburg Water Board, which owned the dam, also declined—after all, the dead cow was in a tree, not in the water.

So for five weeks, the dead cow remained where it was, until finally, workers from the state Division of Highways, along with local volunteer firefighters, removed it.

The Second Commandment of Bureaucracy:
Force the public to do as you say, not as you do.

Who says bureaucracies are hypocritical? Not us. They just want the best—for themselves.

Cases in Point: First, the Los Angeles Department of

Water & Power, which spent $1 million in an advertising campaign to convince Angelenos that the city has top-quality tap water—while spending another $88,000 on commercial bottled water for their own offices

Second, the U.S. Environmental Protection Agency, which was asked to respond officially to a congressional report charging that the agency was using too many outside contractors. The agency gave an official response—written by an outside contractor who was paid $20,000.

THE THIRD COMMANDMENT OF BUREAUCRACY:
Treat yourself well—and don't worry about the expense!

Why suffer? In particular, why suffer if the taxpayers are paying for it? They can afford it, or if they can't, what are credit cards for?

Case in Point: Even *dogs* in bureaucracies get gold-carpet treatment.

During President Bush's March 2006 trip to India, he was accompanied by 17 Secret Service Labradors and German shepherds (each with its own police rank, such as lieutenant). All were housed in *five-star* hotels. [Disclaimer: On a recent overseas trip, we were housed in two-star hotels; so maybe we're jealous.] Interestingly, some Indian police dogs, which assisted the American police dogs, had to go home to dog kennels after a long day of guarding the president of the United States, but then again, India is a less developed country with a less developed tax base.

THE FOURTH COMMANDMENT OF BUREAUCRACY:
Take everything literally.

We're all for following the law, but sometimes we think bureaucracies maybe, just maybe, get a little too *literal* . . .

Case in Point: Henry County in Illinois

According to the federal Americans with Disabilities Act, government can't discriminate. And so Henry County was required to install special voting machines for people with disabilities, specifically, 49 machines costing a total of $260,000. The number of voters who used the machine(s): 1 (one).

Yes, one.

At the cost of $260,000, plus several thousand dollars and many man-hours installing and testing the machines, one disabled voter was accommodated. And he only needed 1 (one) machine, not 49.

In nearby Rock Island County, over $760,000 was spent, but there were more eligible voters there. Like maybe 2 (two) or 3 (three).

THE FIFTH COMMANDMENT OF BUREAUCRACY:
Never say it's bad news.

Case in Point: After the number of rat complaints in New York City rose sharply, many people were upset. But an expert New York City bureaucrat, unfortunately nameless, explained the bureaucratic outlook on this: "Complaints have gone up, but we look at that as a positive thing, because more people know how to contact us now."

THE SIXTH COMMANDMENT OF BUREAUCRACY:
Numbers should softly and covertly and gently be massaged to prove your point and get the money you need.

The key idea: With a proper massage (a deep massage is sometimes necessary), numbers can prove *anything*.

Case in Point: Say you're a rich college town. Say you want to get a lot of federal dollars designated for poor communities. What do you do? *Count all of the students who attend your colleges as poverty-stricken citizens in need of federal help.*

In short, the Census Bureau counts low-income (less

than $9,800 a year) students who aren't living in dorms as being below the poverty line even if their parents are paying their college bill in full. And because of this, rich college towns such as Ann Arbor, Michigan (University of Michigan), and Berkeley, California (University of California at Berkeley), are considered "poor." Just for comparison's sake, the median home price in Berkeley is $591,000—almost six times higher than the national average. But because it's "poor" it can get some of the $3.7 billion in Community Development Block Grants, designed for things like homeless shelters—and business loans for inner-city areas like Camden, New Jersey, and Detroit, Michigan.

THE SEVENTH COMMANDMENT OF BUREAUCRACY:
It all depends on what your meaning of "is" is.

In other words, if the facts sound unpleasant—define the facts differently.

Cases in Point: First, with the dramatic and nasty increase in violence between Iraqi Sunnis and Iraqi Shiites, the Bush administration was faced with a public relations problem: what to call all the fighting. After all, *civil war* sounds so *violent* and *brutal.* So instead, President Bush insisted it wasn't a civil war at all. It was *sectarian strife.*

Sounds a lot nicer.

Second, with the steady decline of manufacturing jobs in the United States, the administration was faced with another public relations crisis. Declining manufacturing jobs doesn't sit well with voters; they want the high-paying jobs for themselves and their children. But how can you get a voter-friendly increase in manufacturing jobs if they're not increasing? Easy: redefine what a manufacturing job is. According to an economist for the National Association of

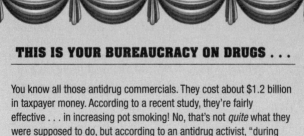

THIS IS YOUR BUREAUCRACY ON DRUGS . . .

You know all those antidrug commercials. They cost about $1.2 billion in taxpayer money. According to a recent study, they're fairly effective . . . in increasing pot smoking! No, that's not *quite* what they were supposed to do, but according to an antidrug activist, "during some periods and for some subgroups, exposure to the ads was significantly associated with an increased tendency to smoke pot." Way to go, guys!

Manufacturers, some administration officials were angling to count McDonald's hamburger-flipping jobs as manufacturing (as in *making—or manufacturing—a Big Mac*). This would show a nice increase in manufacturing jobs.

IMPORTANT GOVERNMENTAL PROCEDURES

We're often not aware of the extremely detailed, multilevel work that goes on behind the scenes of our state and federal governments.

Unsung heroes of bureaucracy have spent hours, nay, *years* developing highly important procedures to cover the many challenges and questions facing society today.

HOW DO I DESTROY MY OFFICIAL USDA FOREST SERVICE WOODSY OWL COSTUME?

According to the USDA, there are certain mandatory steps to take:

Destroying Old Woodsy Owl Costumes—Guidelines

1. Incinerate the complete costume with the oversight of an official USDA Forest Service law enforcement officer.*

2. The entire Woodsy Owl costume including each of the separate pieces is to be destroyed beyond recognition.

* If you do not have access to an official USDA Forest Service law enforcement representative, arrangements will be made for dealing with your costume by contacting the USDA-FS Washington Office at:

Woodsy Owl
c/o National Symbols Program
P.O. Box 96090
Washington, DC 20090-6090

WHAT DO I DO WITH MY OLD TEXAS FLAG?

Texas lawmakers tell us what to do:

Decommissioning of the Texas Flag

Sec. 6.　(a) A state flag, when it is no longer used or useful as an emblem for display, should be destroyed, preferably by burning, in a ceremony or other dignified way that emphasizes its honor as a fitting emblem for this state.

(b) A retirement ceremony for a state flag should be conducted with the honor and respect inherent in the traditions of this state. While the state flag may be retired in a private ceremony, it is encouraged that a retirement be a public ceremony under the direction of uniformed personnel representing a state

or national military service or a patriotic
society.

(c) During a retirement ceremony, a person
in uniform should render the military salute
at the appropriate time as designated by the
ceremony. A non uniformed individual present should stand at attention with the right
hand over the heart. When not in uniform,
an individual who is wearing a headdress
that is easily removable should remove the
headdress with the right hand and hold the
headdress at the left shoulder, with the right
hand over the heart. An individual who is
not a citizen of this state should stand at
attention. . . .

(e) The official retirement ceremony for the
state flag encouraged for public use is:

> I am your Texas flag!
> I was born January 25, 1839.
> I am one of only two flags of an
>   American state that has also served as
>   the symbol of an independent
>   nation—The Republic of Texas.
> While you may honor me in retirement,
>   the spirit I represent will never retire!
> I represent the spirit of Texas—Yesterday,
>   Today, and Tomorrow!
> I represent the bravery of the Alamo and
>   the Victory at San Jacinto.
> My spirit rode with the Texas Rangers in
>   the streets of old El Paso and herding
>   cattle through the Fort Worth

stockyards. I have sailed up Galveston
Bay.
My colors are in the waters of the Red River and
in the Bluebonnets of the Texas Hill
Country.
You'll find my spirit at the Light House of Palo
Duro and in the sands of Padre Island;
I am in the space station at Houston and atop
the oil wells of West Texas.
From the expanse of the Big Bend to the
Riverwalk of San Antone—all of Texas is
my home!

(Etc. There is indeed more. Quite a bit more. Plan
on spending the better part of your day retiring your
Texas state flag.)

WHAT ABOUT MY OLD *ILLINOIS* STATE FLAG?

Legislators suggest burning—and accompanying the ceremony with some meaningful words . . . the long version or
what they amusingly call "the short version."

Short Version or Appropriate for Gathering of War Veterans

I am the Illinois Flag. I represent just one out of fifty
states and what a remarkable State it is. Throughout
the years, the land which I represent has seen wars between nations and between brothers and sisters.

The name Illinois came from an Indian nation
called Illiniwek, meaning the people. The Indians
were the first people on my land just like any other
state and they played a big part in my history. In the
Indian world, Cahokia was one of the biggest cities in

the world. Many Indians on my land built villages like Cahokia with burial and temple mounds. They built Woodhenge, which was used as a sun calendar. Some Indians invented flint hoes for tilling soil, bow and arrows, and began composing poetry. Then people from lands far away settled in my territory and the Indians had to move. One Indian named Black Hawk would not move and this started the Black Hawk Wars. Ten years after the Black Hawk Wars, President Polk called for volunteers to serve in the war with Mexico. Three thousand troops from my state volunteered.

Then the Civil War began and divided a great nation . . .

(Note: The "short" version goes on . . . and on . . . from here. Plan on spending the better part of your day *and* night retiring your Illinois state flag. As for the long version, don't even think about it.)

WHAT SONG CAN I SING TO EXPRESS MY JOY AND LOVE OF THE FOOD AND DRUG ADMINISTRATION?

We'd like to suggest the official FDA Centennial Anthem (found on the FDA website). The opening stanza:

> One century past, a people's hope fulfilled
> By an act conceived for safe medicine and food
> Protecting rights that our founding fathers willed
> To life and liberty, to happiness pursued.

IS THERE AN OFFICIAL CHECKLIST I CAN FOLLOW WHEN WEARING MY OFFICIAL SMOKEY BEAR COSTUME?

Why, yes, there is!

(1) The person wearing the costume must exhibit appropriate animation to be effective. Express sincerity

and interest in the appearance by moving paws, head, and legs.

(2) There shall be at least one uniformed escort to accompany the Bear. The escort shall guide the Bear at the elbow.

(3) After donning the costume, the escort shall inspect the suit. Check for the following:

> Is the drawstring tucked in?
> Is the zipper out of sight?
> Are the buttons fastened?
> Is the belt firmly fastened to the pants?
> Are the pant cuffs neat?
> Is the hat crown up?
> Is the head straight on the shoulders?
> Is the fur brushed generously?

. . . The costumed bear should not force itself on anyone.

THE "MICHAEL BROWN COMPETENCE IN ACTION" AWARDS FOR BUREAUCRATS

When we think of competence, of tough minded, "can-do," good old-fashioned American know-how, the name "Michael Brown" does not immediately pop up. In fact, after an hour or two of thinking about the most competent Americans east of the Mississippi, the name of the former head of the Federal Emergency Management Agency still doesn't come up. But who cares? We *admire* a man who can focus on his television makeup and think about what a fashion god he is while the biggest hurricane in a century is ravaging the Gulf Coast and thousands are being rendered homeless. That takes single-mindeness, focus, stern devotion. . . .

American pioneer virtues.

And so we've decided to use Mr. Brown's name for our first annual "Competence in Action" Awards, the ever-so-prestigious Academy Awards for bureaucrats.

In the "Houston, Uh, We Have a Problem" Division, the winner is . . .

NASA

. . . for losing—yes *losing*—the most iconic film footage of the 20th century: that of astronaut Neil Armstrong's first footsteps on the moon.

The broadcasts of the first man on the moon were flashed back to earth in 1969 and recorded; parts were shown on television to over 600 million people. But rather than prizing this absolutely priceless original historic tape, NASA filed it away. And then, as the people involved retired—the location was lost. "This is what happens when you have a large government bureaucracy that functions for decade after decade," said Keith Cowing, editor of the website NASAWatch.com, and maybe being a little too kind. "It's not malicious or intentional, but I think it's unfortunate that NASA doesn't have maybe just one more person whose job it is to look back at its history."

We ask: Couldn't someone have, like, put a little Post-it note by the watercooler saying "Man on Moon tapes in front drawer"? We guess not.

A preliminary search through the NASA archives determined that the tapes were forwarded to the U.S. National Archives before being called back by NASA to be stored at the Goddard Space Flight Center. But from there the trail goes cold. A spokesman for the space agency said: "We're trying to track them down through the paperwork created at the time. But it's 35 years ago, so it's a challenge."

In the "Beam Me up from These Coordinates, Scotty"
Division, the winner is . . .
I. Lewis "Scooter" Libby

. . . for personally and most important, *creatively,* directing
the search for weapons of mass destruction (WMD) in Iraq.

Scooter Libby, the federally indicted and convicted former
aide to Vice President Dick Cheney, has long been known as
an Iraq War hawk—and as an avid *Star Trek* fan. As a friend
of his once pointed out admiringly, "he could remember not
only all 79 *Star Trek* episodes, but all the titles, too. I think he
always liked fantasy." Libby's love of fantasy came in handy
when it came to giving America reasons to send young
Americans to die in Iraq, but once they were there and the
WMD weren't found, Mr. Scooter had to put his creativity to
work again. So Mr. Libby, who also apparently happens to be
an amateur CIA satellite spy/analyst (it's a fun hobby), decided to call David Kay, then in charge of the hunt for WMD
in Iraq. Said Scooter, "The vice president wants to know if
you've looked at this area. We have indications—and here are
the geocoordinates—that something's buried there." Kay and
his experts plotted the coordinates on the map. It was in the
middle of Lebanon.

And so for that we proudly salute Scooter "I'm a convicted felon!" Libby, who doesn't let pesky reality get in the
way of an agenda.

In the "What Me Worry?" Division, the winner is . . .
*Dale Ray, staff project officer at the Consumer Product
Safety Commission*

. . . for spending over 10 years of personal job time (and cu-
mulatively earning over $1 million plus benefits) trying to
come up with a flammability standard for furniture—and
still not coming up with it.

It doesn't seem to us that it would be all that hard to write a few pages of standards for manufacturers, particularly on an annual salary of about $100,000—and with a team of experts. Hey, government! Give us a shot—we'll do it for $50K!

These standards are vital. Every year burning furniture causes an average of 380,000 fires, 360 deaths, and $22 billion in damages. For this reason, the National Association of State Fire Marshals petitioned the Consumer Product Safety Commission (CPSC), where Ray works, to come up with a flammability standard for upholstered furniture: a guide so that manufacturers can make and consumers can buy (and lawyers can sue about) safer furniture. The CPSC put Ray in charge. That petition from the fire marshals came way back in 1994, and still *nothing* has happened. Furniture keeps burning, standards keep being "forthcoming"—and Ray keeps on collecting his government paychecks.

And so a nice hand for Dale Ray, heading up a key management position for 10 to 12 years—and brilliantly, absolutely brilliantly, getting no results.

IN THE "JUST POSSIBLY *TOO* FAIR AND BALANCED" DIVISION, THE WINNER IS . . .
the U.S. government's Arabic-language satellite television network, Al-Hurra

. . . for broadcasting two rather eye-opening speeches. The American backed Al-Hurra network (meaning Freedom Network in Arabic) strives to give Arabs in the Middle East the American side of things—putting a true-blue American spin on the news in order to win friends and influence people to see things the American way. So what was the network doing broadcasting a virulent speech by Hezbollah leader Hassan Nasrallah, inciting people to fight against Israel? And why did Al-Hurra allow Hamas leader Ismail Haniyeh air time for the fascinating theory that the Holocaust was a myth? (Incidentally, it wasn't a myth. Take it from us.)

We may speculate that Al-Hurra wanted to show how *free* the American press is—i.e., you can say ANYTHING—or maybe, just maybe, it all happened because there were no supervisors who actually spoke Arabic and understood what was being said. In the time-honored bureaucratic way, Joaquin Blaya, of the Broadcasting Board of Governors, offered her succinct explanation. "Mistakes were made," she said.

That's good enough for us.

IN THE "HEY, NOBODY'S PERFECT" DIVISION, THE WINNER IS . . .

Johnnie M. Burton, of the Minerals Management Service of the Department of the Interior

. . . for neglecting to collect as much as $10 billion in royalties owed to the U.S. government by oil and gas companies.

Ms. Burton somehow neglected to find an error that let deepwater drillers escape paying *billions* of dollars in royalties from leases signed in 1998 and 1999. (Let it not be said that the current administration were the only dolts—these leases were signed by Clintonistas.) Though lower officials spotted the mistake in 2000, Burton and her associates at Interior never mentioned the mistake, and didn't even try fixing the leases until 2006.

In July 2006, *Republicans* (her own party) of the House Committee on Government Oversight and Reform accused her agency of stonewalling their investigation and of making too many concessions to oil companies.

The courageous Johnnie Burton, called to testify before a Senate committee, sent her assistant instead, Lucy Querques

Denett, who had only worked at the agency for four months. Denett doggedly defended her boss: "Her direction to staff has always been to perform our mission in conformance with the laws and regulations. She has also clearly impressed upon us that we are responsible for collecting every penny due and owed the American public."

Oh, we see. *Pennies,* not dollars.

Burton is also the target of three other investigations. But there the money is only $12 million or so; chump change.

"She always tried to be perfect at everything she did," said Thomas Strook, a retired oilman from Wyoming who was close friends with Burton. And in terms of helping private oil companies, you've got to admit, he's right. She's about perfect.

IN THE "SUCK MY BIG JUSTICE" CATEGORY, THE WINNER IS . . . *the U.S. Department of Justice*

. . . for providing American Indians with employment discrimination claims a toll-free number that connected them with an adult porno chat site.

As part of a federal lawsuit settlement, which alleged that the city of Gallup, New Mexico, had discriminated against American Indians, the Justice Department gave the city of Gallup a phone number to publish for the plaintiffs to call.

When some of the American Indians called this number this is what they heard: "Get together with others like you now," said a friendly voice that directed them to a second number. It sounded innocent enough—until they called the next number: "Hey there, sexy guy," a hot feminine voice greeted them, "go one-on-one with hot, horny girls from around the country."

That was *one* way of compensating them, we wish to point out.

IN THE "UH, IS THAT, YOU KNOW, *APPROPRIATE*?" DIVISION, THE WINNER IS . . .
the Special Committee of the District of Columbia City Council

. . . for cleverly rescheduling the annual Martin Luther King Day parade to April 1, after having been asked to move the date from January to a "warmer date." Committee members later said they hadn't realized that April 1 was April Fool's Day.

IN THE "BE AN ICE CUBE AND SEE AMERICA" DIVISION, THE WINNER IS . . .
the Federal Emergency Management Agency

. . . for sending 91,000 ice cubes to *Nebraska* for the victims of Hurricane Katrina—who were in New Orleans.

Although not as important as the hundreds of other examples of Michael Brown's management (if it can be called that) of FEMA, the ice cube incident has a certain *frisson,* as the French might say.

First of all, FEMA overordered ice cubes, which were intended to cool the victims and their food and medicine. But rather than let the cubes melt, or deliver them to the New Orleanians to use anyway, the ice cubes were sent around the country on various jaunts. One truck, for example, picked up 20 tons of ice in Greenville, Pennsylvania, drove it to a Carthage, Missouri, FEMA facility, then on over to Montgomery, Alabama, for a day and a half, then to Camp Shelby in Mississippi, then to Selma, Alabama, then to Emporia, Virginia (where the truck idled for a week to keep the ice frozen), and finally to Fremont, Nebraska, where the ice was put up for storage. It never reached New Orleans, but there was a silver lining to the ice cube cloud—when Hurricane Wilma hit Florida a few months later, FEMA had plenty of ice ready for Floridian hurricane victims.

NINE

YOUR GOVERNMENT AT WORK FIGHTING TERROR AS USUAL AND TO THE BEST OF ITS ABILITY

Which Isn't Necessarily That Comforting (If You Know What We Mean)

How CAN WE CAST ASPERSIONS AT A GOVERNMENT THAT IS doing amazing things to protect its citizens, is funneling money to all sorts of truly necessary programs to keep our happy homeland free of terrorism, *and* is spreading democracy at the same time?

Well, we can because the government makes it pretty easy to do so . . .

STUPID GOVERNMENT TERRORIST-RELATED ACTIVITIES

Let us begin by detailing some of the things the government is doing to fight terrorism. Are they stupid? Ask yourself a question: Just how important do you think a toilet seat museum is in the fight against terrorism?

We rest our case.

IRAQ WAR/ANTITERRORISM APPROPRIATIONS BILL PAYS FOR ABSOLUTELY ESSENTIAL WAR/TERRORISM-RELATED THINGS LIKE, YOU KNOW, ABSTINENCE EDUCATION IN ALLENTOWN

The $78.5 billion War Supplemental Appropriations bill in 2003 was, of course, intended to pay for the war in Iraq and antiterrorism programs. But Citizens Against Government Waste found that, with time-honored "Let's add pork!" gusto, Congress managed to finagle funding for 29 projects that don't *quite* seem war- or terrorism-related to us. Among them:

- $110,000,000 for the National Animal Disease Center in Ames, Iowa
- $15,000,000 for the Equal Employment Opportunity Commission
- $1,100,000 for the architect for the U.S. Capitol
- $1,000,000 for the Geisinger Health System in Harrisburg, Pennsylvania, to establish centers for excellence for the treatment of autism
- $1,000,000 for the Department of Labor for the Jobs for America's Graduates program
- $437,000 for the construction of wastewater treatment facilities in Huntington, West Virginia
- $231,000 for Daikon Lutheran Social Ministries of Allentown, Pennsylvania, to fund abstinence education and related services
- $225,000 for the Mental Health Association of Tarrant County, Fort Worth, Texas
- $200,000 for Light of Life Ministries in Allegheny County, Pennsylvania, to renovate a homeless service center in Pittsburgh

BINGO HALLS ARE PROTECTED FROM TERRORISTS (THANK HEAVENS!)

Lest you laugh, let us assure you that the bingo threat is VERY real. At least according to John Holiday, enforcement director at the Kentucky Office of Charitable Gaming, who pointed out that while he didn't know of any terrorists connected to Kentucky bingo, "the potential there, to me, is just huge. I actually went on the Web and did a lot of research about this. There are articles that have linked terrorism to charitable gaming."

So we all can be very relieved that the Department of Homeland Security gave a $36,300 grant to the above-mentioned Kentucky Office of Charitable Gaming to protect bingo halls from terrorists. Frankly, we only wish that the DHS had given them more.

UTAH DOG BOUTIQUE GETS NECESSARY SMALL BUSINESS LOAN SINCE THEY WERE OBVIOUSLY HURT BY THE 9/11 ATTACKS

Yes, even though the 9/11 attacks took place in New York City and the Pentagon, a dog boutique in Utah qualified for an emergency loan from the Small Business Administration—a loan program designed to help businesses adversely affected by 9/11. So did a perfume shop in the Virgin Islands, a radio station in South Dakota, and over 130 fast-food restaurants, dentists, and chiropractors, among others, even though they were miles away from Ground Zero. This, while many businesses right by Ground Zero got zip.

U.S.-BUILT BAGHDAD POLICE ACADEMY IS CALLED "SUCCESS STORY" (WELL, EXCEPT FOR THE FECES AND URINE DRIPPING THROUGH THE CEILINGS . . .)

Lieutenant Colonel Joel Holtrop of the Army Corps of Engineers Gulf Region Division's Project and Contracting

Office summed it up in a July 2006 press release: "This facility has definitely been a top priority. It's a very exciting time as the cadets move into the new structures."

"Exciting" might not be the right word, though. After the cadets moved in, it turned out that the building wasn't quite the success that had been hoped for. Floors were buckling and cracked, water dripped through the ceiling so badly that one room was called "The Rain Forest," and, worse, the plumbing was so substandard that urine and feces inundated the building. One light fixture didn't work because it was so full of urine and feces that had seeped through the ceiling. And the buildup of human waste got so bad that it threatened the building's stability.

For this, the government had paid U.S. construction company Parsons Corporation (which got more than $1 billion for various Iraqi reconstruction projects) a cool $75 million. Was the company fired? Umm . . . no. The contract for this particular project was terminated for "the government's convenience."

BARNEY SMITH'S TOILET SEAT ART MUSEUM IS PROTECTED FROM TERRORISM! (AND, MAN, ARE WE RELIEVED!)

The Department of Homeland Security, anxious to prevent another 9/11, set up a "Freedom Budget" to allocate funds to protect national monuments that are likely targets. You know, as the World Trade Center was.

Kind of.

Among the landmarks the DHS is determined to protect:

- The World's Largest Ball of Paint in Alexandria, Indiana ($12 million)
- Barney Smith's Toilet Seat Art Museum in Alamo Heights, Texas ($10 million)

- The Museum of Bad Art, Dedham, Massachusetts ($31 million)
- Carhenge, Alliance, Nebraska ($25 million)
- and, of course, the Giant Lava Lamp, Soap Lake, Washington ($143 million).

They also listed other rather arcane "landmarks" in their National Asset Database; such "icons" as: Dinosaur World, Plant City, Florida; Old MacDonald's Petting Zoo, Woodville, Alabama; and the Mule Day Parade in Columbia, Tennessee. (Not to mention "Nix's Check Cashing," "Mall at Sears," "Ice Cream Parlor," "Tackle Shop," "Donut Shop," and "Bean Fest.")

As for New York City? On June 1, 2006, the DHS released their Terrorist Threat Assessment of the city—and determined that there were *zero* national monuments and icons . . . certainly nothing equal to Bean Fest. (After a hue and cry, they did change their minds later—and admitted that perhaps there *were* a few important icons in N.Y.C.)

57 Army Forts Have Gates Protected by Convicted Felons

With soldiers needed for war duties, the Army has had to look elsewhere for people to guard the gates at domestic installations such as Fort Bragg and West Point. Like convicted felons.

Contractors employed by the Army have been hiring convicted felons to man the gates. The Government Accountability Office has not been pleased, so they've warned the contractors to stop this hiring practice.

Pentagon Defense Threat Reduction Agency Closely and Carefully Monitors Potentially Dangerous Scottish Whiskey Distillery

In 2003, the top-notch Defense Threat Reduction Agency began monitoring a suspicious facility on the Isle of Islay,

Scotland, after they noticed webcam shots from the firm that appeared to be those of a chemical weapons lab. After much time and much surveilling, the agency came to an important conclusion: Gosh. It wasn't a chemical lab after all, but a whiskey distillery.

SECRET HOMELAND DEFENSE HOTLINE GETS TONS OF TELEMARKETING CALLS

The homeland defense hotline is a top-secret telephone line that will ring only when a national catastrophe occurs. Or so it was designed. But numerous governors began complaining to the Department of Homeland Security that the phone kept ringing even when there was no emergency. "Every time that phone rings, it's telemarketers," said Delaware governor Ruth Ann Minner. The DHS got quickly on the case and registered the super-secret hotline numbers on the Do Not Call Registry.

U.S. EMBASSY IN AFGHANISTAN IS EAGER TO ACCEPT INFO ON TERRORIST THREATS—TWO WHOLE HOURS A DAY (BUT NOT FRIDAY OR SATURDAY, OF COURSE)

The U.S. Embassy in Kabul knows that part of fighting the war on terrorism is listening to informants. So they make it easy for anyone who wants to tip them off. They've posted a sign—written in English, Pashto, and Dari—outside of the embassy: "The U.S. Embassy would be grateful if any of our friends who have information on terrorist activity or threats inform us between 10 a.m. and 12 p.m. on Sunday through Thursday."

BORDER GUARDS ARE TOO BUSY GUARDING NATIONAL GUARD TO GUARD BORDER

It was a brilliant idea (well, sort of): President Bush decided to deploy National Guard troops along the U.S.-Mexico border. This way (theoretically) Border Patrol agents could be free to do their stopping-illegal-aliens thing. But then, due to rising border violence and the fact that most of the National Guard can't carry loaded weapons, it was decided that the National Guard needed bodyguards. And who were the bodyguards? Why, U.S. Border Patrol agents, of course!

Yup, the Border Patrol agents got pulled from their own regions to be within five minutes of National Guard troops because of standing orders the agents call "the nanny patrol."

WE FEEL REALLY SAFE NOW, PART 1:
VERY DANGEROUS THINGS WE'RE BEING PROTECTED FROM

Yes, in the post-9/11 world, the U.S. government has been doing its darnedest to keep its citizens safe.

But you may not be aware of some of the dangers that only constant vigilance and adherence to the highest of safety standards have thwarted. Breathe easy . . . and read on to learn about some of the truly frightening things that our ever-cautious government is zealously protecting us from.

Dangerous Threat: Small American flags on sticks

Yes, we have been ably protected from the dreaded stick to which a tiny American flag is attached, thanks to the vigilant police force of Davenport, Iowa. Well, actually—and more precisely—*Vice President Dick Cheney* was ably protected from said dreaded stick to which etc., etc.

About 120 people were holding little American flags on sticks as they marched to a home where Cheney was doing a fund-raiser for a Republican candidate—and the police (who were described by one protester as "very courteous and very embarrassed") took away all their flags. You see, they were a potential *weapon,* according to Davenport Police Chief Michael Bladel: "These were fairly long wooden sticks with points on them, they thought they might be a threat to the vice president. This could be considered a weapon."

Safe Outcome: Dick Cheney was not attacked by a little flagstick, as all small flags were confiscated. And we now know how potentially dangerous an American flag is.

Dangerous Threat: Canadian rock bands

You will be relieved to know that attentive U.S. border guards have rid us of a scourge from the north.

Canadian rockers.

Rock band the Grey was detained by American border guards after the members said they weren't performing while in the States. The guards checked the band's tour schedule online and found they had lied. Clearly this was worrisome—so the guards split them up and interrogated them separately for six hours. As Hayden Menzies of the Grey explains it, "When we first went, one by one, into the room with the interrogating officer, they used that line about 'America is at war, and Canada may not take that seriously . . .' and 'Since 9-11, we take these things seriously.' Then they realized that we were not making any money doing what we do, and that we were more naïve than anything else."

Safe Outcome: All members of the Grey were deported as illegal aliens and have been banned from entering the United States for five years.

Dangerous Threat: Senator Edward Kennedy (D-MA)

We doubt you thought of Ted Kennedy as a danger. (Well, perhaps you did. Particularly if you are a conservative Republican. But that's not the kind of danger of which we speak here.)

Apparently others disagreed. While discussing the No Fly list with the rest of the Senate Judiciary Committee, Kennedy said that he had repeatedly been delayed at airports because the name "T. Kennedy" appeared on the list. There are roughly 7,000 American men whose legal names could be written as T. Kennedy. (And of course the senator's name would more properly be rendered "E. Kennedy.")

Safe Outcome: Ted Kennedy's name was removed from the No Fly list, thanks to his personal appeal to the Homeland Security secretary. To date, he has not blown up an airplane.

Dangerous Threat: Babies

The No Fly list has also protected the American public from other possible terrorists—of the infantile kind. Literally.

While the Transportation Security Administration (TSA) has issued instructions to airlines that children under 12 whose names appear on the list should be allowed to board and not be subjected to extra security checks, zealous airline security officers often don't follow suit. As a result, infants are detained before boarding. In a stunning example of flexibility, they *are* allowed to stay with their parents while their passports and other documents are faxed to the authorities just to make *absolutely sure* that said babies aren't baby terrorists. (Note: They are also not subjected to interrogation.)

Safe Outcome: As with Ted Kennedy, to date no baby has committed a terroristic act on an airline, domestic *or* international.

Dangerous Threat: President of Bolivia

Yet one more potential threat we're safe from: Bolivian president Evo Morales—whose name (or variations thereof) appears three (THREE!) times on the No Fly list, along with his correct birth date.

Safe Outcome: As with Ted Kennedy *and* babies, the president of Bolivia has not committed any acts of terror on American planes.

Dangerous Threat: Marine on his way for training before serving in Iraq

Alert TSA screeners hit a jackpot when they stopped a man who had gunpowder residue on his boots. Terrorist alert! Granted, said terrorist was in Marine uniform, but still . . .

The supposed terrorist was Marine staff sergeant Daniel Brown, who explained that he was in the Marines, was going for training in California, and probably had the residue on his boots from a previous two-month tour in Iraq.

Not good enough. His bona fides had to be checked (even though he was in uniform) and he ended up missing his flight.

NO NEED TO WORRY ABOUT DEAD TERRORISTS *OR* SADDAM HUSSEIN— THANKS TO THE NO FLY LIST

Among the names (other than Ted Kennedy, babies, or the president of Bolivia) that appear on the No Fly list: 14 of the 19 Sept. 11 hijackers (who have been dead since 9/11), convicted terrorist Zacarias Moussaoui (imprisoned since 2001), and Saddam Hussein (now dead).

When questioned as to why so many nonthreats appear on the watch list, Homeland Security secretary Michael Chertoff sagely noted that the list wasn't perfect. And, hey, we pay this guy for that sort of insight!

Safe Outcome: Well, we're actually not quite sure since the TSA wouldn't comment on this case. For some reason.

Dangerous Threat: The *same* Marine returning from his tour of duty

Let's face it: A uniformed Minnesota reservist who was returning from an eight-month tour of duty in Iraq could *well* have been a terrorist. Even if he was with 26 other reservists (also in uniform). After all, his name was on the— you guessed it—No Fly list.

Yet again Marine staff sergeant Daniel Brown was delayed; he had arrived in Los Angeles en route to Minneapolis after his name appeared on the watch list—probably due to the gunpowder incident. He had to wait until Northwest Airlines representatives could call somebody to clear him.

Safe Outcome: Let's let Brown tell you in his own words: "A guy goes over and serves his country fighting for eight or nine months, and then we come home and put up with this crap?"

Dangerous Threat: Members of Congress

We have heard much about security on the U.S.-Mexico border. In case you have been too busy to hear it, basically Border Patrol agents are there guarding against illegal immigrants and other threats.

Apparently, Homeland Security has determined that members of Congress are also a threat, since Border Patrol agents are now required to file Significant Incident Reports— typically used to detail shootings and other serious border incidents—whenever a congressperson comes to talk with them.

Safe Outcome: Thus far, no member of Congress has illegally crossed the border and taken away jobs mowing the lawn from hardworking Americans.

SPECIAL TERRORISM INTELLIGENCE SECTION—

OR, THE WORD "INTELLIGENCE" CAN BE TAKEN IN TWO DIFFERENT WAYS

As any military strategist would tell you, half of winning a battle is knowing the enemy. So when reading the following, try not to panic, okay?

REPRESENTATIVE SILVESTRE REYES (D-TX), CHAIRMAN OF THE HOUSE INTELLIGENCE COMMITTEE, SHARES HIS INSIDE INFO ON MAJOR TERRORIST GROUPS

> REPORTER JEFF STEIN, *Congressional Quarterly:* "Al-Qaeda is what? Sunni or Shia?"
> REYES: "Al-Qaeda, they have both. You're talking about predominately?"
> REPORTER: "Sure."
> REYES: "Predominantly—probably Shiite."
>
> (WRONG. Al-Qaeda is 100% Sunni. They consider Shia as apostates.)
>
> REPORTER: "And Hezbollah? What are they?"
> REYES: "Hezbollah. Uh, Hezbollah . . ."
> (Laughs. Pauses.)
> REYES: "Why do you ask me these questions at five o'clock? Can I answer in Spanish? Do you speak Spanish?"
> REPORTER: *"Poquito."*
> REYES: *"Poquito?!"*
> REPORTER: "Go ahead. Talk to me about Sunnis and Shia in Spanish."
> REYES: "Well, I, uh . . ."

Reyes added that the issues were "complex," and that "we ought to expend some effort into understanding them. But speaking only for myself, it's hard to keep things in perspective and in the categories."

REPRESENTATIVE BILL SALI (R-ID) KNOWS THAT IRAQ HAD WEAPONS OF MASS DESTRUCTION—HE SAW THEM ON TV

Most Americans now believe that Iraq didn't have WMD when we invaded, but Representative Bill Sali has insider knowledge that proves this wrong. He *knows* there were WMD, dammit.

> "I know that I saw it on the TV station. It might have only been on Fox, come to think of it."

> That's good enough for us, sir!

PRESIDENT GEORGE W. BUSH—JUST TWO MONTHS BEFORE IRAQ INVASION—ALLEGEDLY DISCOVERS THERE ARE TWO (COUNT 'EM, TWO!) MAJOR BRANCHES OF ISLAM IN IRAQ

In his book, *The End of Iraq: How American Incompetence Created a War Without End,* Ambassador Peter Galbraith claims that Bush was a little . . . vague . . . on the religious setup in the country he was planning to invade. Galbraith reports that three Iraq-Americans met with Bush, briefing him on Iraq. When they explained that there are two major sects of Islam, Sunni and Shiite, the president allegedly responded, "I thought the Iraqis were Muslims!"

Hey, he got that part right!

WILLIE HULON, CHIEF OF FBI'S NATIONAL SECURITY BRANCH, PROVES FBI IS SO ON THE BALL WHEN IT COMES TO GRASPING MIDDLE EASTERN POLITICS

> REPORTER JEFF STEIN: "Do you think it's important for a man in your position to know the difference between Sunni and Shiites?"

HULON: "Yes, sure, it's right to know the difference. It's important to know who your targets are."

REPORTER: "Can you tell me the difference?"

HULON: "The basics goes back to their beliefs and who they were following. And the conflicts between the Sunnis and the Shia and the difference between who they were following."

REPORTER: "What about today? Which one is Iran— Sunni or Shiite?"

(*Pause.*)

REPORTER: "Iran and Hezbollah. Which are they?"

HULON: "Sunni."

(WRONG. They're Shiite.)

REPORTER: "Al-Qaeda?"

HULON: "Sunni."

(RIGHT! His score is now 50%. No WONDER he has a high-ranking position at the FBI!)

REPRESENTATIVE TERRY EVERETT (R-AL), VICE CHAIRMAN OF THE HOUSE SUBCOMMITTEE ON TECHNICAL AND TACTICAL INTELLIGENCE, ADMITS SEMI-TOTAL IGNORANCE OF HIS JOB

REPORTER JEFF STEIN: "Do you know the difference between a Sunni and a Shiite?"

EVERETT: "One's in one location, another's in another location. No, to be honest with you, I don't know. I thought it was differences in their religion, different families or something."

(RIGHT! Something!)

After being told by the reporter what the differences were, Everett—with laser-like focus—replied: "Now that you've explained it to me, what occurs to me is that it makes what we're doing over there extremely difficult, not only in Iraq but that whole area."

WE FEEL REALLY SAFE NOW, PART 2:
WELL, DON'T WE?

Maybe it's because all those folks in the federal government are just so busy fighting terrorism that they let a few teeny-tiny things slip. Maybe they're just so absorbed in all those threats that their minds wander and, to quote the T-shirt slogan, shit happens.

But there have been a few bungles security-wise that make us wonder how well we really are being protected, in spite of the chest-thumping of the feds.

Or are we just being paranoid?

U.S. MILITARY SELLS FIGHTER JET PARTS, MISSILE COMPONENTS TO AXIS OF EVIL (OOPSIE!)

With a laudatory urge to save money, the Defense Department holds auctions for its surplus equipment. "Right Item, Right Time, Right Place, Right Price, Every Time. Best Value Solutions for America's Warfighters," says the Defense Reutilization and Marketing Service website (the self-proclaimed "place to obtain original U.S. Government surplus property").

Somehow, though, in the money-saving enthusiasm, the U.S. military has managed to sell so-called "forbidden equipment" (i.e., things that can help the "bad guys" get us) to, well, the so-called "bad guys"—including current super-bad-guy Iran, part of the Axis of Evil!

At least six times, middlemen for countries including Iran and China managed to get their hands on such things as helicopter engine parts, missile guidance parts, and F-14

"Tomcat" fighter jet parts. (One interesting fact: Iran is the only country currently flying F-14s.)

U.S. MILITARY SELLS BODY ARMOR, TRACKING DEVICES, AND ALL SORTS OF OTHER SENSITIVE EQUIPMENT ON OPEN MARKET—WHERE IT CAN THEN BE SOLD TO AXIS OF EVIL (OOPSIE AGAIN!)

Undercover investigators for the Government Account-ability Office reported in July 2006 that they were able to purchase, on the open market from Pentagon contractors, surplus body armor, mounts for shoulder-fired missiles, an aircraft tracking antenna, and missile radar test devices. Not to worry, though. Alert customs agents are doing their best to catch the outflow of these potentially dangerous pieces of equipment. For example, in 2005 they confiscated F-14 "Tomcat" parts that were headed for Iran and returned them to the Pentagon. Unfortunately for us, though, the Pentagon sold them again (they didn't even bother removing the cus-toms evidence tags). Who bought the parts? Yet *another* buyer who is a suspected broker for Iran.

One final note: The U.S. military isn't even good at mak-ing money out of these sales. They were selling a $344,000 unit to manage global positioning for a cut-rate $65.

U.S. MILITARY MEANS TO DEMILITARIZE DANGEROUS WEAPONS HELD AT SURPLUS SITES, BUT SOMETIMES MAKES A TEENY MISTAKE

Defense consultant Randall Sweeney visited a Defense Department surplus site five years ago that was (supposedly) filled with items that had been demilitarized, i.e., made inef-fective for military purposes. And *most* of the items he looked at were indeed de-milled. But there was one item he stumbled upon: an intact heat-seeking missile warhead.

Oops.

As he said, "This shouldn't be in here." He added that it would be easy for military-savvy buyers to spot something like that. "I'm not the only sophisticated eye in the world." The problem? Surplus items are catalogued by number and if one digit is off, something still working (and still dangerous) could wind up at a surplus site. But, hey, we should be understanding. A one-digit mistake? It could happen to anyone . . . particularly if he or she is working for the Defense Department.

HANDGUNS MYSTERIOUSLY DISAPPEAR FROM SUPER-SECURE DEPARTMENT OF HOMELAND SECURITY VAULT

The Department of Homeland Security might want to take the old saying "Physician, heal thyself" to heart. Case in point: Four handguns were missing from the security vault at its headquarters in Washington. The department spokesman, Jarrod Agen, helpfully explained that the guns didn't belong to the DHS, but rather to Paragon Systems, a company that provides security for the DHS and that "the DHS is investigating the report. Paragon guns do not belong to DHS nor are they under the control of DHS." In other words, just because they were stolen from a DHS security vault, it had nothing, absolutely *nothing* to do with the DHS. Boy, that makes us feel better.

WANT TO GET PAST THE MAIN SECURITY CHECKPOINT AT DEPARTMENT OF HOMELAND SECURITY? NO PROBLEMO!

Yes, it's the DHS again, that incredible department ostensibly responsible for the country's (i.e., homeland's) security. Unfortunately, their *own* security is a tad dicey, it seems. A retired New York City police officer passed through their main headquarters checkpoint by casually flashing his one piece of

ID on hand: an old Mexican consulate card. We are sure that the card looked very official, though.

PENTAGON HELPFULLY POSTS ENTIRE COUNTERINSURGENCY "WAR ON TERROR" MANUAL ON THE WEB FOR ANYONE TO READ

The Pentagon (theoretically) knows its stuff when it comes to fighting terrorism. In fact, it wrote the manual on fighting terrorism . . . literally. Experts put together a very complete counterinsurgency manual designed to help U.S. forces fighting in Iraq and Afghanistan with all sorts of super-special tips—282 pages with subject matter like Intelligence, Surveillance, and Reconnaissance Operations; Human Intelligence and Operational Reporting; Counterintelligence and Counterreconnaissance; Intelligence Collaboration; Intelligence Cells and Working Groups; Protecting Sources; Executing Counterinsurgency Operations; and Targeting.

Now that's just super-duper and we're thrilled the Pent seems ("seems" being the key word here) to know what they're doing. So we're sure, absolutely *sure,* that they knew what they were doing when they decided to make the "War on Terror" manual approved for unlimited distribution. They've even helpfully posted it on a number of military websites . . . where anyone can read it. Granted, the people against whom the U.S. forces are fighting can read it, too, but perhaps we're being unwarrantedly nitpicky.

AIRPORT SECURITY TO BE HANDLED BY COMPANY THAT CAN'T HANDLE IT (BUT AT LEAST IT'S IN KENTUCKY!)

Representative Hal Rogers (R-KY), chairman of the House Subcommittee on Homeland Security, decided it was *vital* to have tamper-proof biometric ID cards—designed to improve airport security—produced at a factory in Corbin, Kentucky. (It must have been coincidental the factory was in Kentucky, *non*?) Sadly, the factory wasn't up to the job. So he had the government cough up $4 million to test the factory's technology . . . and, by gum, one of the small companies that was involved with the testing just happened to employ his son. The factory failed . . . but Rogers didn't give up. Next step: The new card prototypes *still* had to be produced in Kentucky.

Rogers also pushed for a no-bid airport security contract to be awarded to a trade group that had no applicable experience. The group did have experience in paying for Rogers's six trips to Hawaii and one to Ireland, however. (The contract was ultimately opened up to bidders.)

For these actions, conservative *National Review* called Rogers a "congressional disgrace." Decorum prevents us from telling you what nonconservatives have called him.

INDIANA'S SPECIAL HOMELAND SECURITY EMERGENCY-ONLY HIGHWAY MESSAGE BOARDS ADVERTISE FISH FRIES AND SPAGHETTI DINNERS

The whole point of state homeland security emergency-only highway message boards is, as you may surmise, to warn of state homeland security emergencies. Perhaps we should stress this point to the officials of Vermillion County, Indiana. Lacking a homeland security emergency to put on the highway message boards, they were cleverly using them to advertise charity fish fries and spaghetti dinners.

COVERT CIA OPERATIVES FORGET TO BE COVERT (BUT GET CRITICAL FREQUENT FLIER MILES)

CIA operatives are supposed to be pros at covering their tracks. We assume that many of them are. But we *know* some of them aren't—such as the CIA operatives who work secretly transferring terrorism suspects from U.S. custody to foreign governments. Or should we say theoretically secretly? A report found numerous instances where ostensibly covert operatives allowed themselves to be fairly overt instead. For example, operatives in Milan, Italy, forgot to take the batteries out of their cell phones—which allowed others to electronically track them. And there was one budget-minded operative who, rightly, booked all of her reservations at hotels under aliases. But she had the hotels credit the frequent-flier miles she earned by staying at them to her personal frequent flier account . . . which was listed under her actual name.

Airport Shoe X-Ray Machines Meant to Detect Explosives Look Really Spiffy But, Sadly, Can't Detect Explosives

Let's get something straight: The much-ballyhooed airport shoe X-ray machines do work. Really, they do. They *do* x-ray. Unfortunately, though, they can't detect explosives . . . which, of course, is the whole point of them. But the Transportation Security Administration—even after learning of this—still stuck with their insistence that all airline passengers had to remove their shoes and run them through the machines. We can only assume this is due to a perverse sense of humor.

Feds Post Helpful "How to Build an Atom Bomb" Info on the Web

Congressional Republicans wanted to "leverage the Internet" to prove there was a reason for invading Iraq, so they pressured the Bush administration to set up a website and let the public see many of the Iraqi documents captured during the war. But then a little problem arose on the site, snappily named "Operation Iraqi Freedom Document Portal" . . . or should we say a problem mushroomed?

Among the documents posted were detailed accounts of Iraq's secret nuclear research dating back to before the 1991 Persian Gulf War, including . . . a handy-dandy primer on how to build a bomb. (Which the feds didn't even know about until *The New York Times* told them.)

Interestingly, the same website had earlier posted handy-dandy instructions for making the deadly nerve gases tabun and sarin—and pulled that document after U.N. arms officials complained. But, hey! Gotta give the government credit for trying to make their case, right?

Secret Service Can't Keep Bush Daughter's Handbag from Getting Stolen

The Secret Service's mission statement is: "Building on a tradition of excellence and meeting the challenges of the future." You'll note there is nothing about preventing your basic purse-snatching in there. Small potatoes, perhaps, but it does make one wonder a tad about how tough those Secret Service guys really are. . . . President Bush's daughter Barbara was in Buenos Aires with a full entourage of Secret Service agents when someone (no one saw who) stole her bag and cell phone. The red-faced agents admitted they hadn't even noticed the bag being stolen, but there was no official statement made.

It could have been worse . . . and, well, maybe it was. A few days earlier, one of the agents who was visiting Buenos Aires as part of the Bush daughters' advance team was mugged. There *was* an official statement for this one. It was "an attempted mugging"—and it happened while the agent was on his own time. So it didn't really count.

WANNA ATTACK A NUCLEAR PLANT? GO TO THE PUBLIC LIBRARY!

It is a well-known fact that terrorists or would-be terrorists don't go to the library. Ever. This is, apparently, what the feds think. An NBC News investigation found that sensitive documents from the Nuclear Regulatory Commission (NRC)—packed full of information such as what the most vulnerable part of a nuclear plant is in terms of aircraft impact, how one can get the maximum damage out of an attack, how to get past the security barriers outside nuke plants, and so forth—are available at the public library.

After 9/11, the NRC pulled documents of this sort off their website, but gosh-darn if they kinda forgot to ensure that the same sensitive documents were pulled from NRC document collections in public libraries across the United States. The NRC, of course, says not to worry: "the usefulness of this information is minimal given its age and subsequent changes to and improvements in security programs and physical modifications that have been made to nuclear facil-

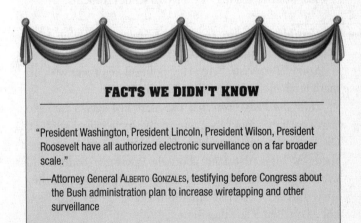

FACTS WE DIDN'T KNOW

"President Washington, President Lincoln, President Wilson, President Roosevelt have all authorized electronic surveillance on a far broader scale."

—Attorney General ALBERTO GONZALES, testifying before Congress about the Bush administration plan to increase wiretapping and other surveillance

ities. . . . [We want] to assure the public that information directly related to the security programs and protection of nuclear power plants is not in the public domain." But a nuclear safety engineer with the Union of Concerned Scientists, Dave Lochbaum, said the information was "very explicit, very detailed, and would be very useful to the terrorists planning out such an attack."

Whom to believe? The people who forgot to pull documents? Or a concerned scientist? Hmm . . .

WE FEEL REALLY SAFE NOW, PART 3:
HOW THE FEDS ARE PROTECTING US FROM THOSE SCARY HIGH SCHOOL STUDENTS

As we have already pointed out, the U.S. government is vigorously protecting the citizenry from potential terrorist threats.

But perhaps you aren't aware of one specific subset which the feds apparently think deserves special scrutiny because the people in it have done all sorts of very, very scary things.

Yes, we are speaking of U.S. high school students.

Possible Terrorist: 16-year-old junior at Calvine High School, Sacramento, California

Scary "Terroristic" Act: Had political argument with his math teacher, then wrote "PLO" on his binder

How the Feds Protected Us: Alert FBI agents came to Calvine High School to question the high school student. Okay, so it was two years *after* the junior (as a freshman) argued with his math teacher about the Palestinian conflict and wrote "PLO" on his binder, but they were there because they knew this act deserved attention. Besides, they had been tipped off. Better late than never . . .

The FBI agents pulled the young man out of his classroom and questioned him in a private room, asking him about the PLO and, according to the *Los Angeles Times,* "whether he had pictures of suicide bombers stored on his cell phone." The student explained he wasn't a terrorist and, no, had no snaps of bombers on his phone.

Possible Terrorist: 14-year-old freshman at McClatchy High School, Sacramento, California

Scary "Terroristic" Act: "Threatened" President George W. Bush on her MySpace page (and also called him an idiot)

How the Feds Protected Us: Alert Secret Service agents first visited the girl's home and questioned her mother. Mom text-messaged her daughter, writing: "there are two men from the secret service that want to talk with you. Apparently you made some death threats against president bush." Replied the potential terrorist: "Are you serious!?!? omg. Am I in a lot of trouble?"

Yes, she was. See, her MySpace page, which she had put up as an antiwar message, not only said "Kill Bush," but also showed a cartoon with a knife stabbing Bush's hand. And, to make matters worse, the page was titled "So Bush is an idiot but hey what else is new?"

OMG, thought the feds upon seeing these blatant plans to attack the president. So the alert Secret Service agents tracked down the threatening gal in her freshman molecular biology class and took her for questioning. The agents didn't mince words. According to the girl, the agents told her she could be sent to juvenile detention for death threats against the president. And "they yelled at me a lot. They were unnecessarily mean."

Possible Terrorist: Senior at Currituck County High School, Barco, North Carolina

Scary "Terroristic" Act: Took anti-Bush photo for Bill of Rights school project to be developed at Wal-Mart

How the Feds Protected Us: Alert Secret Service agents got the pressing call from the alert Kitty Hawk, North Carolina, police department who had, in turn, gotten a call from an alert Kitty Hawk Wal-Mart employee: Someone had handed in a photo to be developed. Said photo was a composite showing President George W. Bush with a red thumbtack through his head next to a hand making a thumb's-down sign.

Clearly this was a death threat, so clearly the Secret Service agents had to pull the student—and his teacher—out of class for individual close questioning. Said the teacher about the photo, "They asked me, didn't I think that was suspicious? I said no, it was a Bill of Rights project!" The agents, apparently, were not convinced. The incident had to be interpreted by the U.S. attorney who would decide if the student would be indicted. Interestingly, he wasn't.

TEN BRILLIANT AND INNOVATIVE IDEAS FROM THE PENTAGON

Ya gotta love that Pentagon! While other governmental departments opt for the old tried-and-true ways of getting things done, the DoD goes that extra mile and comes up with truly creative solutions. Note: The word "creative" does not necessarily mean "good."

While some of the Pentagon ideas below were indeed enacted, many, sadly, never saw the light of day. We can't imagine why.

CLEVER PENTAGON IDEA #1: *Let's shoot high-power microwaves at American citizens to see how well they work!*

A brilliant combination shot—this covers weapons testing, cost cutting, *and* press relations in one fell swoop. The microwave devices use "active-denial technology," in Pentagon parlance—which means that they are designed to "inflict intense pain on human skin."

As Air Force Secretary Michael Wynne convincingly explained, "If we're not willing to use it here against our fellow citizens, then we should not be willing to use it in a wartime situation."

Was the idea used?: Yes. And all the volunteers got a 15-second cool-down period between shots.

CLEVER PENTAGON IDEA #2: *Let's topple Saddam by projecting a picture of Allah into the clouds!*

Back when Saddam Hussein was still in power, the great minds of the military came up with a way of ousting him without involving U.S. troops: projecting a holographic image of Allah in the sky above Baghdad. While Allah was hovering in the air, He would command the Iraqi citizens to overthrow Saddam.

Was the idea used?: No.

CLEVER PENTAGON IDEA #3: *Let's turn enemy troops gay!*

This was just one of the truly groundbreaking ideas that came out of a lab at Ohio's Wright-Patterson Air Force Base as part of their six-year, $7.5 million nonlethal chemical weapon research—in a report snappily titled "Harassing, Annoying and 'Bad Guy' Identifying Chemicals."

This particular idea—the "gay bomb," which they termed "a distasteful but completely non-lethal example"—involved developing an aphrodisiac that would, with some luck, make enemy troops get a little hot and bothered about each other. In other words, it would "foster homosexual behavior." As a result, to quote the proposal: "discipline and morale in enemy units is adversely affected."

Was the idea used?: No. After this report was made public by a military watchdog group, the Sunshine Project, Defense Department spokesman Lieutenant Colonel Barry Venable of the Army said, "This suggestion arose essentially from a brainstorming session, and it was rejected out of hand." However, this idea (and the following three), while initially floated in 1994, somehow also showed up as under consideration in 2000 and 2001. Hmm . . .

CLEVER PENTAGON IDEA #4: *Let's use rats as a weapon— or . . . maybe wasps instead! (Or something else! Whatever!)*

Those same folks who floated the "let's make 'em gay" idea also came up with this one: developing and spraying chemicals on enemies that would attract wasps and other stinging and/or biting insects, rats, and other rodents, and larger animals.

Was the idea used?: No. Well, not yet. Not as far as we know.

CLEVER PENTAGON IDEA #5: *Let's give our enemies really, really bad breath!*

Yet another from the lab at Wright-Patterson Air Force Base: creating a way of inflicting "severe and lasting halitosis" on enemy fighters. No, this wasn't to affect their morale, but rather to "mark" them—so they would stand out if they were trying to blend in with civilians.

Was the idea used?: No.

CLEVER PENTAGON IDEA #6: *Let's help stressed-out military families by teaching them how to laugh more!*

U.S. troops are dying overseas; families are tense about their loved ones in Iraq and Afghanistan. What can the Pentagon do about this? No, not stop the war, of course. Something seriously helpful. Or rather, not seriously. In other words, hire a "laughter instructor" to hold therapy sessions for National Guard families. Included in the sessions are exercises in which family members blurt out "Ha ha hee hee ho ho" and walk like penguins.

Was the idea used?: Yes. The "laughter instructor" explained that it works so well because "the guiding principle is to laugh for no reason."

CLEVER PENTAGON IDEA #7: *Let's fill the hole left in the families of troops overseas with a two-dimensional cutout!*

Another way to help worried families—supply them with a "Flat Daddy" or "Flat Mommy" cutout. It's a surefire way to calm down kids who wonder when they're going to see their 3-D parent again. Or so thinks the Maine National Guard, which dispenses life-size cutouts of deployed service members to their families.

Was the idea used?: Yes.

CLEVER PENTAGON IDEA #8: *Let's spray cattle with deodorant!*

An oldie but a goodie that was only revealed in the late 1990s, but was born during the Cold War: Worried that the Soviets might be able to poison the U.S. meat supply by breaking into stockyards and infecting cattle with hoof-and-mouth disease, the U.S. Army came up with a way to determine how easy it could be. They would break into stockyards and stealthily spray cattle with plain-old deodorant.

Was the idea used?: Yes. In 1964 and 1965, sneaky scientists sneaked into stockyards in six different cities and sprayed cattle with deodorant.

CLEVER PENTAGON IDEA #9: *Let's make troops into projectiles!*

The Defense Advanced Research Projects Agency—the Pentagon's hotshot research agency—has been considering a human-cannonball weapon. More specifically, it is a human-launching device that could, with precision, fire special forces troops into hard-to-reach locations.

Was the idea used?: Not yet. But it's still in the works.

CLEVER PENTAGON IDEA #10: *Let's fight terrorism with the Three Stooges!*

How to win the hearts and minds of the citizens of Iraq and Afghanistan? How to steer people away from terrorism and convince them that the United States is in the right?

Yes. Of course. The Three Stooges. (Come on. That's what you were thinking, weren't you?)

This was one idea that came out of the psychological operations unit at Fort Bragg, North Carolina—where they produce news, TV spots, articles, and more to support U.S. government objectives in those countries and, if possible, neighboring countries. Some might call this by the old-fashioned term "propaganda," but the officers in charge call it "truthful messages."

One plan: to produce an anti-terrorist comedy based on *The Three Stooges.* In this case, Larry, Moe, and Curly (or perhaps Ahmed, Mahmoud, and Khalid) would be bumbling terrorist knuckleheads who can't pull off their jobs.

Was the idea used?: Nyuk-nyuk, no. They also nixed a variation on the old sitcom *Cheers* and on the satirical newspaper *The Onion.* But they have placed thousands of "news" articles, editorials, and the like.

POLITICIANS TAKE A PERSONAL INTEREST IN TERRORISM

Terrorists may indeed threaten certain important people, but why would Alan Hevesi, the comptroller of New York state, assign a personal security detail to his wife? The wife of the New York state comptroller being targeted by terrorists? Isn't that kind of overdoing things to think of *her* as a target?

We think so. Maybe we're going out on a limb here, but we wonder if some of our ego-inflated gasbag politicians (nothing personal) are just acting a teeny-weeny bit over the top on security issues. Maybe they're getting a little bit PARANOID?

Paranoic #1: Governor Jim Gibbons (R-NV)

Why He's Maybe Just a Little Paranoid: Based on absolutely no evidence, had himself sworn in at midnight to be immediately ready to handle any major impending danger: *a possibly imminent, potential, possible Iraqi terror attack on Nevada that would nefariously take advantage of the state governmental transition.*

Gibbons had himself sworn in just seconds after midnight on January 1, 2007, in the living room of his Reno home because of these important "security concerns." He issued a terse statement that said that even though state agencies "know of no credible threat, recent world events and New Year's celebrations raise the potential for problems during Nevada's first government transition since the terror attacks of 9-11." According to Gibbons spokesman Brent Boynton, "recent world events" referred to the execution of former Iraqi dictator Saddam Hussein. (He didn't say why terrorists would target Nevada and not, say, Washington, D.C.) Gibbons added melodramatically, "Nevadans should be assured that their leaders are in place, ready for any emergency." (Note: And his wife was also ready for any emergency—dressed in an Armani gown. Take *that*, Osama!)

Paranoic #2: Representative James Bunning (R-KY)

Why He's Maybe Just a Little Paranoid: Based on no disclosed evidence, got security detail to follow him around to protect him from al-Qaeda

Why would al-Qaeda be interested in *specifically* targeting a Republican congressman who isn't particularly influential and hails from the bluegrass of Kentucky? Congressman Bunning didn't exactly explain—he didn't even sort of explain. But he indicated his firm conviction that, indeed, members of al-Qaeda had targeted *specifically him* for elimination. "There may be strangers among us," Bunning darkly informed a Paducah TV crew.

Strangers . . . ahhh . . .

Paranoic #3: Senate Majority Leader Bill Frist (R-TN)

Why He's Maybe Just a Little Paranoid: Had such elaborate mail security it took up to four weeks for constituent mail to reach his office

It's one thing to protect yourself from anthrax and letter bombs, it's another thing to be part of the Bill Frist protective mail detail.

His senatorial office warned that their security restrictions would "cause considerable delay in processing postal mail" and they were most definitely not joking. Mail addressed to Frist's D.C. office was first sent to a processing unit in Virginia, where it spent about four days; then it was forwarded to Lima, Ohio, for irradiation under an X- or gamma-ray machine; for another 10 to 14 days, it was then sent to yet another processing center, where all nonpaper contents were removed and tested. After another wait of 7 to 10 days for test results, the mail—or what remained of it—was finally delivered.

Paranoic #4: Senator Mark Dayton (D-MN)

Why He's Maybe Just a Little Paranoid: Dayton is not exactly the calm "Everything's going to be all right" kind of guy. He seems to us to be more of the "Help, fire! Thieves! Bugs! Bears!" kind of guy. Even though the FBI and CIA said there were no new threats whatsoever in 2004, Senator Dayton closed his office during the election week, saying that he would keep his kids away from Washington due to fear of a terror attack.

Dayton claimed he had received some juicy top-secret information from Senator Bill Frist (who didn't close his office, however, and didn't comment on the terror info). He added, "I do so out of extreme, but necessary, precaution to protect the lives and safety of my Senate staff and my Minnesota constituents, who might otherwise visit my office in the next few weeks. I feel compelled to do so, because I will not be here in Washington to share in what I consider to be an unacceptably greater risk to their safety." No other member of Congress followed suit and in fact a parade of senators and congresspeople made a point of saying how their offices would stay open.

But then again, thanks to Senator Dayton, *not one* of his Minnesota constituents or office workers was killed in this nonexistent election terror nonthreat.

Paranoic #5: New York state comptroller Alan Hevesi

Why He's Maybe Just a Little Paranoid: Got antiterror personal security guard for wife

First of all, let's establish what a comptroller is—he's the head *accountant* of an organization. In this case, Alan Hevesi is the chief accountant for New York state. Comptrollers, even of large states like New York, tend not to figure all that high on terrorist lists of preferred assassination targets—although we can *certainly* imagine Osama in his cave boasting "I killed their chief accountant! No longer can he arrange laddered loan portfolios for the state pension fund!" But to our knowledge Osama bin Laden has not *ever* directly threatened to kill *any* comptroller, and even more important, he has *never* to our knowledge targeted any accountant's spouses. Or kids.

Which makes us think that maybe Mr. Hevesi was going a little over the top when he authorized a personal antiterror bodyguard for his wife. But given allegations about Mr. Hevesi's high-living ways on the taxpayer dollar (see page 24), maybe the whole bodyguard thing was not paranoia at all. After all, it's *prestigious* to have bodyguards. And we hear they're very handy for carrying shopping bags.

OVERKILL: TOP POLS WEIGH IN ON THE JOYS OF TORTURE

There's a big debate going on: *Should America torture people?* This debate is always centered around some captured hypothetical terrorist who knows where a nuclear bomb is hidden that is about to explode and totally destroy New York, Los Angeles, or Washington, D.C. What do we do? Should we turn the thumbscrews or play Kathie Lee Gifford songs until this evil terrorist reveals to Keanu Reeves where the bomb is—so that some hero bomb squad person can defuse the thing just as the LCD combined bomb-oven timer flashes "6, 5, 4" seconds and then stops and we all breathe a collective sigh of relief?

So far, this hasn't happened (only in movies, but that's our new reality)—and the debate goes on about all the other (nonhypothetical) people we've captured. Should we torture 'em? Here some top U.S. pols weigh in on the debate.

WE SHOULDN'T TORTURE TERRORISTS AT ALL; INSTEAD, WE SHOULD *HELP* THEM.
—*President George W. Bush*

Yes, we were surprised, too. What about Gitmo? The president probably didn't even *know* about it; or else, why, on April 4, 2005, did he say, "It's in our country's interests to find those who would do harm to us and get them out of harm's way." Is the president saying that he doesn't even want to *harm* terrorists?

Wow. Talk about turning the other cheek!

WE SHOULDN'T EXACTLY TORTURE TERRORISTS, BUT WE CAN DO *OTHER* PAINFUL THINGS, LIKE WATERBOARDING.
—*Speaker of the House Tom DeLay (R-TX)*

DeLay feels that things like waterboarding (where the victim—oops, terrorist—is submerged or has water shot up his or her nose and mouth until he or she almost drowns) isn't torture at all. He cogently explains: "I don't think waterboarding is torture. My definition of torture is you physically harm someone by cutting them, cutting their fingers, sticking things in their eyes, sticking their fingers in electric sockets. Waterboarding is a frightening experience. But the person does not have physical damage."

WE SHOULDN'T TORTURE TERRORISTS—WE SHOULD ELIMINATE THEM *BEFORE* THEY BECOME TERRORISTS.
—*Department of Homeland Security Secretary Michael Chertoff*

This is the maximal preemption strategy, the "terminate with extreme prejudice" mode of dealing with the problem.

In other words, why go through all the angst of even discussing torture when you can get rid of the problem before it even starts? Said America's brave defender of the homeland Michael Chertoff during an interview on National Public Radio: "Clearly at the end of the day, we've got to eliminate that pool of people who are susceptible to becoming killers."

"Eliminate"? "Susceptible to becoming"? Who decides who's a susceptible killer and who's not? What if someone's just cranky that day?

Of course, this also raises the question: "Is killing *potential* terrorists worse than torturing them after they become terrorists?"

But we're just being nitpicky (again).

WE SHOULDN'T TORTURE TERRORISTS, BUT WE CAN "WHACK THEM AROUND."
—President Bill Clinton

This is the "It all depends on what your definition of 'is' is" analysis that Clinton, ever the word parser, loves to trot out. Like Tom DeLay, he has definitional attitudes about torture. Chopping off fingers with an ax is not okay. Whacking—whatever that is—is okay. Or in his precise words, "whacking around" suspects is acceptable, particularly if there were an imminent terrorist threat. Helpfully, the former Master of the Bureaucracy adds that a law like the Foreign Intelligence Surveillance Act could be used to allow the government to get approval after the whacking is done; i.e., the government can cleverly and legally cover its collective butt. Clinton is, however, against blanket approval for "whacking around," only *specific* whacking is acceptable, apparently.

I'M FOR—AND AGAINST—TORTURE.
—*Senator Hillary Clinton (D-NY)*

Hillary "Captain Renault of Vichy" Clinton, known for her bold principled stands made without regard to which way the political wind is blowing, first declared on the Senate floor that she was against torture. "Have we fallen so low as to debate how much torture we are willing to stomach?" she asked, leaving most people with the general idea that she was against torture.

But *then*, at a New York *Daily News* editorial board meeting, Hillary started discussing the ol' Keanu Reeves "ticking time bomb" scenario. She said that there was actually a place for "severity," all in what the *Daily News* said was "a conversation that included mentioning waterboarding, hypothermia, and other techniques commonly described as torture." So "severity" seems to be torture.

Hillary added, "I have said that those are very rare but if they occur there has to be some lawful authority for pursuing that. Again, I think the president has to take responsibility. There has to be some check and balance, some reporting. I don't mind if it's reporting in a top secret context. But that shouldn't be the tail that wags the dog, that should be the exception to the rule."

That clears things up for us. Torture should be banned, except when it shouldn't be.

TEN
POLITICAL
PUNDITS

POLITICAL PUNDITS ARE PEOPLE WHO ARE BEST DEFINED negatively, i.e., as to what they are not: They are not politicians. They are not policy-makers. They are not government bureaucrats.

So what are they?

Well . . . they talk a lot. About politics.

FAR-SEEING PUNDITS

Let's face it: People listen to political pundits because the latter know so darn much. And they're almost always right.

Brilliant Far-Seeing Pundit: Pat "God Talks to Me" Robertson

Pundit Prediction: According to God, storms (and maybe a tsunami, too) would wreak havoc on the U.S. coastline in 2006.

What Really Happened: Nothing out of the ordinary. In fact, 2006 saw fewer hurricanes than usual. But Pat said that heavy rains and flooding in New England counted. Well, partially.

Brilliant Far-Seeing Pundit: William "I Know Everything and I'm Not Afraid to Tell You That" Kristol

Pundit Prediction: In 2003, said 1) all would be copacetic with Sunnis and Shiites following a U.S. invasion of Iraq. "We talk here about Shiites and Sunnis as if they've never lived together. Most Arab countries have Shiites and Sunnis, and a lot of them live perfectly well together." Added that 2) "very few wars in American history were prepared better or more thoroughly than this one by this president." And 3) it would be cheap, too! Only $100–200 billion for the whole Iraq shebang.

What Really Happened: 1) War between Sunnis and Shiites in Iraq. 2) You call that preparation? 3) Estimates for the cost of the war are ten times that—or about $1.2 trillion.

Brilliant Far-Seeing Pundit: Dick "I Like Dem Girlie Toes" Morris

Pundit Prediction: In late 2005, said: "You know, George Bush basically believes the federal government should do two things: fight wars and help people recover from disasters [referring to Hurricane Katrina] and now he's got both on his plate. I think that his ratings are gonna soar! Not necessarily in the next three days, but over the next year he's gonna look so good doing all this stuff. The people who said this storm is gonna hurt Bush's presidency are just wrong. He can get all the money he wants out of Congress 'cause of this disaster, the people will be solidly behind him, the media will cover it like crazy, and he's gonna look like Santa Claus."

What Really Happened: People thought Bush looked more like the Grinch—and his popularity ratings plummeted.

Brilliant Far-Seeing Pundit: Jonah "Superior Person According to Himself" Goldberg

Pundit Prediction: In 2004, said, after University of Michigan professor Juan Cole predicted that Iraq would fall into strife: "I do think my judgment is superior to his when it comes to the big picture. . . . So, I have an idea: Since he doesn't want to debate anything except his own brilliance, let's make a bet. I predict that Iraq won't have a civil war, that it will have a viable constitution, and that a majority of Iraqis and Americans will, in two years' time, agree that the war was worth it. I'll bet $1,000 (which I can hardly spare right now). This way neither of us can hide behind clever wordplay or CV reading."

What Really Happened: Civil war (or "sectarian violence") in Iraq. As for the constitution? Yes, but no one seems to be following it. And as for a majority of Iraqis and Americans feeling the war was worth it? Well, if 30% of Americans is a majority, yes. And you can't tell in Iraq since it's too dangerous to conduct a poll.

Brilliant Far-Seeing Pundit: Bill "Falafel" O'Reilly

Pundit Prediction: Just before the U.S. invasion of Iraq, said: "I will bet you the best dinner in the gaslight district of San Diego that military action will not last more than a week. Are you willing to take that wager?"

What Really Happened: Person made bet with must have won since war took a bit more than a week. Like four years and counting.

Brilliant Far-Seeing Pundit: Charles "Sauerkraut" Krauthammer

Pundit Prediction: Just after the U.S. invasion of Iraq, in early 2003, said: "Hans Blix had five months to find weapons. He found nothing. We've had five weeks. Come back to me in five months. If we haven't found any, we will have a credibility problem. I don't have any doubt that we will locate them. I think it takes time."

What Really Happened: No WMD found so far. But, hey, it's only been four years.

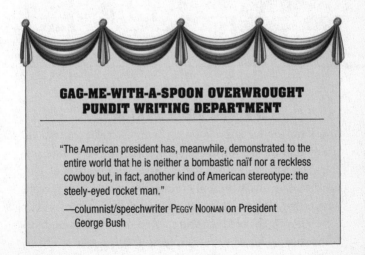

GAG-ME-WITH-A-SPOON OVERWROUGHT PUNDIT WRITING DEPARTMENT

"The American president has, meanwhile, demonstrated to the entire world that he is neither a bombastic naïf nor a reckless cowboy but, in fact, another kind of American stereotype: the steely-eyed rocket man."

—columnist/speechwriter PEGGY NOONAN on President George Bush

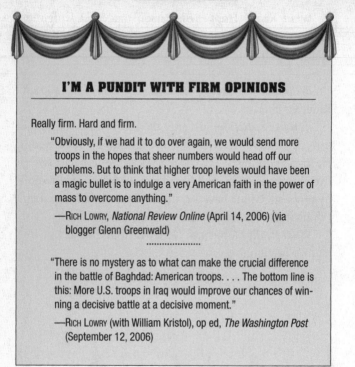

I'M A PUNDIT WITH FIRM OPINIONS

Really firm. Hard and firm.

> "Obviously, if we had it to do over again, we would send more troops in the hopes that sheer numbers would head off our problems. But to think that higher troop levels would have been a magic bullet is to indulge a very American faith in the power of mass to overcome anything."

> —RICH LOWRY, *National Review Online* (April 14, 2006) (via blogger Glenn Greenwald)

....

> "There is no mystery as to what can make the crucial difference in the battle of Baghdad: American troops. . . . The bottom line is this: More U.S. troops in Iraq would improve our chances of winning a decisive battle at a decisive moment."

> —RICH LOWRY (with William Kristol), op ed, *The Washington Post* (September 12, 2006)

THE PUNDIT PUNISHMENT CHART

You have to give some modern pundits credit. Instead of mealy-mouthedly voicing tepid opinions about politicians they take issue with, like the old-style wimpishness of Edward R. Murrow (who only brought down Senator Joseph McCarthy), they go all red-meat. Big-time.

Herewith, the reddest meat spewers of them all—and the somewhat . . . lurid . . . punishments they suggest for their political targets.

PUNDIT	TARGET	MEANS OF DEATH	IN OWN WORDS	COMMENTS
Michael Savage	Gay person calling into show	AIDS and/or pork ingestion (not sexual, but parasitical)	"Oh, you're one of the sodomites. You should only get AIDS and die, you pig. How's that? Why don't you see if you can sue me, you pig. You got nothing better than to put me down, you piece of garbage. You have got nothing to do today, go eat a sausage and choke on it. Get trichinosis."	Savage was fired from his MSNBC show after this aired, but still flourishes on the radio.
Bill O'Reilly	Hypothetical person strolling down the streets after 7 P.M.	Gunshot through head	"See, if I'm president, I got probably another 50–60 thousand with orders to shoot on sight anybody violating curfews. Shoot them on sight. That's me . . . President O'Reilly. . . . Curfew in Ramadi [Iraq], seven o'clock at night. You're on the street? You're dead. I shoot you right between the eyes. Okay? That's how I run that country. Just like Saddam ran it. Saddam didn't have explosions—he didn't have bombers. Did he?"	

PUNDIT	TARGET	MEANS OF DEATH	IN OWN WORDS	COMMENTS
Bill O'Reilly	Bloggers who are not pro-Bush	Being blown up with grenade	"[I know] for a fact that President Bush doesn't know what's going on in the Internet. . . . I have to say President Bush has a much healthier attitude toward this than I do. Because if I can get away with it, boy, I'd go in with a hand grenade."	
Bill O'Reilly	Financier George Soros	Hanging	"Where does George Soros have all his money? Do you know? Do you know where George Soros, the big left-wing loon who's financing all these smear [web]sites, do you know where his money is? Curaçao. Curaçao. They ought to hang this Soros guy."	

PUNDIT	TARGET	MEANS OF DEATH	IN OWN WORDS	COMMENTS
San Francisco talk show host **Melanie Morgan**	*New York Times* executive editor Bill Keller	Gas chamber	"If he were to be tried and convicted of treason, yes, I would have no problem with him being sent to the gas chamber. It is about revealing classified secrets in the time of war. And the media has got to take responsibility for revealing classified information that is putting American lives at risk."	Interestingly, were Morgan to get her wish, Keller would have to be executed in one of the five states—Wyoming, California, Maryland, Missouri, and Arizona—that technically retain this method (though all allow lethal injection as an alternative).
Ann Coulter	*New York Times* executive editor Bill Keller	Firing squad	"I prefer a firing squad, but I'm open to a debate on the method of execution."	Perhaps aware of the logistical problems of gas chamber execution, Coulter proved more flexible than Morgan regarding Keller.
Ann Coulter	*New York Times* staffers	Execution (did not specify mode)	"[*New York Times* staff members should be] executed."	Coulter shows admirable populist leanings with this broad-brush approach to death.

PUNDIT	TARGET	MEANS OF DEATH	IN OWN WORDS	COMMENTS
Ann Coulter	ALL people working in the *New York Times* building	Fertilizer bomb	"My only regret with Timothy McVeigh is he did not go to the *New York Times* building."	
Ann Coulter	Members of the media in general	Bombing, sniper attacks, etc., etc.	"Would that it were so! . . . That the American military were targeting journalists."	
Ann Coulter	Rep. Jack Murtha (D-PA)	Fragging, i.e., being killed by own troops	"Jack Murtha? The reason soldiers invented 'fragging.' "	
Ann Coulter	Entire population of North Korea	Explosion of nuclear fissile material	"I'm getting a little fed up with hearing about, oh, civilian casualties. I think we ought to nuke North Korea right now just to give the rest of the world a warning. I just think it would be fun to nuke them."	

PUNDIT	TARGET	MEANS OF DEATH	IN OWN WORDS	COMMENTS
Ann Coulter	Former senator Lincoln Chafee (R-RI)	Assassination—means unspecified	"They killed the wrong Lincoln."	Justified herself by calling him a "half-wit" and a "silver-spooned moron"
Ann Coulter	Supreme Court Justice John Paul Stevens	Poisoned dessert	"We need somebody to put rat poison in Justice Stevens's crème brûlée."	
Writer Matt Taibbi	President George W. Bush	Big hook through balls	"George Bush should be hung up by his balls. No kidding. He should be grabbed from behind, restrained, forcibly stripped below the waist, and a big hook should be pushed through his scrotum. Then the rope attached to the hook should be dragged through a pulley at the top of a flagpole, and the president should be hoisted up and left to swing in the breeze, 60 painful feet above the ground."	Wins points on creativity and detail

PUNDIT	TARGET	MEANS OF DEATH	IN OWN WORDS	COMMENTS
Michael Reagan	Democratic National Committee chair Howard Dean	Hanging	"Howard Dean should be arrested and hung for treason or put in a hole until the end of the Iraq War!"	Note charitable nature of Reagan, who offered Dean the option of spending time in a hole rather than being hung.
Glenn Beck	CNN pundit	Nuclear bombing	"Blowing up Iran. I say we nuke the bastards. In fact, it doesn't have to be Iran, it can be everywhere, anyplace that disagrees with me."	Rather tiresome and clichéd at this point—and a bit selfish
Tom Friedman	Serbians	Unrestricted bombing, unspecified type	"Let's see what 12 weeks of less than surgical bombing does. Give war a chance."	Referring to the U.S. bombing campaign against Serbia. To be fair, does not seem to mention *killing*, just bombing and war.

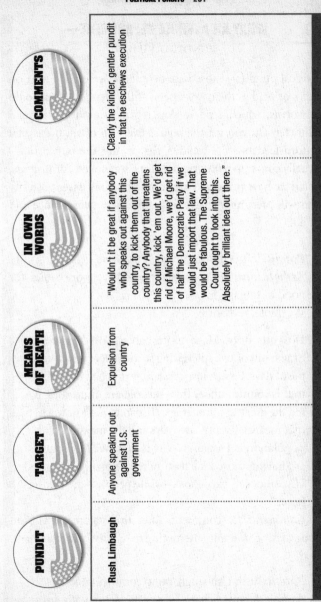 PUNDIT	TARGET	MEANS OF DEATH	IN OWN WORDS	COMMENTS
Rush Limbaugh	Anyone speaking out against U.S. government	Expulsion from country	"Wouldn't it be great if anybody who speaks out against this country, to kick them out of the country? Anybody that threatens this country, kick 'em out. We'd get rid of Michael Moore, we'd get rid of half the Democratic Party if we would just import that law. That would be fabulous. The Supreme Court ought to look into this. Absolutely brilliant idea out there."	Clearly the kinder, gentler pundit in that he eschews execution

WHAT AN ASSHOLE DEPARTMENT—

PUNDIT DIVISION

Political pundits—those wise people we see on TV, hear on radio, or read in the newspapers—fill a vital function. So do pinworms, which tend to congregate around the human sphincter. Do you get the segue? Every so often, these vital bottom-feeders—the pundits, that is, not the pinworms— actually come up with original ideas, statements, or insights, which we have preserved here for a hopefully wiser posterity who will presumably have forgotten these people once and for all.

Pundit: John Gibson, anchor, Fox News

Asshole Idea: White people should have more babies, for the good of the nation.

We quote, verbatim:

> "Do your duty. Make more babies. That's a lesson drawn out of two interesting stories over the last couple of days. First, a story yesterday that half of the kids in this country under five years old are minorities. By far, the greatest number are Hispanic. You know what that means? Twenty-five years and the majority of the population is Hispanic. Why is that? Well, Hispanics are having more kids than others. Notably, the ones Hispanics call 'gabachos'—white people—are having fewer."

Comment: No comment. After this statement, Gibson made many comments attempting to "clarify" this statement.

Pundit: Rush Limbaugh, radio commentator

Asshole Idea: Michael J. Fox, the actor with advanced

Parkinson's disease, was *acting* when he shook uncontrollably on a television ad calling for stem cell research.

Limbaugh said that Fox (during his shaky appearance for the Claire McCaskill [D-MO] campaign) "was either off the medication or he was acting. He is an actor, after all." Rush added, "This is the only time I've ever seen Michael J. Fox portray any of the symptoms of the disease he has. He can barely control himself." Rush Limbaugh, who dropped out of Southeast Missouri State University, seemed to be in substantial disagreement with various medical doctors, who are probably more authoritative sources for Parkinson's than Rush. (MDs tend to take a number of years of higher education beyond the two semesters and a summer session that make up Rush's entire higher education.) In fact, one MD opined:

> "The chorea that Michael J Fox has in that ad comes from chronic use of dopamine agonists in the context of Parkinson's. They're movements from the medicine, not the disease itself. Although he might have odd movements off of his meds, they wouldn't look like the ones in the ad. They'd look like the Parkinson's-like presentation of Muhammad Ali's dementia pugilistica. In addition, those movements are hard to imitate accurately because they stem from circuits between the basal ganglia and cortex that you can't just turn off or on. Those aren't volitional circuits. There is little chance he was acting, and if he was, he could only accentuate slightly movements he already had. In other words, this is as tragic as it looks."

Added Elaine Richman, a neuroscientist and co-author of *Parkinson's Disease and the Family,* "Anyone who knows the disease well would regard his movement as classic severe Parkinson's disease."

Rush then cleverly tried a different tack. "Michael J. Fox is allowing his illness to be exploited and in the process is shilling for a Democratic politician," the pundit stated.

Comment: Interestingly, due to his *own* little disability, an anal cyst, Limbaugh got a deferment from fighting in Vietnam. We wonder if he was faking, too. Maybe he should release a photo.

Pundit: Rush Limbaugh

Asshole Idea: Polar bears stranded on ice floes are just "playing around."

In response to widely circulated photos of polar bears stranded, due to global warming, on ice floes, Rush—who apparently studied the physics of climate change and mammalian Arctic zoology as well as medicine during his two semesters (and summer session) at Southeast Missouri State University—confidently asserted that the bears weren't stranded, they were just playing around. Rush has "weighed in" on the fact that global warming is a myth.

Pundit: Christopher Hitchens, writer, former Trotskyite, current pro–Iraq War, anti-God pundit, author of *Why Orwell Matters*

Asshole Behavior: Showing off his new method of informed *literate* debate, a mode that would make polite writers like Orwell proud

We quote from Hitchens at a party, as published in *The New Yorker*, speaking to someone with whom he disagreed.

"Fine, now that I know that, to you, medical ethics are nothing, you've told me all I need to know. I'm not trying to persuade you. Do you think I care whether you agree with me? No. I'm telling you why I disagree with you. That I do care about. I have no further interest in any of your opinions. There's nothing you wouldn't make an excuse for. You know what? I wouldn't want you on my side. I was telling you why I knew that Howard Dean was a psycho and a fraud, and you say 'That's O.K.' Fuck off. No, I mean it: fuck off. I'm telling you what I think are standards and you say, 'What standards? It's fine, he's against the Iraq War.' Fuck. Off. You're MoveOn.org. Any liar will do. He's anti-Bush. Fuck off. . . . Save it sweetie, for someone who cares. It will not be me. You love it, you suck on it. I now know what your standards are, and now you know what mine are, and that's all the difference—I hope—in the world."

Comment: In his younger years at the *New Statesman,* the rotund Trotsky-loving scribe, according to his friend Martin Amis, called for "rule by yobs." It looks like he got his wish.

Pundit: David Brooks
Asshole Statement: "One of the things I've found in life is that politicians are a lot more sincere than us journalists and we are more sincere than the people that read and watch us." So said Brooks on *The Chris Matthews Show.*
Comment: Was this a joke, or the product of a seriously disordered mind?

Pundit: Tucker Carlson, host of *Crossfire*
Asshole Statement: "If Pol Pot came on the show and was charming and witty and good-humored and had a good inscription, I'd say, 'Well, Pol Pot, charming guy.' "

This cute genocidal-maniac joke came from Tuck after he cleverly announced he'd eat his shoes and tie if Hillary Rodham Clinton's book sold more than one million copies, and after Hillary so cutely appeared on the show with a chocolate cake in the shape of a shoe along with her autographed book. Tuck stated he was impressed by Clinton in person, and then made the witty Pol Pot comparison.

Comment: Oh shut up, Tucker!

Pundit: William Kristol

Asshole Idea: Barack Obama would have been proslavery if he had been born in Lincoln's time

Yes, you read that right. According to Bill Kristol, presidential candidate and *African-American* Senator Barack Obama would essentially have supported slavery. Kristol stated that Obama's opening campaign speech on the steps of the Illinois statehouse (where Abraham Lincoln made a famous speech) "is a can't-we-get-along speech—sort of the opposite of Lincoln. He [Obama] would have been with Stephen Douglas in 1858." Douglas was in favor of letting slavery continue; he argued that Lincoln was a dangerous radical who advocated racial equality, something we presume Obama is somewhat in favor of as well. The historically astute Kristol is employed by Fox, for some reason.

Pundit: Michael Ledeen

Asshole Idea: Many U.S. soldiers in Iraq are essentially lazy; they should be out getting shot

Believe it or not, here is Michael Ledeen writing in *National Review Online:* "We've got lots of soldiers sitting on megabases all over Iraq. They should be out and about, some of them embedded, others just moving around, tracking the terrorists, hunting them down. I don't know how many guys and gals are sitting in air-conditioned quarters and drinking designer coffee, but it's a substantial number. Enough of that."

Ledeen also observed that "the level of casualties is secondary. I mean, it may sound like an odd thing to say. But all the great scholars who have studied American character have come to the conclusion that we are a warlike people and that we love war."

Comment: Speak for yourself, Mike! We kind of prefer peace.

ABOUT THE AUTHORS

KATHRYN PETRAS and ROSS PETRAS are siblings, and the authors of the national bestselling "Stupidest" series as well as other humor books. Their titles include *Unusually Stupid Celebrities*, *Unusually Stupid Americans*, *The 776 Stupidest Things Ever Said*, *Stupid Sex*, and *Very Bad Poetry*. Their work has received the attention of such personalities as David Brinkley and Howard Stern; publications including *The New York Times*, *Playboy*, *Cosmopolitan*, *The Washington Post*, and the London *Times*; and television shows including *Good Morning America*. They are also the creators of the number one bestselling *365 Stupidest Things Ever Said Page-A-Day Calendar* (now in its thirteenth year).